Hard Scrabble ≋≋≋≋≋≋≋

HARD SCRABBLE

Observations on a Patch of Land

JOHN GRAVES

ALFRED A. KNOPF New York 1974

THIS IS A BORZOI BOOK
PUBLISHED BY ALFRED A. KNOPF, INC.

A portion of this book originally appeared in *Esquire* Magazine.

Library of Congress Cataloging in Publication Data

Graves, John, (date)

Hard scrabble; observations on a patch of land.

1. Country life—Texas—Somervell Co.   2. Somervell Co., Texas.   I. Title.
S521.5.T4G7 1974   917.64′521′036   73–21857
ISBN 0–394–48386–3

Manufactured in the United States of America

FIRST EDITION

For Sally

Who knows the creatures that live under rocks, and where wildflowers grow, and the things that goats can say to you, and how to laugh . . .

It is storied of that Prince, that having conceived a Purpose to invade Italy, he sent for Cineas, a Philosopher and the Kings friend: to whom he communicated his Designe, and desired his Counsel. Cineas asked him to what purpose he invaded Italie? He said, To Conquer it. And what will you do when you hav Conquerd it? Go into France said the King, and Conquer that. And what will you do when you have Conquerd France? Conquer Germany. And what then? said the Philosopher. Conquer Spain. I perceive said Cineas, you mean to conquer all the World. What will you do when you have conquerd all? Why then said the King we will return, and Enjoy our selvs at Quiet in our own Land. So you may now said the Philosopher without all this adoe.

THOMAS TRAHERNE: The Centuries, I, 22

A part of this book was written on time made available by a grant from the Rockefeller Foundation, for which I am lastingly grateful.

Contents ⋙⋙⋙⋙⋙⋙⋙

Hard Scrabble ≈≈≈≈≈≈≈≈≈

1 ≋ By Way of Introduction ≋≋≋≋≋≋≋≋≋≋

In Southwestern terms, it is not a big enough piece of land to be called a ranch without pretension, though that title is more loosely awarded these days than it used to be. Nor is enough of its surface arable to qualify it as a serious farm. It is something less than four hundred acres of rough limestone hill country, partly covered with cedar and hardwood brush and partly open pasture, with some fair trees of various kinds and a few little creekbottom fields more or less amenable to cultivation. It has a name, Hard Scrabble, which is not shiningly original and appears on no signboard and in fact gets little use, but does reflect the way I feel about the work I have put into it and the existence it has imposed on other owners and occupants over the years. Mainly I call it "the place," the old term for just about any rural property that is its owner's main holding. Unconnected to it physically, though theoretically a part of its economics, is a separate hundred acres of gentler land a few miles away called usually, when anything, Soft Scrabble or just "the other place."

Until lately I lived on the place only part of the year,

3

spending summers here with my family and going down in other seasons as often as time and energy permitted, and sometimes more often than that. I would poke around after quail or dove or whitetailed deer, study birds or vegetation or the way rain works its way into and across the land and down the watercourses, stare at a liveoak fire and listen to the windowpeck of sleet borne along on a January norther, puzzle over traces of old human presence—or, more usually, plunge into one phase or another of the harsh labor that adapting such a property to even minimal use requires. Fences, pens, garden, house, outbuildings, livestock, roads, brush control, a little forage farming . . .

We inhabit a time of electronically amplified human crisis and change, of possible permissive delights of many descriptions, of geometrically burgeoning mortal millions creating geometrically burgeoning mortal problems that demand obsessive concern, of disappearing quiet hard rural ways and the triumph, or so they say, of easeful technology. And if at some point in his perusal of this book a perceptive and thoughtful reader should ask why the hell, in such a time, anyone even half aware of the currents of the world would choose to spend heavily out of his allotted time on such archaic irrelevances as stonemasonry, the observation of armadillos, vegetable gardening, species of underbrush, and the treatment of retained afterbirth in ruminants, with very slight expectation of even crass cash gain, he will be asking the same thing I have often asked myself. In part the book itself is an attempt to scratch through to an answer, and if one emerges to view it is almost certain to be irrational by general standards. But it is a known if little heeded fact that people's most passionate activities never have rational, reasonable roots. *Porque si* is the unequivocal and comfortable Spanish answer to such questions, and it may not be a bad one to start off with. Because yes.

Anyone who seeks to find here and share a deep wide

knowledge of rural and natural things is a little bit out of luck. The book is concerned with my part of the world insofar as I have a part, and I know a few things about it and into some subjects have dug deeper perhaps than most people have. But in none am I truly expert, nor have I sought to seem to be. The ways in which I accomplish various bucolic purposes, for instance, lack the glow of perfect rightness that shines through in most writings on the soil and country life and related subjects, from Junius Moderatus Columella on down through Louis Bromfield to contemporary fertilizer admen and the literati of the hippie communes. I do some things in a traditional manner, some more or less according to other people's written-down ideals, and a good many in my own way which is occasionally ingenious but often slipshod makeshift, both temperament and the question of available time and money having entered into this. . . .

Thus, while there are expert books on many of the concrete and unconcrete matters considered here specifically or in passing, and thank God for them, this book is not one. It is not the account of a triumphant return to the land, a rustic success story, but mainly a rumination over what a certain restricted and unmagnificent patch of the earth's surface has meant to me, and occasionally over what it may mean in wider terms.

For the most part, I hope, it is unpolemical and does not seek to grind large axes or to give large answers. The Unco Guid and the Rigidly Righteous, in one or another not necessarily religious hue, dominate our time as shrilly as they ever dominated Burns's Scotland. The conservative old and the arrogant young and the scratchily earnest of all ages are at one in this. Uncomfortable company they tend to be, for one who has too often in his life seen skulking from treetrunk to treetrunk behind him the specter of his own and his people's imperfection. I would as soon not add much to the chorus of indignation. Yet one does have indignations and pieties of

5

one's own, which may willy-nilly at some points bubble up to the surface of things in the form of outrageous opinions.

Though it is a place book rather than a people book, people inevitably edge into it from time to time, the tales about them shuffled about and fictionalized a little or much. Hard Scrabble is not wilderness by a long shot, not by something over a century of grinding Caucasian use. Like the pocket of country of which it is a part, it is weighted with human remembrances and ways of being, afflicted by them, rich with them, inseparable from them. The region is not much like Europe, dominated by men back to a time before men's records begin, the feel of their layered migrations and conflicts and great moments and desperate eras striking at you through architecture, through accents, through the usefully arranged stones and sticks and trees of a landscape, through the very slant of an eye seen as you walk along a street. It is not even like the Atlantic South, where on an aboriginal shell midden along the shore of a tidal river you can kick up English colonists' brickbats and winebottle shards from the 1600's. It is like Texas, where the civilized layers are shallow, but the traces and shades of people who have been here—as well as many who have not—matter so much that there is small chance of understanding the land without taking them a little into account. Nor in truth have I, your genial author and observer, ever been able for very long at a time to view the earth and its ways without considering what it may mean in human terms.

On said genial author and his quirks and foibles there is no point in dwelling further here, those things tending to out in books for better or worse, particularly in personal books like this one. Of such quirks and foibles, like most men, I have my own fair share. . . .

2 ≋ *A Comment* ≋≋≋≋≋≋≋

It was May and evening and the chuck-will's-widows and screech owls had begun to call and toads to answer, for there had been rain. In clean dusk light, sweetclover glowed green and solid in the little field across the branch from the house, and its vanilla scent tinged the air. Beyond were the dark trees along the main creek, and across it more green small fields and then the hills rising up to a sky with two stars in it. Somewhere a Spanish doe with a tightening udder wailed for a misplaced kid, and from somewhere else the kid called back. The lawyer had had three beers with me there on the screen porch, or maybe more. "It's a pretty place to be," he said. "I won't pretend I don't envy you, having it."

"But you wouldn't want it yourself."

"The hell I wouldn't," he said. "I'd take it in a minute. But I wouldn't run it the way you do."

"No," I said, and grinned. We were old friends and had seldom seen life alike.

"You're too much *into* it," he said. "You ought to get somebody living here on the place that could tend to all this little crappy carpentering and farming and just let you enjoy things. What'd you go to college for, and travel around and all that stuff? The way you're doing it, it's like . . . I don't know."

"Like work."

"Well, I don't know," the lawyer said again after a pull at his beer can. "What it makes me think about—it's like some old fart at the edge of town in one of those junk suburbs that just kind of grow up before the city reaches out that far. Watering his Super Sioux tomatoes. Reading magazines about making compost and how to build things out of hunks of busted concrete. Crooked tin sheds all over the back end of the lot and his banty hens not even all the same color."

"You see any crooked buildings around here?"

"It's the principle," the lawyer said. "All this do-it-yourself. You know what I'm talking about."

"Never you mind about that old fart," I said. "He's a friend of mine—kinfolks, sort of. I'm built a little different, but he's all right. You let him alone."

"Oh, I wouldn't bother him if I could," my friend said agreeably. "Which I can't. He's got it made. I expect he and his kind will watch me and my kind pass right on out of existence, and they'll still be out there by the highway among the junkyards and the beerjoints and the asbestos-shingle Baptist churches, chopping johnsongrass and bragging about how they slaughtered the cucumber beetles with cold goat pee or something."

"Marigolds."

"What?"

"Marigolds repel cucumber beetles," I said. "At least they're supposed to."

"Jesus," said the lawyer. "That's exactly the kind of thing I mean."

3 ≋ *Used to Be* ≋≋≋≋≋≋≋≋≋

Maps that split country into zones of topography, climate, vegetation, and such things have much more neatly sweeping lines of demarcation than nature has usually been willing to go along with. Nor do the ones generally available to a Texas layman always jibe with one another. In terms of both country and people, for instance, it is a moot question whether North Central Texas goes with the American Southeast or with the Great Plains, and in fact it goes with both and in some ways with neither. It is traversed by the ninety-eighth meridian, Walter Prescott Webb's "institutional fault" line between East and West, woodland-and-prairie ways and Plains ways, which passes about ten miles to the west of Hard Scrabble, unnoted by bird or beast or indeed by many people. It is traversed even more significantly by the thirty-inch isohyet of average annual rainfall, one county west of us, along and beyond which in Texas the dependability of rain for ordinary crops becomes a more and more dubious proposition.

Physiographically Somervell County, where my place lies, is a part of the Comanche Plateau subdivision of the Great Plains Province. In terms of soils and vegetation, the little county is a crossroads, having stretches of Brazos bottom, much sandy postoak land identified with the Western Cross Timbers, and—on the place and probably through most of the area—darker calcareous soils mainly shallow but sometimes deep over limestone, typical of the rolling Grand Prairie that stretches north and south from the county. The Grand Prairie is a sort of prong of the rich Blackland Prairie Province that extends from around San Antonio northward through Texas. A good bit of it is a quietly prosperous, long-productive belt, its farming based mainly on cotton through most of history, with ranching in the rougher parts. The trouble with the Somervell County portions of it is that they constitute part of its hilly fringe, and in the past that fact has led not to quiet prosperity and long production but in the other direction.

To a layman who cares about country, most of Somervell regardless of what the maps call it looks like a northern counterpart of the Texas Hill Country at the eastern edge of the Edwards Plateau near Austin and San Antonio. It has relatively rugged terrain carved by the millennia out of slightly shelving limestone layers that are the beds of successive ancient seas, and a network of clear streams—most of them classified "intermittent" nowadays—that run over ledge rock and gravel and are bordered by willows, elms, oaks, walnuts, pecans, cottonwoods, and the ubiquitous cedar. Along these watercourses are strips and patches of level farmland, narrow except in some of the bends of the Brazos that undulates from north to south across the county's richer eastern section. On the uplands are thick dark brakes of cedar and scrub brush, scattered liveoaks and other trees, and some open grassland that lately has been increasing in extent as the brush is bulldozed away and piled and burned.

We have an average rainfall upward of thirty-two inches a year, much of which comes in thunderstorms during the usually lush springtime and the long yellow-and-blue autumn. Summers are customarily drouthy and hot, with sometimes two or three weeks in a row during which each day the thermometer stretches its scarlet thread above a hundred degrees. But generally during such spells the southwest winds are strong off the Mexican desert, and you can work outdoors all day in a shirt that stays dry but is nevertheless crusted with sweat-salt by evening. In good summers waves of storms work across the region periodically, keeping field crops and grasses and gardenstuffs alive, along with the bugs that thrive on them and you; in the worst ones fitful, hot, damp but rainless east or southeast airs keep us steaming for weeks on end. Winters are rhythmic and frontal, the big Plains northers ramming Arctic cold at intervals down across the land and the relatively warmer Gulf wetness or dry Mexican air flowing back up betweentimes. The temperature can, though rarely, drop uncomfortably close to zero or even below it in a rough January, and nearly any year sees spells of twelve- to fifteen-degree weather, usually just after a strong norther has shoved through, perhaps with rain or snow along its edge. Behind the front the new clear frigid air sits calm upon us, intensifying its cold through frozen starry nights, but within days most often the insistent southern warmth has moved back in again.

What this type of Texas country was like in its later natural state, before white men came to stay, is a matter for some difference of opinion, mainly among people with different axes to grind. Charles Pettit, who devoted all his vigorous middle and elder years and much oil money to the shaping and reclamation of his big Flat Top Ranch in Somervell and Bosque Counties a few miles south of Hard Scrabble—a sort of pilot project, and a model that others have followed—was wont to maintain that it had been a grassland paradise, with no cedar at all and only occasional liveoak mottes besides the timber along the streams. The late Lyndon B. Johnson, who grew up in the similar Hill Country farther south and used to refer to it often in speeches, tended to describe it as a tough inhospitable land whose inhabitants from the very start had had to hang on by their teeth.

You can find evidence to support either view, depending on what bit of ground you are looking at, for the Texas limestone country at the western edge of the black-dirt prairies varies from rolling to rugged and back again all up and down its length, and the land's vegetation and productivity must always have reflected this variance to some extent. There was a time within the memory of old people I have talked to, dead now, when the gentler parts of Somervell and Bosque Counties had hardly any cedar, but the rough sections seem always to have been adorned with thick brakes here and there. Memoirs like those of the intrepid ranger Buck Barry, who settled in a good part of Bosque in the 1850's when there were still just about as many Indians as whites around, tell of going up with wagons into the country near the Paluxy where my place is, to camp and cut big loads of cedar posts and rails for fencing.

Even here, though, old people remember—or rather remember their parents and grandparents saying—that most of the land was covered with lush tall grass in virgin times and for a good while thereafter. Outside the brakes and mottes and bottomland woods stretched mainly that humble, magnificent, green-and-tawny vegetation upon which Nebuchadnezzar in his madness did feed and Texas was largely built. The Somervell hills undoubtedly rolled more smoothly then, with fewer jags and gullies and less bald white rock showing through, for the grass over ages of time had built a rounded pad of soil upon them and had held it in place. Wind-driven fire cleansed them from time to time, singeing back encroaching brush and giving the quick-sprouting bluestem and indiangrass and gramas and other species a head start toward new thick-woven stands. Fed by rainwater that soaked into the vast mat of grass and trickled out slowly and constantly at the bottoms of slopes, and by springs welling up from deep

artesian aquifers, the region's network of streams ran clear
and cool through the years, almost immune to the occasional
long drouths that burned the grasses beige and to hot southwest summer winds from off the Chihuahuan Desert. The
early account of George Wilkins Kendall, who rode through
not far away with the ill-fated Santa Fé Expedition sent out
by the Republic of Texas in 1841, has a lyrical if gastronomic
ring:

> . . . Grapes, plums, and other fruit were found in profusion;
> honey could be obtained in almost every hollow tree; trout
> [the old Southernism for black bass; real trout are not native
> here] and other fish were plentiful in the small creeks in the
> neighborhood, and the woods and prairies about us not only
> afforded excellent grazing for cattle and horses, but teemed
> with every species of game.

Good country, it does seem to have been, free of the
malaria and damp windlessness of the forestlands to the east,
seldom parched and thirsty like the big country farther west.
It had supported populations of men of various sorts for thousands or perhaps tens of thousands of years before Kendall's
time, as have most livable regions on the earth's long-trodden
face. For most of those sorts of men there are no names except the broad place or era labels scientists use to impose
order on their scanty leavings of bone and baked clay and
flint. It it said that some of the earliest, with what must have
been a combination of huge courage and huge hunger, used
spears to hunt great beasts that no longer exist—elephants and
mastodons and ground sloths and giant bison and such things
—through a landscape and a climate nothing like today's.
And if you squint back through the haze that far, you inevitably look back farther still, into the unhumanly mindless,
unimaginably long eons of geological time when over and
over again the restive earth would wrinkle itself or shake or
rise and subside, and the rains and winds and rivers and frosts

and questing roots would carve it, and the wide shallow seas would creep in and recede, and galaxies of living species would thrive and change and perish or migrate, to make room for others still. Less than a mile from my house, in a stratum of limestone exposed by the little Paluxy River, are tracks imprinted in seashore mud a hundred million or so years ago by great saurians—latecomers, really, in the whole scheme.

(Clearly enough, things have been going on around Hard Scrabble for a good long while. In that perspective, a man's interest in any particular people's effect there, and his study of any particular community of wildlife and vegetation, and his groping efforts to "restore" the land to any particular sort of human use, are bound to look a little bit petty. And yet a man tries, anyhow. . . .)

In latter pre-Columbian times the region's people appear to have belonged—as far as I can judge from the literature—to a hunting-and-gathering culture that archaeologists call formally the Toyah Focus of the Central Texas Aspect. These were likely the ancestors of the tribe known as Tonkawa, which dominated much of Central Texas in the immediately pre-horse, pre-white period and took up a horseback life when horses came their way. But by the time that Kendall and other whites first viewed the region, besides "Tonks" it held also scraps and bits of other red peoples—some who had fled the white frontier from sometimes distant homes and now were fleeing it up the Brazos valley, and others who had left their old territories for other reasons, often driven out by Plains Indian warriors made terrible by the acquisition of horses and horsemanship.

Among these relatively peaceful refugees, many of them farmers by habit, were Caddoes, two or three kinds of Wichita, some Lipan Apaches probably, Delawares, Kickapoos, and the like. There were not very many of either them or the Tonkawas, and good records of where most lived and in what manner are lacking. But they pop up in the old frontier annals.and memoirs, sometimes as farmers of beans and squash and corn in bottomland villages, sometimes as corrupted hangers-on about the white trading posts and settlements, sometimes as volunteer scouts against the Comanches. Practically always as victims . . .

For a while before whites and Comanches started to clash in this area and to make mincemeat out of everyone else, the Tonks and their refugee neighbors may have found some security here, but it cannot have been more than relative. For this was the southeastern rim of the Comanchería, within the sometime sway of that Comanche subdivision called Penateka, which is translated Honey-Eaters or sometimes Wasps. They had kept Spanish colonists out of it and for the most part Apaches, and in the days of their imperial power they seem to have used it mainly as a wintering ground. Winter in the empire's Plains heartland to the northwest could be bitter, but the territory along the middle Brazos had timber for firewood and shelter, plenty of game, and sweet limestone water for long encampments. A man I know had a Comanche grandmother, captured by whites in childhood and raised by them, who had been born at a Wasp wintering place where the Paluxy runs into the Brazos in present Somervell County, and whose mother and grandmother had both been born there too.

Anglo-Americans began to elbow into the neighborhood of the lower Paluxy in the 1840's and '50's with a fierce land hunger that intended to brook no interference. To the south they had been in increasingly harsh armed conflict with Comanches for years before this, but their forerunners had been in harsh armed conflict with one kind of Indians or another since the 1600's, and they were neither easily disheartened nor any more inclined to see injustice in what they were doing than the Comanches had been as they extended their bloody horseback empire a century or so before. . . . The conflict was a way of life by now, a means of getting land, either because you had none or because you had worn out the patch that belonged to you where you came from—seeing the crops grow shorter and skimpier year by year on the tiring soil, seeing the land itself wash thickly away under rain and the gullies bite deeper into subsoil, seeing the wagons and the people headed for new country. . . .

Some early trading posts and a line of federal forts set up in the Comanchería provided a modicum of protection and encouragement, and a modicum was all the hard-shoving white individualists required. Just past the middle of the century the outer line of their settlements and farms and ranches was a good fifty miles beyond present Somervell County. Enough of them rooted themselves along the lower Paluxy and its environs that one of the Barnards—Yankee trading-post people, much involved in the area's history—found it worthwhile to build a handsome limestone mill on the little river to grind their meal for them.

Ground worse than meal, the gentler red tribes faded quickly into that foggy limbo where history's victims go. The Comanches and allied Kiowas fought back hard for a while, though there is not much point in pausing here for a new recountal of their stormy and rather magnificent displacement and decline, a story that has been told and told again. Opposing aggression to aggression, as imperial warriors should, they shrank in effective numbers and ceased rather soon to be capable of real warfare, turning into hit-and-run mounted raiders and thieves in usually small parties. But they managed to keep on fighting, even while losing, for two decades or more after their fate must have been fairly clear even to them. (To feel the spirit that kept them going, you need only look at a few old photographs of deadly-unsmiling Comanche and Kiowa bucks and then compare them with the looser, softer, thoughtful or bewildered faces that show in pictures of other less warlike Indians.) During the Civil War when military protection waned, they stabbed repeatedly within the line of settlement and made the frontier recoil on itself, and a pattern developed in which settlers would make up retaliatory parties and trail the raiders into the wild Plains country, sometimes catching up with them for a fight but more often not. Nor did all this stop till the seventies when hide hunters on the Plains had done their dirty work with the buffalo, cutting off the Comanches' sustenance at its source, and U.S. cavalrymen had herded what was left of the Wasps and their fellow bands, nearly horseless again after more than two centuries of arrogant equitation, onto an Oklahoma reservation to eat tame beef and pork and to assume the reluctant ownership of agricultural implements.

The whites who supplanted them and the other Indians in the Paluxy country—"taking it up," as the phrase went then—show but dimly over this span of years, few among them having been much addicted to record-keeping. The earliest probably derived mainly from the turbulent, thrusting, cotton-and-slave South, coming either from southern and eastern Texas (where they might have been born or might only have paused a while in their westering; one friend of mine's Alabama-born grandfather left five children dead of malaria along the Louisiana border before he came on west) or direct from the older states. Few appear to have brought with them much recollection of magnolias, classical porticoes, and smiling black chattel servitors. But neither did many among these early ones issue from a background of sour restrictive poverty. Most belonged to that basic Scotch-Irish yeoman class of Southern whites whose ancestors had swarmed to Pennsylvania, Maryland, Virginia, and the Carolinas from the early eighteenth century onward, after the expiration of Cromwellian leases in North Ireland turned thousands of Protestant Scots farmers adrift.

Of that breed it has been said that they feared God so much they had no fear left over for any man. They were not much afflicted with doubt concerning their own abilities and righteousness, not even when the God-fear curdled in them and turned them into boarish drunken brutes, as it sometimes did. By the time they reached Texas, many had taken on admixtures of other blood—English along the Eastern seaboard, French or Spanish in the cotton states and sometimes Indian too, Choctaw or Cherokee or whatever, showing up still in some families' eyes and jaws and hair. But the basic type remained Anglo-Hibernian, suited to the frontier as the frontier was suited to them, abrasive toward Mexicans, Comanches, and just about anyone else who got in their way.

There were families and individuals from other ethnic strains as well, but in Somervell County no identifiable groups of them who clove to their ways against the Scotch-Irish way of being. The Germans who form so staunch an element of the South Texas population never came here in numbers, nor Catholic Czechs, nor the Scandinavians who have whole towns a few miles to the south, nor the Mexicans to whom the new inhabitants of the Comanchería seemed as unwelcoming, perhaps, as ever the old ones had. Of Negroes very few had ever been brought here, and none stayed on for long.

Somewhere along the line—early or late or both—another kind of Scotch-Irish-English showed up in numbers, people who had followed a different, rougher route from Pennsylvania and Virginia westward and south. Someone must have published a good account of the highland Tennesseans and other Appalachians who flocked to Texas in the middle nineteenth century and after, but if so I have not seen it. Enough came to leave a mountaineer flavor along most of the Texas farming frontier. The manner of men's speech in my part of the state, for instance, and in all of West Texas, is classed by linguists as a subdialect of "Hill Southern," and a nonlinguist has a hard time telling the difference between it and other subdialects. I once spent a couple of weeks in a hospital, far from Texas, within earshot of a multiply-fractured, good-humored, loudmouthed fellow across the hall, and just about when I had figured out for myself what part of my home state he came from and how he had probably developed all that lungpower at Texas A. & M., a nurse told me he was from West Virginia.

A certain amount of impermanent friction created heat between the first-comers and the hill people, as witness this grump by an old-timer, quoted in one of the books of James K. Greer of Bosque County:

> . . . I do not recall that we had many poor whites from the hills of Tennessee, Alabama, and Kentucky: people who were clannish, who hated or loved fiercely, and who were quite as prolific as wild animals. This type of people came in years later. They used such words as "ary," "nary," . . . words which if used by early native sons, I cannot recall ever hearing. Nor do I recollect hearing any native Texas son say "I done it" and "I seen 'em." . . .

But first-comers tend by nature to look down on those who show up later, whether the place in question be New York City, the Texas frontier, or a Mediterranean resort. The hill people seem to have fixed themselves most solidly in the rougher parts of the country, probably because by the time they arrived earlier settlers had occupied most of the best bottomlands and prairies. Thus the Appalachian flavor is stronger in Somervell County than in less rocky nearby regions—the stouter dialect even now, the recent tradition of white-whiskey distillation, the solidity of families and clans, the emphatic morality or its emphatic absence. . . .

At any rate they came, the early Somervellians, some leaving only wornout land behind them where they came from, others leaving bad trouble or wives who spelled the same thing, or the bitterness of competing as yeoman farmers in an economy based on black slave labor. Moving along south and west as people moved then . . . The land they "took up" they usually had to buy from entities or individuals or families that had received or bought title to big hunks of it from the state before the wave of settlement had washed that far west, and who often had never laid eyes on it.

On these purchased, usually small tracts of homestead land they put up houses of postoak logs or sometimes limestone, though within a couple of decades East Texas pine boards, brought in on wagons or on railroads passing not far to the north and south, became the main material. The life the early whites lived was built around mixed subsistence farming and range stock raising, a pattern that had been evolving along the Texas frontier "fault line" and was both reminiscent of life in the woodlands east to the Atlantic, and prophetic of life as it would be lived on the untimbered plains west of Ninety-eight, west of thirty inches of rain. Most had cornfields and kitchen gardens, bees and chickens and hogs and milk cows, smokehouses and log barns and dug wells and the rest of the Eastern things. But many too were heir to the violent horseback skills of Mexico and South Texas, and ran a few or many longhorned beef animals on the open range that included the whole region except for fenced-off croplands, until barbed wire came into general use in the eighties and nineties. The Chisholm Trail passed not far away, carrying cattle north. Feeling its tug, young men sometimes rode out with a herd to savor the joys of the Kansas railroads, crossing the fault line into the new Western way of being and maybe never coming back.

Around 1870 the prairie soils and rainfall were proved suitable for cotton-raising. Since burgeoning civilization had brought with it a civilized need for money, that king cash crop was shortly being sowed wherever there was enough dirt to sprout a seed. It brought some fluctuating prosperity to the county during three or four decades, along with some panics and turbulences of the sort that any farming community based on one single crop is prey to. In the nineties when resentful Populism reached its unvictorious high tide in Texas, it was stoutest of all in a few counties of North Central Texas like Somervell, where white small-farmers made up most of the population and cotton had established its capricious, demanding rule. Subsistence farming went down the drain. So did much else. The main thing that cotton, along with open-range grazing practices and other frontier institutions, did to the erstwhile grassland paradise of the Tonks and the Comanches and the teeming wild creatures was to play hell with it. By the time Scotch-Irishmen reached Texas, they were a long way in miles and years from careful European husbandry, and a longer way mentally. Good land by then meant new land, not an old place nurtured through generations. The guiding principle, sanctified, was use it up and move along. Wear out and get out. . . .

Some kinds of land resist human misuse better than do others. The Fertile Crescent of Mesopotamia sustained a long succession of early exploitative civilizations. Not even the excesses of old-time tobacco culture kept the Virginia coastal plain from bolstering up a century and a half of social magnificence before the American Revolution and furnishing us with an Enlightenment gentry to start the republic on its way. Nor did the soils of our Midwest wear out before modern knowledge developed to save them, or the Mississippi's famed alluvia. But those regions are mainly flat and Somervell County, Texas, is not.

If, in this rough pocket at the far western edge of the old Cotton Kingdom, sturdy individualistic yeomen during the final decades of the nineteenth century and the early ones of the twentieth sowed year after year the one cash row crop they knew would pay, and sowed it wherever their mules could tug a plow, whether in the valleys, on the slopes, or atop the hills, and sowed it furthermore without heed or knowledge of such soil-saving measures as contour plowing, crop rotation, fertilization, terracing, stripcropping, cover-cropping, and the like, then the result was foreordained. The soil, seldom thick above bedrock or clay, lay naked during much of each year, growing more powdery all the while as cropping ate up its humus content. Big plains winds hissed across it when it was dry and lifted it in swirls and walls of dust to the next county, the next region, the next state. The characteristic heavy, hard, infrequent rains of the area pounded down on it and sloshed away along the casual uphill-downhill plow furrows or across them, carrying millions of tons of dirt down draws and branches to the creeks, down the creeks to the Paluxy, down the Paluxy to the Brazos, down the Brazos to the Gulf.

And all the while, in places too steep or rocky for plows and mules to work, the multitudinous cattle were eating down the grass as fast as it could grow and faster, leaving nude soil in those places too, to blow or wash away. Over wide stretches of the county, in a few decades, the padded grassy hills turned into a landscape of gullied clay and caliche and white rock, and what had once been a legitimate if rough part of the Grand Prairie was so no longer. Cedar and other brush and weeds that livestock would not eat moved in to cover the nudity as best they could, and since the land was less and less worth defending and bollweevils and other things had started making cotton a riskier crop, men did not fight the invaders back and they thrived. Streams, robbed of the steady supply of rainwater the grasses had trapped and fed out to the subsoil, grew "flashy"—more subject to spates and flooding in wet seasons, but shrunken and warmed and changed the rest of the year. What happened here happened up and down the continent, if more slowly in most other places. It was inherent in the frontier's view of land, and we are told by those who view such matters with philosophy that it was needful if our nation was to buy industrialization and pay for its rising might. To some others of us the price may look a bit high, but we see it with jaded modern hindsight. . . .

I was talking once with a federal fisheries man about whales, which as everyone knows are vanishing fast as factory ships armed with scout-planes, chase-boats, sonar, and much of the other deadly gadgetry of our time harry them across the several seas. International compacts for their protection have not worked; a whale is a large tempting chunk of protein and oil. Probably the only hope for their survival, the federal man said, was what he called "economic extinction"— meaning that after whales have been so thinned out that the catch won't pay for all that hardware, maybe whaling nations will not mind signing some meaningful papers toward their preservation.

It is a good enough phrase, I guess, for what happened to the rougher part of Somervell County. It reached economic extinction, at least in American terms. Steady cash cotton farming and stock raising, frontier style, so depleted its possibilities that on much of it even frugal people could no longer make a living in that way. In the early years of this century the little county held around 4,000 people and, I am told, sixteen cotton gins. In 1970, after a half-century in which the world's population had, God help us, approximately doubled, the county had some 2,800 residents and no cotton gins at all, nor anything else that represented that sort of widespread production.

If the earlier whites here had been Old World peasants in their outlook, with mystic attachment to the fields they worked and scant migratory tradition to carry them elsewhere, most probably would have stayed on, to revert to a tough herding life and to finish the job of turning the region into a moonscape, or else possibly to work out better and more permanent ways of making it serve them. You can find innumerable rough-land pockets and regions of Europe and Asia where hundreds or even thousands of years ago men did one or the other of these things after disposing of the land's virginity. Mainly if they could they worked out better ways, even if it meant resoiling whole mountainsides with dirt hauled up in baskets and dumped behind stone terrace walls. There was nowhere else for them to go.

23

These weren't Old World peasants, however, but people removed from the prodigal frontier by only a generation or so, if that. Droves left, not in a mass migration but by trickles, as individuals and families. Some found new farms to the west while that possibility still existed, some drifted to the big cattle country and another kind of life, some ended in towns and cities far away. They went where Americans go. . . . Many sold their ruined hilly farms for small change when they went; others abandoned them or turned them over to mortgage holders. As late as 1940 much of the cedar hill land was for sale at five dollars an acre or even less, with hardly any takers in sight.

The natives who did stay on, kinsmen often to those who left, were the lucky ones whose forebears had come early enough to get hold of good flat land that had not washed or blown away, some townsmen at the county seat of Glen Rose (erstwhile Barnard's Mill), and a thick sprinkling of rugged hill folk, mountaineers in type whatever their ancestry had been, who had lived in intimacy with hardship for so long that they took pride in their ability to stand it, and had the pessimistic certainty that if they went elsewhere they would simply find more hardship of an unfamiliar sort. Aloof from the world's currents, they stayed on at the little hill places they sometimes owned or rented but often just occupied, not trying to mold the land into new forms of usefulness but molding themselves to its shrunken possibilities. They raised what corn and vegetables the little fields would still grow and sometimes another skimpy crop of cotton, tended pigs and gaunt cows, cut cedar fenceposts for sale from the brakes that covered the hills more and more densely over the years, became some of the world's best worn-out-car mechanics, ran hounds at night after coon and fox and cat, worshipped an

24

austere Old Testamental God or resisted Him, and at moonshine stills back in the cedar sometimes made raw white whiskey for solace and courage and cash.

The demand for this latter product soared with Prohibition, and in the twenties stills proliferated in the hills, turning out a beverage that was more like rum than whiskey by now, for less grain went into its making than bought sugar. Some of it was aged in barrels for a time; much was not, but dripped from copper worms into jugs and mason jars and found its way quickly to Glen Rose, a sort of spa in those days with some fine malodorous sulfur springs and a pretty location on the little Paluxy between the dark hills and a good many chiropractors and "rubbing doctors," some with a reputed magical healing touch. There the liquid result of the cedar people's ancient Hibernian craft furnished fuel for big drunks by healthseekers from Dallas and Fort Worth and Waco and Abilene and points between, or was transshipped to those and other cities for distribution by the jovial underworld of the era.

Much of the county's folklore derives from the old white-whiskey boom, which did not end entirely with Repeal in 1932—a lot of West Texas stayed Dry on through the thirties and forties and even later, and remained a market. There were Rangers and federals and stoolpigeons and moonshiner heroes and bloodshed and jail terms and quite a bit of money bouncing around, more of which reached the pockets of town middlemen and bootleggers than reached those of the cedar folk who made the stuff. Not that all were involved, by any means, for some people's Old Testamental God looked darkly on strong drink and its manufacture and its social effects. . . . But many a native today can tell you fondly about the intricacies of brewing mash, and who got moderately rich off of selling kerosene burners that made no smoke to guide lawmen to a still site, and how a big barbecue was given for a group of citizens newly returned from a year's sojourn in the penitentiary at Huntsville, and of such quaintnesses as the little train of burros someone had taught to march untended up into the hills carrying sacks of sugar, while he watched their approach from hiding and made sure they were not followed.

Of how the arbitrarily delineated little patch of slopes and creekbottom whose ownership I now claim figured directly in all these things that were, I know only a little. The dinosaurs and the other great reptiles walked here in the layered limy mud that lies flat somewhere beneath its contours, transmuted into stone. The galaxies of other creatures thrived and perished. The seas crept in and ebbed, leaving new layers of mud to turn to stone or shale, and to be worn down with time to hills and valleys, to which ancient carnivorous men found their way from the Bering bridge or elsewhere, seeking their quarry large or small across Hard Scrabble's surface. Later men, red ones, must have hunted and foraged here frequently over the ages, and camped sometimes or often beside the sweetwater stream that still runs well, most years, and ran more copiously then. Maybe they even farmed a little if they were farming types. My own farming sometimes flips bits of worked flint to the surface of the small fields. They are often of the whitish hue of the nodules occurring in association with the Edwards limestone strata of the Chalk Mountain ridge a few miles west and south, which divides the Paluxy and Bosque river basins and marks more or less the line where Somervell's roughest country gives way to rolling land.

One section up against that ridge, probably rocky and barren even in Indian times, used to be known in the county as "the Tonk Nation," though whether the name had reference to real Tonkawas who certainly inhabited the hills within old remembrance (not highly esteemed Indians despite their services as scouts, for they sometimes ritually cooked and ate defunct Comanches with glee), or whether it was applied later, by townsmen and richer farmers, to the hard-bitten whites who settled and lingered there, I do not know. The phrase is somehow quite descriptive of the country itself, and it has often seemed to me that as erosion and agricultural ruin spread down through the lower hills, Tonkishness spread with them, and in later days the name came to fit the whole hill zone, including Hard Scrabble. I use it that way in my mind. The Tonk Nation wherein we dwell . . .

Comanches lived in no single place, but they must have known and used this piece of country in the days of big grass, for the land and its crannies were their book, and in unheroic reservation times surviving old warriors could describe with accuracy to white interviewers hills and creeks and groves four hundred miles away that they had not seen for fifty years. I believe I remember once reading somewhere of a raiding party whose trail showed white pursuers it had driven its stolen horses down the valley of my creek to where it joins the Paluxy. But neither these nor any others left traces of the kind that tell stories, or if they did I have not had the eyes to see and read them.

Passed over for land along the Brazos and the Paluxy and for the more level expanses of prairie, the broken parts of Somervell County were probably not farmed much till cotton came, though it is not possible now to find out exactly about such things, for squatters or neighbors sometimes cropped places for many years before resident owners moved in, and these owners themselves had often been living there for a decade or more, making payments, before they got recordable titles to the land. Hard Scrabble is made up of two homesteads taken up in the eighties out of a large tract granted earlier as wild country to the Galveston County School Board, to ensure the education of pupils three hundred miles southeast.

But its decline from virginity had begun long before the homesteaders came. As open range in a neighborhood of small-farmers and ranchers each of whom had as much hoofed stock as he could lay his hands and brand upon, it had undoubtedly already been hard-grazed. And here and there on the scattered eighty or ninety acres of the place that have been plowed and cropped in the past—whether ideally they should have been or not—you can find traces of early use. In brush alongside one old field, for instance, stands a fragment of wall with some enormous pieces of ledge rock in it, three or four hundred pounds in weight, that someone must have dragged there and laboriously levered into place before barbed wire came into general use. Its function could only have been to protect a plowed and planted patch against wandering stock, and it was probably supplemented by some sections of rail or brush or stump fence, long since moldered away. But who it was that thus presumed on the unwitting hospitality of the Galveston County School Board, or the state, or the Comanches, or the Tonks, or when, or where he went from here, God only knows. . . .

In about 1884 a Confederate veteran and surveyor from Virginia named George Booker moved his family to that part of my present place locally still called after them—"the Booker"—and at some point in the same era or before, a family named Lee, who lived on adjoining property, acquired the other 140 acres or so now within my fence, turning it over afterward to the ownership of a Lee daughter and her husband named Kyle. Virgin or not, this was still pretty good country then; surviving Bookers, some of them born on the place before the family moved to Glen Rose in 1896, remember their parents telling of abundant deer and bear and turkey, and their father ran as many as two hundred cattle on the open range roundabout. Feral hogs foraged here too, descended from razorback stock brought in by the earliest settlers; in the fall, when they were fattest, people would hunt them by riding out horseback early on cold mornings and watching for the steam that rose from the bowers they had wallowed out for themselves in the deep thick grass. A road that no longer exists wound across the hills and through the valleys to Glen Rose five miles away, and passed through no cedar at all. Even after the Bookers had moved away from the place, a tenant family one year harvested thirty-five bales of cotton from what cannot have been more than forty acres or so of field land. . . .

The Bookers built a substantial home for the time and place—board and bat, with a good limestone foundation and chimney and stout outbuildings. It burned down around 1930, long before my time on White Bluff Creek. Years before I owned the place bulldozers smashed across the house site on their mission of renewal, scraping away the cedar and scattering archaeological traces not only of Bookers but of Indians and moonshiners and everyone else, far and wide. But in a thicket beneath a big liveoak is a trench walled with good hewn rocks (I sometimes sit there and watch for deer) that once was a well-constructed storm cellar's entranceway, and strewn about the area of the old dooryard, in and under rank bermudagrass, are other squared and faced blocks of native stone that show George Booker had a Virginia sense of permanence about his clan's presence there, even if his health and the practice of his profession did take them away from the place to town rather soon.

The Kyles—at least I have assumed it was they—built a different sort of dwelling for their own relatively short stay on the other, rougher, smaller tract. Their house was not for sybaritic living or the ages' admiration but for quick and simple shelter—one room with a lean-to kitchen, never painted inside or out, its walls of upright wide planks without studs to stiffen them or battens to cover their cracks, its floor raised off the ground on a few piles of unworked, unmortared flat rocks stacked high enough to make a biding place for dogs and to discourage rattlesnakes. They set it on a hillside looking south toward the Bookers, between two liveoaks. It was still standing after a fashion when I took over the place, lost in thick cedar, dangerously aslant beneath the weight of an ingenious sort of roofing—Portland cement plastered over flattened Model T hoods—that subsequent occupants had contrived on the kitchen part when the original shingles got leaky.

You could tack newspaper over the wallcracks in a house like that, and put up a muslin ceiling to contain your wood-stove's heat a bit, but at best it was a minimal sort of shelter against shoving, probing Plains northers and driven rain. It was built by and for a tough outdoor people. Its aspect summed up an era's lingering frontier casualness about comfort, and the quick exploitation of land, and the disappearance of even frontier craftsmanship after cotton and cash began their reign and cheap lumber started coming in from the East Texas piney woods, to take the place of the stubborn native logs and stones. In truth there was nothing much worth a damn about it, nor had there ever been.

Yet it had served three or four vigorous families as a home. And it also had great beauty in its gray diagonal defeat—rotten, a haven for snakes and rats and spiders and wasps and wary Angora goats escaped from ranches farther up the creek when spates washed out the fences' watergaps. After I had robbed one stone too many from its shaky piers for my own projects, a big wind finally blew it flat, and on a damp day I set the whole nostalgic jumble afire and later cleaned away the tin and nails and cement that remained in the ashes. Now old human presence on that low hill is indicated only by a goat-ravaged lilac bush, a scabrous cholla cactus not native to the region, a heap of accumulated stove ashes melted almost level with the ground, a shallow pit where an earthen storm cellar caved in, a collapsed stovepipe casing where there was once a drilled well, a square of decayed logs that held hogs for salted summer meat, and an impressive, embedded midden of jars, snuff and medicine and condiment bottles, glass and crockery chips, rusty wire and nails and flattened cans and pots, barrel hoops, shoe soles, wagon hardware, and automobile parts up to and including whole bodies, though all these treasures have dwindled greatly in sporadic cleanup campaigns and under the scouring blades and grinding treads of bulldozers. I lately hauled off three large trailerloads to the dump in a gully on the Booker. . . . Thus transits glory.

A few years after the Bookers moved to town, the Kyles left White Bluff too, selling out, and both farms continued their long slide downhill toward extinction, cotton-farmed by tenants. Cedar furred the erstwhile grassy hills and pushed at the edges of the fields; old boundary fences rusted away and were not replaced; and much of the neighborhood became again for practical purposes open range, minimally sustaining a population of random kine. The Tonk Nation expanded its boundaries down White Bluff's watershed, its weapons cedar and erosion and exhaustion. Whiskey and posts and a little subsistence farming—those were what you could do in the hills, after the cotton and the grass played out and the cedar moved in. . . . The cedar people asked less of the land and of life than those who had come before; the land had much less to give.

Not that they were all tamely alike, the cedar folk; they had the frontier too close behind them for that. They were a number of different possible things in a number of different combinations—religious, pagan, upright, debased, drunken and brawling, sober and withdrawn, hardworking, lazy—in short, human. There was a narrower gamut of things for them to be in that small world, of course, but they tended to make up for that by being what they were far more emphatically than most people these days are anything. If a man was broilsome, he was likely to go whole-hog about it, utilizing tire irons and stones and teeth. If he liked you, he was a rock of loyalty, but his grudges were durable also. If a family was reclusive and looked darkly on the world of men, its members might act as did the "big old boys" of a tenant clan that inhabited the Booker for a while—bearded and longhaired and barefoot, it is said, they would scatter to brush like quail if you drove up to the house and would stare out at you from hiding. . . .

What the cedar people were was sort of more so. What they were not was washed-out, inept, red-clay poor whites of the sort that were common in parts of the older cotton states. It was that era and conditions were similar, but the people were somehow not like that. If some were sour or desperate or drunken or violent or degenerate, they generally were so energetically. Maybe the absence of Negroes or of a strong class structure made a difference; maybe the minerals in greens and things from limestone soils, thinning though they were, maintained Tonk Nationals' vigor. . . .

Six or eight old whiskey-still sites from the moonshine era have turned up on my place, mainly uncovered by bulldozers clearing brush, and I have no doubt others are around. There is not much to them—a few pink-scorched slabs of stone that held the pot above the fire, often some barrel hoops, a scatter of mason jars intact or shattered, the creek or a branch nearby for water. The stills themselves were too valuable ever to have been left. Hearty old moonshiners' legends involving big drunks and fights and lawmen's raids and harrowing horseback chases and escapes attach to a couple of the sites, but I don't know who practiced his craft at the rest. One family that lived on the place for a time had skill in that profession, but both homesteads were sometimes vacant, and people from miles away might set up an operation there to avoid being identified with it if it was found. "Joints," they were called, by those who ran them.

Hearty tales aside, it was not a truly jovial trade, what

with alien armed lawmen snooping about the country in disguise, and the armed hill folks' short-fused belief in people's minding their own business. Killing was uncommon, and there was a set of fair-play rules accepted by most of the lawmen and lawbreakers that avoided some bloodletting, but for a good many years it was fairly easy to get hurt back in the cedar. Near the lower end of my property, White Bluff Creek cascades off an eroded ledge into a shallow pool, a pleasant spot where children like to splash in summer and their elders can watch from the thick shade of an overhanging elm. Once an enterprising deputy—sniffing around without his bosses' knowledge, the story says (there being moral subtleties in these things)—found a still in the cedar nearby, poured out its contents, and was toting it off down the creekbed when, just above the fall, a twenty-two bullet ricocheted off the stone beside his moving feet, in warning.

"Shoot!" he called back over his shoulder without even breaking stride, whereupon they fired a twelve gauge loaded with birdshot, spattering him from afar.

"Shoot!" he yelled still walking, and that was when they unlimbered the thirty-thirty. He was hit, reports agree, "square in the butt," and survived. . . .

That was thirty or forty years ago, but remembrance lingers in the cedar; I was told a year or so since by an aging native that he could if he wanted, which he did not, lead me directly to a stone on one of my brushy steep hills beneath which rested the cartridge case belonging to that bullet. He hadn't fired it, but he knew where it was. . . . Wandering up there among cedar and shin oak and poison ivy, I have rested in the spot where the outraged snipers must have sat to fire, a bald ledge with a fine view down the creek eighty or a hundred feet below, and have, to confess a childishness, drawn a bead with a rifle on a boulder in the streambed. I have not searched for the shell case, but it is somehow comforting to know it is there. And since bulldozers will probably never

33

scale and scour those heights, there it will likely remain.

All the cedar natives were first-rate axemen in the tradition of their woodland forebears, though long restriction to cedar specialized them like yucca moths or koala bears, and now that the cedar is disappearing, so are they. Those who are not disappearing are changing into something else. . . . Nor is the dwindling of the cedar so much a cause as a symptom of the change. Outsiders like me buy up the old homesteads and lump them into larger holdings, clearing and fencing and replanting and arranging them as stock farms or ranches. Wars and conscription and boom and recession stir the nation with great spoons. Fat wages in cities far and near pull the people from the land in that general urban drift of our time, strongest out of hardship country like the Tonk Nation. Women tug their men toward the world the TV lays before them, in the belief that it exists. Thus fewer and fewer natives cut posts full-time these days, even where there are posts to be cut, and more leave each year, though many keep on living here while holding down city jobs, driving a hundred miles or more every day. For the old attachment to the hills is tight—maybe tighter, paradoxically, in these people born in the hard cedar times than it was in their predecessors and kinsmen who knew the country fresh and strong, and used up the freshness and strength with long-horned cows and cotton, and moved along elsewhere without many backward glances.

The cedar-choppers you see at present are often migratory unlocal types, working up and down the cedar regions of the state from near the Rio Grande to the Palo Pinto country northwest of Somervell. These are a strange and gypsy breed, some of them Mexicans now but more out of the old Hibernian stock, cut loose from whatever local roots they may once have had but tied by long habit to a single species of vegetation and the hills on which it grows. Like koala bears and eucalyptus trees, or the little bird called the golden-cheeked warbler, which nests only in the Texas cedar and is shrinking in numbers as the cedar regions shrink and change, just as it must have burgeoned when they were spreading.

Among such post-cutting migrants the old Scots family bonds, always stout, sometimes grow crazily tight against a hostile and incomprehensible outside world. Many refuse to put their children into schools, hauling them up and down the hills in decrepit flatbed trucks, to live for a few weeks or a few months in some rented or preempted shack near where there is cedar to cut. Whole clans show up in the brakes to work as a crew, father and mother and grown sons and their wives and a taciturn tangle of smudge-faced barefoot young ones. At noon the women build little fires and cook, and in the evening the old truck grinds out of the brake sitting on its axles under the burden of a great load of aromatic posts and of the people perched on top, not looking at you. . . .

A family like that frequented my place for a time, getting the posts out of an area that was to be bulldozed. One day I was working through the cedar, lopping off limbs with a light camp axe to make a line of markers to guide the dozer man when he came. The patriarch of the chopper clan came over to talk, ostensibly about the dachshund I had with me, for anything that looks like a hound has fascination for those folks. But while he pulled the little dog's ears and crooned to it, he watched me corneringly with long, shapely, slightly mad, pale-blue eyes as I hacked at twigs and branches, an alien amateur.

He said finally, unable not to: "Shame you got to work with a little old shitty play-toy axe like that. And hit not even sharp."

4 ≈ The Forging of a Squireen ≈≈≈≈≈≈≈≈≈≈

It was during an odd good interim time of life when I first noticed this piece of land. Years before, I had left Texas more or less for good, I thought, but I had come back now because of sickness in the family and was unsure, without worrying about it much, where I would go next or when. Not a real traveler but a moseyer and sojourner who had bogged down in a number of different places for a while, mainly pleasant places, to live and work till something pulled me elsewhere, I knew there would be other places to live and work, but just now I was in between.

It was a time of looking again at the part of the world I had known in youth, and learning with some surprise that I would never know any other part as well, and learning too how much I still did not know about it. I was reading a lot—books of local lore and natural history and such things for the most part—and was doing a good bit of floating down rivers and poking through stretches of country I had known well or slightly long before. These are juvenile activities, I suppose, in a businesslike nation and time, and certainly having the leisure on your hands for them is a juvenile sort of privilege these days. But you learn to make certain swaps in life if life lets you do so and if you are built that way—leave me out but let me be, is the most common of such arrangements—and the fact is that such juvenilities can mean a lot more to you grown than they ever did when you were young.

The pretty, exhausted Paluxy hills were one piece of country I frequented then. Periodically I spent days at a time on a friend's ranch there, camping with a bedroll on the shaky floors of abandoned little farmhouses, broiling wild or bought meat in their limestone fireplaces or over coals on the ground outside, sometimes with a typewriter and a few books for self-justification, often with just a shotgun and maybe a fieldglass and an urge to walk through the cedar and down the stony creeks and branches and to loiter beneath china-berry trees in erstwhile dooryards. The ranch was being cleared of brush and put back to grass piece by piece, old homestead by homestead, and in some of the newly bared pastures, with the seedy herbs and weeds that sprang up first from the torn earth, bobwhite quail were thick. But mainly by myself I sought less formal game if any. Most of the pastures, like the ruined houses in which I stayed, had old family names attached to them that the foreman and others of the region used, the Alabama and Tennessee and South Texas surnames of people who had once owned them and farmed those parts that could be farmed.

There was one January day of solid milkwhite scudding clouds, with a cruel steady wind off the plains to the northwest and a temperature in the twenties. After lunch I put a crotch of liveoak on the fire to keep it going, and went out. I stuck to cedar, which stops the wind and is a good place to be on a day like that, though suffocating in summer. It stopped sound too, the big wind itself only a susurration in the bending treetips overhead. I ran across a few scrub cows, someone's, snorty and shy as cattle in brush nearly always get to be, and once disturbed a deer, hearing its alarm-cough and seeing only its rump and flag as it thumped away through the interlocked evergreens. Occasionally juncoes and cardinals and other small finches twitted as I passed, and in one deep flat-bottomed draw thousands of robins were feeding on cedar berries, but even their yelping seemed quiet because of the kind of day and place it was.

On a hillside in a bald rock-and-caliche clearing, I stopped and looked out over the valley of the Paluxy at people's fields and barns and watertanks and houses far away, and felt the fine privacy that aloneness and the cedar and the hostile shoving wind overhead had compounded among them. I had long since gotten off of my friend's property into country where I had not been before, a trespasser, but in those years old owners and tenants had mainly left the hills and few new ones had yet showed up. The places I was crossing were abandoned, their rusty fences down, their little fields thick with brush, occasional old roads through the cedar over-grown, washed out, impassable except on foot.

At the bottom of that hill, having thrashed down through a thicket of scrub oak and elbow brush, I struck a stream that had to be White Bluff Creek, running fast and clear over solid ledge rock, with skim ice at the fringes of its pools. I followed it down a way, north into the wind, then crossed it on some strewn dry-topped boulders and headed up a shel-tered branch. Out of a triple-boled elm in a flat beside the branch I shot two squirrels and missed a third that ducked into a hole or a hollowed crotch, and I built a little hot dead-stick fire to warm myself while I skinned and cleaned the kill. Afterward I looked around, and farther away from the branch on the same flat of good dark soil that the elm was rooted in, found that the cedar dwindled to scrub size and the land rose gently westward in what had once been a field. At that lower end someone had had a garden long before; a piece of crumpled netwire fence had been interwoven with cedar branches and bits of tin and old car parts to keep rabbits and other nibblers out. It had the melancholy and mystery and unlikelihood of old human things found in wild places, and the pathos.

That was on the old Kyle part of what is now Hard Scrabble. The garden is now my garden, though fenced less picturesquely, and my house is notched into the lower hillside just above. For air and grass and for safety from fire most of the cedar just there has been dozed out or cut, but on summer mornings when I wake on the screen porch I study out faces and figures shaped by the big triple elm's thick-leaved branches, and those of the liveoaks all around. I have seen Adolph Hitler there, and Queen Nefertiti, and a grinning Mexican vaquero, and dozens of other personalities and fantasms. Once discerned through a musing morning eye they meet the gaze clearly on subsequent mornings, old friends, until leaf growth or a windstorm or the autumn wipes them out. Few last over from year to year, though I remember one skull-like miser countenance that endured for two or three summers. . . .

Late that cold afternoon as I came out of the cedar on the place where I was camped, the wind had turned arctic and bitter and was flecked with sleet that stung my face. Despite walking, the meat of my legs and buttocks felt cold two inches in as I slogged across new-cleared land among dry sunflower stalks and charred snags where bulldozed cedar had been stacked and burned. A half-mile from the house the foreman of the ranch came bumping out in his pickup across a gullied old field and I got in with him gratefully to ride the rest of the way.

"Worst blow this winter so far," he said. "He promised to send out a load of hay. Hit don't get here tonight, we're fixing to lose some cows. Radio says it's supposed to snow and snow some more and get down to ten by morning."

Unspecific "he" in those conversations was always the

friend who owned the ranch; I was close to both of them and never took sides in such matters. We talked about cows and weather a little, and got to the old house where my things were. I stirred and fed the fire and got the squirrels browned and put them to boil in a pot with potatoes and onions and bacon. The foreman said by God he recollected old Alec Barcus had kept some whiskey hid out around that place when he was staying there and building fence the year before.

I agreed it was a whiskey sort of evening, and going out he came back in a while with a two-quart mason jar half full, slapping it on the bottom and counting according to some formula as the bubbles rose to the top and disappeared. "Not very stout," he said. "I bet old man Jack Sneed made it, boiling it off too fast. Alec he had it stuck in the goat shed, back of some big old rocks."

Like most of that whiskey it was raw and oily, but it tasted all right with the wind and the sleet outside and the cold on our backs away from the fire, in the old house with broken windows, and doors that would not fully shut. After two or three drinks I felt warmth seeping back into my legs. I do not remember much that we talked about, but we talked. I recall telling Davis how they plugged screw-worm wounds with mud in Mexico, and the taste or smell of the whiskey got him off onto Crossroads, Texas, capital of the Tonk Nation in the thirties, where on Saturday afternoons the hardier elements from the hills would foregather to drink and tell stories and play cards and perhaps to fight, for fun. If someone was running off a batch of whiskey they might meet at his "joint," though more serious distillers did not encourage such assemblies.

"Me a little old kid a watching," Davis said. "Make your blood run cold. You take old Bill McCauley. Tall, them long arms, whitey-blond hair just like a little cottontop shaver. Never used no fists, just circle around till he could get him a bear hug on a man, and then commence to eating. Ear, nose, cheek, anywheres his mouth was at. Just chomp down and turn his old whitey head patooey and spit out a hunk of meat and go back to chomping again. Only he never chomped more than about once till they started hollering calf rope. The thing was to stay outside that bear holt of his. . . ."

From these gentle topics we progressed to others, and then the squirrels were ready and we ate them, and he went off to worry about his load of hay some more. I stoked the fire with cedar stumps and listened to the wind blow outside and thought about what a good day it had somehow been. Then by lantern I read for a while in Scott's *Kenilworth*, which was one of a jumble of books I had brought. Its high derring-do romance and higher language seemed a long way from Somervell County, Texas, except perhaps in ingrained Britannic violence. There were plenty of people in Elizabeth Tudor's England who would chomp your ear, or slice it off with a sword. . . . Finally, even with the fire and a heavy jacket, the bitter air forcing its way through the house's apertures drove me to my bed on the floor. In the morning there was thick snow on the pastures and the cedar, and no wind, and a clear blue sky, and far off I could hear Davis wailing a long long howl at cows to come and be fed. His hay had arrived.

It was a pleasant segment of life, that year or so, one of the unencumbered clear-minded interim times that come after one way of being has ended for you, though you may not yet know that, and before another has set in. They do not last, such times, not unless you have built a better wall against life's insistences than I have ever managed to do. And maybe, for that matter, they are not supposed to last. . . .

To that point in my life I had never much wanted to own anything that could not travel with me or that I could not walk away from, selling it or giving it away or leaving it where it was. There was nothing wrong with sailboats and furniture and books and such things, but if they were worth having you still owned them in your head after you walked away from them. . . . But inside me somewhere there had always been the incipient disease of land, or it seems so now looking back. Land mattered, and even in peasant villages in foreign mountains I had cared to know that a man owned a patch of terrace with vines and olive trees, and what it produced for him, and how the grazing was for sheep and goats on the gnawed slopes thereabout. I had never managed to purge myself of the simple yeoman notion, contracted in childhood from kinsmen looking back to a rural past, that grass and crops and trees and livestock and wild things and water mattered somehow supremely, that you were not whole unless you had a stake in them, a daily knowledge of them.

The casual interim time blended and then changed into what came next—being at home again perhaps for good, married, teaching in a college, wearing a tie and coat most days, restricted by the unjuvenile shape of life from going off to poke around patches of country for days at a time when a whim said that was what to do. . . .

With such relative respectable stability came ownership of various kinds, not merely of portable objects and not solely in the head. And with the acceptance of any ownership, if you are built a certain way, come thoughts of ownership of land. The trouble—I suppose it was a trouble—was that I was thinking then of land in terms of that interim time. Terms of aloneness, of hunting and poking about, of secret cedar places from whence you could peer out at the far world of other men without having to feel yourself a part of it, of enjoyment rather than use. Maybe it is by such vulnerability to mood that romantics and drifters ultimately bare themselves to the scratchiness of a practical world. For sooner or later a mood is going to commit you to something more or less lasting. And if, in terms of land, it commits you not to wide deep flat bottomland fields and grassy rolling pastures all tamed and manageable, such as the practical world has had the good sense to choose unto itself over the ages, but instead to a collection of wild rough rocky cedar hills traversed by water that bubbles and swirls clear over solid ledge limestone, then the practical world is going to get its kicks watching you sweat when the Ownership Syndrome brings you, as it will, to the fevered stage of trying to make your rocky acres useful. . . .

At any rate, I asked about the place where the triple elm stood, and went there once with an old real-estate man and the townsman who owned it then, and walked over the easier parts of it with them, and watched as they knelt ritually and drank from the creek to prove to me it was pure, which I already believed, having drunk from other parts of it often myself. But the tract had lain abandoned for so long that the original road into it had been fenced off and the question of legal access was clouded; therefore I couldn't get a land loan I needed through a state veterans' loan program which had grown puritanically difficult after a period of free-wheeling corruption and some scandals.

Nevertheless I had let myself want that place. From a distance and over a period of time, with some jealousy, I watched it pass into the hands of a new owner, and then into those of a third, though unused still and unchanged. And finally I managed to buy it, after some haggling over price and over a guarantee of access, and also after some family consultation. (We got thoroughly lost searching along criss-crossed old post-cutters' trails for the plank shack on its hillside, and the creek was a tepid trickle because there had been no rain since May, and the horseflies in their hundreds drilled us where clothes clung to our skin, and the hot July wind murmured overhead but did not touch us in the cedar. There-

43

fore the place's private magic did not much dent my wife's awareness until later, when she had been for maybe a year or more, by virtue of the Texas community-property laws, its indisputable co-proprietor. . . .)

One bright cool day in November of that year, 1960, with all the papers signed, I drove in on a bumpy new road dozed out through the cedar to the hillside where the Kyles' disastrous house stood gray and leaning beneath the weight of its years and its ingenious kitchen roof, and put my boots to earth with a mingled set of feelings, some of them new to my experience. There was a kind of resentment, because I had spent most of forty years refusing to own things. Against that, there was a bit of bourgeois pride in possession, a tinge of the territorial imperative at work. And there was something else. Down inside somewhere, I believed that in that sorry, wornout, wrinkled polygon of dirt and rocks and brush I had bought a piece of the unencumbered interim time, to have and hold forever. . . .

Is there (shall we generalize?) in most of us, down inside somewhere, a memory of such a time, maybe not even personal but racial, and a stout yearning back toward it? . . . I know some anthropologists have said they think there is. I know too about the "nasty, brutish, and short" view of primitive life and have no doubt it was often so, but this other thing is something else, not typical perhaps but nonetheless powerfully real. . . . A green-and-golden Eden time before farming and complex societies, when the Old World's climate and human brains and simple tools let Stone Age hunters and gatherers lead an uncluttered hearty life, with spare time to savor what was killed and picked and dug, to develop a little discernment and wonder about forces that worked unseen, and doubtless to chomp off one another's ears and noses, exuberantly . . . It is not hard to believe there may have been more than one or two such eras in the interstices of the European glacial cycles and elsewhere on the earth, and that our genes and guts remember them, with sadness or madness for the most part nowadays.

Not that I claim to have studied out such thoughts beside the Kyle house on that November day, scuffing at fragments of old brown snuff bottles with my heel. I had Hard Scrabble, the first part of it. Or it had me.

5 ≋ *Of the Lay of Things, and a Creek* ≋≋≋≋≋≋≋≋≋

But the land, whither ye go to possess it, is a land of hills and valleys, and drinketh water of the rain of heaven.

DEUTERONOMY 11:11

Of how that conviction of owning a piece of golden unencumbered time fared within the stew of desires and impatiences and satisfactions and commitments that starts to boil in you when you buy land, there may be more to say. Now, though, it may be worthwhile to try to get down a part of what Hard Scrabble consists of as a place, a piece of country, a segment of the rough Tonk Nation.

Made up of the Kyle homestead and the Booker which was added on a few years later, it covers about 380 acres or so, only a part of which has been measured with care—the original surveys around these hills were for the most part loose and generous, and sometimes vary widely from the acreage actually under fence. Outlined on a map or an aerial photograph, the shape of the whole thing resembles nothing much either organic or geometric, though I have occasionally thought to discern in it a sort of flat-topped knight's helm with the visor off, or a grinning idiot robot's head. Part of the east boundary runs more or less along the divide between White Bluff Creek's drainage basin and that of the next watercourse over, and a short segment on the west runs nominally along a branch, but no other stretches of the boundary correspond to natural features. Of the dozen or so noticeable turns and corners in its outer fences, only two even approximate ninety degrees, for while some of the Tonk Nation is sliced into neat American rectangles of ownership, its topography and its shortage of arable field land sometimes dictated less arbitrary lines when it was parceled out in the last century. These parts that were sold off late often came out whopperjawed.

Like the Nile in at least one way, White Bluff flows north, and it snakes across the place well to the west of center, the land on either side sloping down toward it and draining to it either directly or by way of winding draws and branches. From the hump of the high flat in the east "mountain" pasture of the Booker, about nine hundred feet above sea level, to the low point where the creek leaves the property on the north, there is a fall of some two hundred feet. To people accustomed to real hills that may sound like little difference, but there are a good many ups and downs between and all around; you might say that Hard Scrabble makes the most of what difference it has. Like most of the Nation it is not so much hilled as hilly, the carved terrain rising to noses and saddles and ridges rather than to individual protuberances, though down toward Bosque County where the typical Grand Prairie starts and the land flattens and rolls, separate heights often loom alone and have names.

The Nation's general landscape is perhaps best described by the pleasant Spanish word *accidentado*. You can see a long way from high places—thirty or forty miles sometimes, into different kinds of country—but you can seldom see

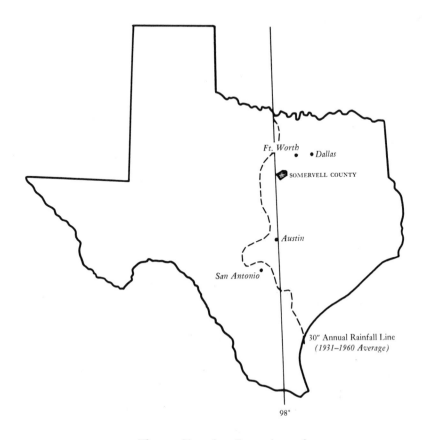

Ft. Worth
● ●Dallas

SOMERVELL COUNTY

● Austin

San Antonio ●

30″ Annual Rainfall Line
(1931–1960 Average)

98°

Texas, Showing Location of
Somervell County

more than a small part of what lies between you and the limit of your vision, because of the folds and gouges in the earth's dissected surface. Thus after years of being in the region you can drive along a road long familiar to you, and at some point can glance in a direction that your eyes happen never to have taken before, and you may find just disappearing behind a nose of land an old house you did not know was there. Early dwellings were often built in valleys, for shelter and for water and for proximity to the best field land; most have privacy, and a view that is not wide but intimate. Standing on one of their drooping porches, or only at a spot where junk and worked stones show that a house used to be, you see the farm's own fields and hillsides and a part of the shape of the valley in which it lies, made crooked by dark heights nosing in from either side.

The high eastern part of Hard Scrabble is one of the terminal prongs of a long rather flat-topped ridge stretching up out of the south. It has good, dark, but not very deep soil over clay and parent rock, but the hillsides dropping off from it are brushy and steep and cut by ravines, with level gray-weathered ledges of differently aged and textured limestone outcropping at intervals from top to bottom, and caliche and clay and soil and brittle talus in between. On the smaller part of the property west of the creek the slopes are easier, except for a long wooded scarp that borders the stream toward the south, called the Booker Bluff by natives, and an abrupt hillside with great tumbled undercut boulders above the waterfall on the north.

On either hand at the bottoms of the hills are intermittent fairly flat strips of soil fit for reasonably unexploitive agriculture. These add up to fifty or more acres in all, including some brushy patches not now in use as fields, though a good deal more than that was farmed on the place in the halcyon past, when the old-timers aimed their mules and walking plows as far up the hillsides as they could go without hitting ledge rock, and sometimes a little farther, to judge by the rusty enigmatic shards of implement iron one finds. But those steeper plowlands are now washed down to rock or gullied subsoil, as it was assured they should be when cotton showed up in the region. The remaining bits of usable field land, all of them with some slope toward the creek or the branches, have been eroded too and in places are sandy or stony. But in most the topsoil still tends toward the original darkish

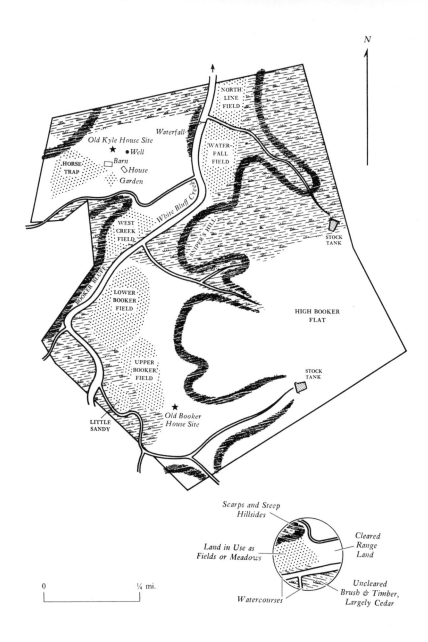

N

Old Kyle House Site
★ • Well
HORSE
TRAP
☐ Barn
◇ House
Garden

Waterfall

NORTH
LINE
FIELD

WATER-
FALL
FIELD

White Bluff Creek

WEST
CREEK
FIELD

SNYPER'S HILL

STOCK
TANK

BOOKER BLUFF

LOWER
BOOKER
FIELD

HIGH BOOKER
FLAT

UPPER
BOOKER
FIELD

STOCK
TANK

LITTLE
SANDY

*Old Booker
House Site*
★

*Scarps and Steep
Hillsides*

*Cleared
Range
Land*

*Land in Use as
Fields or Meadows*

*Uncleared
Brush & Timber,
Largely Cedar*

Watercourses

0   ¼ mi.

HARD SCRABBLE

50

prairie loam, underlain by adobe and gravel deposited by White Bluff in past ages as its course shifted and wavered about in the valley, and deeper down by the thick bed of limestone over which the creek now flows.

Names get attached to the individual fields because you need names as you work them and sow them to different forage crops. In terms of the place's function they matter more than any of the other land, and you tend to watch them closely and to know their varying traits. The West Creek field, for instance, is the flattest and richest of all and the least damaged by old use, with heavy soil that stays unworkable for a good while after rains. The North Line field and the Waterfall field, most recently renovated, are full of hardwood roots that keep sending up sprouts and trying to reestablish the old anarchy, notably oak roots whose solidity defies all implements. The creekside part of the Lower Booker is cluttered with stones that need removal, and the Booker Little Sandy, a two-acre patch surrounded by woods, gets eaten down by deer. And so on . . .

White Bluff Creek's own unspectacular name probably derives from a layered low cliff a mile upstream from Hard Scrabble, at a point where the creek's two main upper branches merge. Its farthest points of origin, in ravines that pleat the northeast slope of the Chalk Mountain ridge, are only about five miles distant from our place as the crow is supposed to fly, though most years in these parts we have few crows, which seem to stay in richer farming regions, wise parasites of affluence. Nearly all the channels in the creek's network slice down to solid bedrock, with frequent shallow accumulations of white limestone gravel and rounded flat boulders, for the steepness of the country and occasional rapid runoff create scouring flows that prevent the formation of long sand- and silt-bottomed stretches of the sort you see in flatland streams. These same rises also smash and carry off those expendable sections of fence known as watergaps, however ingeniously one may erect them.

On Hard Scrabble the creek's cut banks, except in a few shelving grassed and timbered places, are mainly either flaky nodular limestone—known as shell rock in the county—or naked dirt walls up to twelve or fifteen feet high, where you can study the dark topsoil full of roots and the underlying adobe and gravel above bedrock as in a soils textbook. Swallows and kingfishers sometimes have nestholes in the taller dirt bluffs, and here and there at their bases inconspicuous seep springs issue over the rock and into the creek, dependable in all but the worst dry seasons. This is the rain that has entered the soil and is percolating by gravity toward its eternal starting point and destination, the sea.

Where White Bluff makes sharp bends against hills it has gouged out pools up to six or seven feet deep, with shallower ones in other spots like the little basin below the waterfall. The inside banks of the bend pools have humped beaches of sandy gravel, for the fine stuff tends to swirl out and settle in such places while coarser materials are rammed on around the bends and strewn out in long bars and boulder-jumbles, where they block and twist the stream's progress and make it talk. Deposits in the creekbed change unpredictably from season to season and year to year as the big rises work on them, sometimes giving and sometimes taking away, so that where in November you noted with satisfaction a good accessible bed of concrete or road gravel, in April when you go to fetch some there may be nothing but bald stone. A landmark boulder weighing tons, bearing a name bestowed on it by your kids, may vanish utterly. Pools fill with gravel, then scour deep again. I remember one long mound of washed pure sand, a rarity in this creek, that stayed where it was, smoothed and replenished occasionally by rises, for two or three years while I hauled tractor-scooploads and pickup-loads off for mortar and children's playboxes and floorslab padding and such things, and then one spring it was whisked away, and has not since been built again. Maybe it was the quirk creation of some big skew-laid boulder that bounced the current a certain way for a time, but then shifted; deposition is a complex thing. A friend of mine who owned a ranch alongside a wide strong river once shoved a huge tangle of railroad iron and cables and wire into it at a bend to stop bank erosion, and within a year, somewhat to his embarrassment, had picked up about ninety acres or so of new land at the expense of the owners on the other shore.

Our creek is fed by no main gushing springs these days, but gets its flow from many shallow sources throughout the ten thousand acres or so of territory that it drains. Hence it depends not only on rainfall year by year but also on the way the land receives and handles the rain. For where there are good grass and humus—or even terraces and contour-furrowed fields—to slow runoff and soak it up and feed it to the subsoil, rainwater is rationed to a stream system over a long period of time and the stream flows steadily, with fewer flood-peaks and fewer spells of drouthy trickle. In this part of Texas, where a reasonable-sounding thirty-two-plus inches of precipitation per year—not much different from parts of wet England—tend to fall in restricted seasons and in un-reasonable big downpours, with weeks or months of bright windy arid weather in between, the maintenance of this rationing process is crucial for the creeks and rivers, and for the land itself.

Nature, which invented the process, did a pretty good job of maintaining it, as old descriptions of the region testify. Man as usual has not. There exist no long-kept hydrologic records for the Paluxy and its basin, to study and interpret, but the main outline of the train of events that over the past century has degenerated White Bluff and the region's other small watercourses from pleasant useful streams into flashy channels, prone to flood-or-trickle extremes of flow, is not hard to make out. We already looked at it. . . . The hills were gnawed bare and the fields were worked hard and fecklessly, and wind and water had their way with the dirt till finally the land's surface, once spongy, could soak up only a little rain at a time and the rest sloshed away downhill, carrying more dirt with it as it went.

The cedar as it tightened its hold upon the country must have helped a little, shielding the earth from the rain's full pounding and laying down an absorptive mat of shed needles, but it was a skimpy substitute for what had been, for thick grass and humus. So when it rained the streams ran big and muddy and chewed their banks into shapes the Tonkawas had not known. And when it did not rain they ran low or not at all, and their pools stagnated and shrank and stank under the sun, and where did all those fish of George Wilkins Kendall's go? . . .

In recent years our creek has never really flooded— jumped the cut banks and inundated bordering field land. Older neighbors remember times when it did, one being in the twenties or thirties when huge rains backed the Paluxy into swollen White Bluff till water was lapping at the hillside ledge where my house now stands, thirty-five or forty feet above the creekbed and a thousand feet distant from it. But fierce rises within the creek's banks are still frequent enough, coming mainly in spring and fall when big rains hit already saturated land and flow off fast. As the country sheds the falling rain, the creek changes from an innocent clear runnel, where children can paddle and laugh, into a wide brown forceful thrust that sluices over a four- or five-foot waterfall with nothing but a rolling boil to show the bottom is not flat. Vagrant cottonwoods and cedars and sycamores slide down it, catching the bottom from time to time and cartwheeling roots over teakettle as the current lashes them on, and beneath the water's roar you can hear the grind and thump of the gravel and rocks it is shoving along as well.

You can be marooned at Hard Scrabble for a day or so

sometimes when the creek gets up that way, for the entrance road fords it on my northern neighbor's place. Once when I thought I had to get out—there was an airplane to catch, or something—I picked a wide and relatively shallow place and waded. But I lost a pair of boots from under my arm while doing it and nearly lost a good strong-swimming dog, not to mention my own brash self, and I have not since opposed my will to White Bluff's when it roars. Often in wet weather we leave a car on the outer bank, but wait till the stream is wadable before trying to reach it—most often a matter of only three or four hours after the rain has stopped.

If water matters to you (and if it doesn't, I expect you have started thinking about skipping to the next chapter, as you should), you are likely to take occasional sodden rambles during big downpours, studying the branches to see whether they are running clear or muddy and therefore whether you are losing soil, checking terraces and ditches you have built to catch runoff and divert it from land that could erode, perching soaked above the creek itself to watch its maniac force, sloshing through black mud to confirm your foreboding that the middle watergap, an engineering masterwork that took a day to build a month before, has snagged a wandering tree and been washed away entire. At such times I often have a pessimistic feeling that the creek is going to attack its dirt bluffs and cave away great slices from them, menacing the indispensable small fields above. But it seldom seems to do so now, having long ago bullied out enough elbow room for its usual tantrums. With rocks and gravel and sand it does keep grinding away at its own bed, though—cleansing it of algae and weeds and small trees grown during periods of low flow, and making gradual lasting changes in its contours. The shellrock ledge over which the waterfall plunges has been eaten away upstream ten feet or more in the brief period of my ownership, a rate of travel that will move the waterfall clear outside Hard Scrabble's south boundary in another mere five thousand years or so. . . .

For all the drama of these occasional spates, it is during the months—sometimes stretching to a year or more—of puny flow that you can best see the country's plumbing at work, and take the most interest in it. Because it is then that water really begins to matter to people along Ninety-eight and westward, in a way that it can seldom matter to those in regions where moisture levels are more in line with what Anglo-Saxons and North Europeans have been ancestrally used to. (That ancestral view creates a sort of schizophrenia in a lot of us white Southwesterners, I think; you grow up on rhymes and tales both childish and adult that are full of dripping forests and constant clear cold streams and morning dews, but the reality you know—and love in the way you love things that have entered into you—is a land of drouth-hardy grass and rather stunted trees and watercourses that may or may not have water in them.)

During the Big Drouth of the early 1950's—the worst in at least two centuries, according to people who study such things—White Bluff and its tributaries were bone dry for long periods. It was a fierce time when the climate gods wrinkled their noses at men's and beasts' demands, rolled back the "semi-arid" twenty-inch rainfall line far to the east of where it belongs, and left it sitting there for five or six years running. That drouth probably had as much to do with the destruction of old ways of farming and ranching in our part of the world as did World War II with its social dislocations and technological changes. Operations that were marginal on overworked land, as most of the old ones were, collapsed. Thus progressivists in time may look upon the Big Drouth as beneficent, though it is hard for any Texan of rural bent, remembering, to do anything but make a sour face. Angora goats—browsers of deep-rooted brush—were the only profitable form of livestock around Somervell County in those years, profitable at least to those who could afford to build the net fences they require. There were no profitable crops, hardly anyone here having been set up for irrigation.

Lesser drouths occur irregularly every two or three or four years when a few rainless months deplete soil moisture and cause local pessimists, including me, to start saying the fifties are beginning all over again. Then they break, usually with much more rain than anybody wants. . . . In my few years of experience with Hard Scrabble, White Bluff has gone entirely dry only a couple of times, though it has quit flowing for periods during two or three other years, but with water still in its pools. Nearly always it gets quite low in the hottest months, often disappearing from view beneath thick gravel beds on my northern neighbor's place, only to emerge again beyond him, cooled and filtered, where it runs into the Paluxy across a wide hard ledge, a midnight trysting and carousing spot along a county road.

At critical times, when the sources are low or failing, the creek can do peculiar things, sometimes running fairly well on the upper part of the place where the best springs are, and as far down as the lower of the two main bend pools, called by our children the Deep End, but not at all below. Evaporation is a strong subtractive force in these pools and in the channel stretches where the creek courses over bald sun-heated rock. So is transpiration by the leaves of trees and grasses and crops, whose roots suck up water during the hot days before it reaches the seep springs at the bases of the bluffs. At night both these forces are less active, so there are times, again during critical spells, when the creek trickles by night but not by day. Even when it is carrying water all the time you can see a difference. Early in my time here I was camped alone down at the place most of one hot summer, laboring on the first part of our interminable house. In the evenings, bushed and filthy, I would bathe at the waterfall, wetting myself and soaping and then sitting in the tepid gush to let it pummel my shoulders and neck and head. When the sun had dropped low enough to leave the creek in shadow, it would cool almost immediately, taking on the chill of the springs farther up. And in twilight, having toweled and dressed and sat down in a dry spot to smoke and listen to the frogs and crickets and night birds begin their praise of summer darkness, I would hear the waterfall's voice grow a little louder and deeper and would wade out and feel its strengthened cold shove.

In recent years I have thought to see—wishfully, yes—a gradual halting improvement in White Bluff's summer flow. The Big Drouth, together with rising land prices unlinked to climatic quirks or the land's richness, brought a lot of ownership changes to the Tonk Nation in the fifties and sixties. Many new owners are outsiders like me, often absentee, a fact productive of certain sadnesses inherent in the death of any old way of being, which we may consider sooner or later but not right here. Some speculative types leave their new land as it is, often leasing it to a local who, as the saying goes, "loads cows in there till their tails are hanging over the fence." But maybe most new owners come down on weekends and whenever else they can, hacking at weeds and brush, fixing up old houses or building cabins, slowly or quickly succumbing to the Ownership Syndrome affliction that makes them want to bring it back into shape. They clear brush and crossfence and build dams and terraces and corrals and barns; they nurse and cajole old fields and hillsides into stands of coastal bermuda and other fancy grasses; and in general they spend a good deal more money on their places than the IRS is going to want to let them deduct, come April. Many locals who have held onto their land are also bringing it back into condition with these new yet old techniques, forgotten by the forefathers on the long drifting road from Ulster and only available now, in the monstrous degree needed, by courtesy of rampaging Caterpillar dozers and three decades of hard, almost religious work by soil conservationists, governmental and otherwise.

(It is ironic, to a nonprogressivist at least, that most genuine progress in our gadgetful frantic age is likely to turn out to be backward progress toward what ought to be—toward what in fact once was. Maybe, I think, the old red horseback overlords of the region are enjoying that irony a little, if they can see it from wherever they are. Not that it will bring back their buffalo, or them. . . .)

All things natural and rural being parts of a whole, most of this land improvement benefits the watercourses too. So that if in White Bluff's ten-thousand-acre basin there are more good grass cover and fewer cedars and expanses of bare gullied ground than there were ten or fifteen years ago, then the creek is a better creek, a little closer to what the Tonks and the Comanches drank from. The shining seep springs that feed it run a little better than they did; the spates are not so strong. No full restoration is possible; you do not by wishfulness and engineering and machines rebuild the living grassland topsoil that took thousands of years to develop and a scant few decades to ruin. But there has been a little backward progress.

Yet paradoxically the lower parts of White Bluff have a less dependable flow than they had in the 1930's, during the Nation's worst exhaustion. Old folks and some not all that old swear to this, and I believe them. Not only the creek but some of its branches ran all year long in these downstream reaches, every year, a boon to moonshiners and teetotalers alike.

This unprogressive hydrologic fact has little to do with the land's condition, however, but seems to come from human interference with a bigger water cycle than the local one—from use and abuse of the deep aquifers underneath the region, which get most of their recharge water from surface seepage entering the ground in sandy outcrop zones many miles away. The dependable Trinity Sand formation, into which my well and probably most others in the county are drilled, has its upper surface about 140 or 150 feet beneath the creekbed on my place, with many impermeable layers of shale and clay and rock above it. Through much of the county it used to have full artesian force, as it still does in a diminishing section: higher water elsewhere is pushing at it so that when the overlying layers are drilled through, water flows up out of the hole without having to be pumped. But heavy modern use of the aquifer's water for municipal supply and industry and irrigation, in the thirty or forty Texas counties that tap it, has created what hydrologists call an "overdraft" in places, withdrawals exceeding recharge. Hence in areas like ours the artesian pressure is waning, and along lower White Bluff, where wells and deep ancient fracture springs used to flow and feed the stream, pumps and local rainfall now have to furnish all the water. The trouble has come on slowly—I know of one still-flowing well only about a mile down the Paluxy from my east fence—but inexorably. All things natural and rural being parts of a whole . . .

≋≋≋

Besides being a little bit dry periodically, for reasons we have explored perhaps too much at length, Somervell County in recent decades has generally been Dry as well. Among Dryness's more ardent supporters have been the county's bootleggers, who have little to do with white spirits of local distillation ·(which is, in fact, getting hard to find, not that the loss is a serious one except in sentimental terms). What the bootleggers principally purvey is Pearl beer, a San Antonio brand favored in the region, buying it from wholesalers in Wet cities and hauling it home to sell in their own living rooms or high-fenced backyards, impromptu unlabeled honkytonks that nobody worries much about, unless as sometimes happens they foster mayhem or worse.

They also foster beer cans. Faced with an accumulation of empties, the bootlegger tosses them in the back of his pickup and carries them to a deep ravine not far away but preferably not on his own place, and dumps them in. After they stack up for weeks and months and years, finally a big enough rain comes to wash them away. Except that it doesn't truly wash them away, but rather strews them all the way from the dump to Lake Whitney far down the Brazos, bright red-and-gold testimonials to the region's stout brand loyalty. Glen Rose voted Wet this past year, putting a crimp in the bootleggers' style, but I expect the stockpiled empties will keep coming down to us for a good long while. Only rarely do we get any heavy deposit of them, when freak timing has caused a rise in the creek to subside just when the main load of cans has voyaged this far, and the next rise usually washes them on down. But there are always some, jammed under rocks with pieces of barbed wire and posts from up-stream watergaps, or stranded high on shelving banks. They take forever to rust and become picturesque.

This is just about the only emphatic form of pollution to which White Bluff has been subject in my time. Algae build up during low-flow periods, nourished in part by the synthetic soluble nitrates and phosphates that almost every-one uses now to help field plantings along, but it seldom amounts to much. Pesticides are not much of a problem in the Nation, which except for a few small sandy peanut farms has little row-crop agriculture left, though undoubtedly some cattle-spray residues do run off into streams. Nor are there any towns or industries or great jammed accumulations of animals, not that a poultry-processing plant or a beef feed-lot couldn't change that picture fast. In ten thousand acres there must be a few septic tanks and cesspools overflowing, but the Nation's population is sparse and it is certain that whatever foulness manages to drool streamward is easily digested in the creek's sunny rapids and its filtering sand and gravel beds. Because that is one thing that streams are good for, unless you overdo it as we have in just about all heavily peopled areas now.

So White Bluff is probably still clean enough to drink from, though when I get hot out working I go by preference to seep springs or a running branch, both of them cooler than the creek and more certainly sanitary. The water is good, sweetened by the limestone over which it has passed, with no trace of the salt and alkali that the bigger Texas rivers bring with them out of the west. Fit water, White Bluff's, for an Indian encampment of the sort the valley must have known in better times.

In terms of the place's usefulness, the creek is more of a liability than an advantage. It gives stock water, but stock water is easy enough to provide in dammed ponds, called "tanks" around here, or in troughs fed from wells. The creek is a constantly renewed source of gravel and sand and rocks, but in Somervell County these are not excitingly rare commodities. Its fluctuations keep it from building up good populations of fish and make it more or less useless for irrigation, since during the periods when the garden and the creekside fields could most gratefully use water, the stream is usually shrunk to a trickle. Nor, with its huge rises and the permeable soil of its cut banks, have I been able to envision any sort of strong low dam that would impound some of its water cheaply and dependably. Periodically it cuts us off from the world of men and rips out watergaps, creating trouble and strayed stock and a lot of soggy labor reconstructing things. Goats, which hate getting wet, won't cross it when its flow is more than a dribble, so that when kids are small and vulnerable or when outlaw dogs are running, you can't channel the goats on the other side to some pen near the house for enclosure and protection each night. Therefore functionally the creek is not "good for" much, and for reasons such as these in the past many farmers and small ranchers in Texas have preferred places without "live water" crossing them. Some still do.

But for most of us inveterate romantics, economic function has little to do with the meaning of a stream. Hard Scrabble would be a sadly less interesting piece of land without White Bluff. Despite its deterioration from what is used to be, it is an avenue and magnet for all sorts of wildlife, and on hot summer afternoons its cool shallow pools are fine places to take a dip or to watch youngsters splash safely, while sipping something pleasant and listening to birds. It is a pretty creek, and it mirrors in its ways the history of this land. Uselessness notwithstanding, the feel of its presence and its differing flows and moods is one of the central facts of life on the place.

Which is maybe why it has here managed to grab nearly a whole chapter of this book . . .

6 ≋ *Ghosts* ≋≋≋≋≋≋≋≋≋≋≋≋

They used to say he was the fairest of the laws, old
T. J. Mayes. The roughest too, but fair. Ran mostly by himself, a great big man with a government forty-five. Come
easing down through the cedar quiet like some big men are
quiet. Jump out of the brush and lay down on you with that
big old blue pistol and holler, "You're under arrest!" Chase
you like a track star if you tried to run off from him. Never
had to kill nobody I ever heard of, even if he did splash a
little gravel and lead on some folks that was running a mite
too fast to suit him.

He had him a set of rules and he done what them rules
said, or maybe they was rules from higher up, but he was
the only law that always stuck by them. Had to grab you at
your joint or when you was running off, or he wouldn't take
it to no court. Never told no lies to the judge about what he'd
seen you do, the way most of them done. Him and most of
the other laws they split their time pretty much between
here and Fairfield, east in Freestone County. You know it
was sort of the same over there; they made a lot of bust-head
too.

There was a good many folks around that sort of ap-
preciated old T. J. Mayes, they'd done seen so much of the

other kind of laws. Because he was fair. Smashed up some
good stills when he found them or carried them off to town,
but that was part of the way the rules worked too. I was a
little old barefoot shirttail thing but I seen some of it, tagging
along with Papa, and I heard about most of the rest.

First time I seen him it was November and the Spanish
oaks and shoemakes was all red, and me and Papa was
dropping down off the hill to a joint he had that year here
on this place, and we started to hearing somebody whanging
on some metal. Later on it turned out it was one of them Ott
kids in the family that was living here then; he had got a
hold of some old galvanized stuff and was hammering it
straight to build himself a chicken shed. But we never
knowed that then. Sounded like it was coming straight from
Papa's joint, somebody busting up his rig, and he says to me,
"God damn, son, they're raiding on White Bluff."

So we turned ourselves around and headed out for home.
Except that just back over the hill we run smack into old
T. J. Mayes, walking to where we'd come from. He had been
hearing that whanging too. He says, "Well, Tom. You staying busy?"

"Minding my own," Papa says. "Looking for some squirrels."

"Seems like squirrels is scarce," says old T. J., because we
didn't have a sign of a squirrel about us, except Papa he had a
little old twenty-two target cradled across his arm.

Papa he just looked back at T. J. Mayes, and T. J. grins
and says, "They say Stevie Squires and you, you all had your-
selves a tangle."

Papa says, "If we did it wouldn't have been no tangle."

"Don't reckon it would at that," old T. J. says, because
Papa was much man back then. And he says so long, we say
so long, and that was the first time I ever seen T. J. Mayes.
What I noticed about him mostly was that pistol sticking up
out of an open-top holster, the way kids look at guns. And I
was waiting for Papa to start cussing the laws, but what he

said was, "Son, don't ever let nobody tell you that ain't one hell of a man."

Well, a year or so later Papa had him a joint at what we called the Booker Hole. It was a pool of good water a little way down that draw from where you've got your tank. Had him a kerosene burner. Never made no smoke at all but made a hell of a noise. Whoooo. Roared . . . Except you couldn't tell where it was coming from; it come from everywhere, that noise, sort of filled up a piece of country. You'd stand there and you'd listen and you'd say to yourself, It's over yonder. Then you'd listen some more and decide it was plumb behind you. And then you'd say, Aw hell, it ain't no place at all.

But old T. J. Mayes he must have had different ears. He come sneaking down through the cedar that day when Papa was running off a batch and them two old Calhoun boys was setting there with him and talking and tasting the run. Papa had him a horse tied up, and the Calhouns had come there double on a mule. It was a glass-eye paint, Papa's horse, and everybody in the county knowed whose it was. Well, Papa he got to feeling something the way he used to—never could tell you why but he had them feelings and they was nearly always right. Knowed when an old Confederate uncle of his was dying in Albuquerque. Went to Granbury and bought him a train ticket and when he got to Albuquerque he was right. Things like that . . .

Well, this time when he got the feeling he laid right down on the ground and he looked up through the cedar trunks and he seen old T. J. Mayes's boots a creeping down, tippity-tap, fifty yards away. So he pss-ed and he made a sign, and them Calhoun boys knowed what it was, all right. Never even thought about their mule but busted out through the cedar on the downhill side and I guess they run clear out of the country. But Papa he grabbed his horse and he taken out south a loping, three or four miles till he come to the house on the old Barney place, with nobody living in it then.

66

His horse was plumb blowed. He tied it up in the yard and he sort of eased out of there not making no tracks, and he come on home to supper. Put us kids to watching the road till it was dark, but we never seen a soul.

Old T. J. Mayes he heard them busting out of the joint, and he run down there but they had hauled, that old burner still a roaring and the whiskey still a dripping in a jug. So he grabbed that Calhoun mule and he lit out after Papa, cutting sign. He could read sign pretty near as good as Papa could. . . . But none of the Calhouns had ever got that mule out of a trot, and T. J. Mayes he couldn't neither. Went trotting across them hills a whacking on that mule and reading sign, and by the time he reached the Barney place I guess Papa was plumb home.

So T. J. Mayes he untied Papa's paint horse and he led it behind the mule back to that joint, trotting all the way. And he tumped the still over and run the mash out on the ground, and he shot it full of holes and he beat it flat with a green oak club. Busted the jars of whiskey they had done run off and that fancy burner too, except Papa said he never missed that loud old thing. And in a week or so him and Papa they run across each other on the square down in the town, and old T. J. Mayes he said, "Tom, I carried your paint horse back home the other day and put him in your pasture."

But Papa he looks him in the eye and he says, "Crap. You never carried no horse of mine nowhere. . . ."

Had him a heart attact one day when he was chasing a fellow over in Freestone, in a car. That fellow must of felt like Papa did about old T. J. Mayes, because what he done when he seen there was something funny, he turned around and drove back there and carried old T. J. to the doctor. . . .

Oh, there was stories. . . . There was the time Dick Belden whupped old Bill McCauley, sitting straddle him on the ground with rocks in both his hands, whanging him left and then right and old Bill he never did say quit. There was the time Luke Whatley pulled a knife, so they stuck him in a cotton sack and strung it up in a tree till he had done cooled off. There was—well, take that fuss between Papa and Stevie Squires, the one old T. J. Mayes had heard about. . . .

Old Stevie he lived way yonder up where they've got that T-Bar ranch built now, and he never done much but steal. It was the way he was. Steal anything, I mean an old wore-out hame strap hanging on your fence. But whiskey most of all.

Well, one day Papa was plowing that blackland field on our place down along the branch, and one of the Calhouns he come along and says, "Tom, did Stevie Squires come see you? I seen him heading up this way."

And Papa says, "No, I ain't seen Stevie Squires. I ain't feeling bad about it neither."

But when that Calhoun boy was gone, Papa he was walking along behind them mules and watching that dirt roll over and he got to thinking. And all of a sudden he says to himself out loud, "Tom, you old ignoramus. I bet that Stevie run across my whiskey up by the road, and that's why he never come this far." Because he knowed when he put it there he hadn't drug in enough brush to cover it right, wanting to get on with the plowing before it set in to rain.

So he went and he looked and sure enough, it was a half-gallon missing from that batch. And Papa he went back and unhitched his mules and turned them out, and then he hit out walking across the country to Stevie's house, mad every step of the way because there he'd had to leave his plowing. And when he got there and stepped up in the yard, old Stevie he was setting on the porch and sipping on that jar.

"Hey, Tom," he says.

And Papa says, "No hey to you, you son of a bitch. You stole my whiskey."

Stevie he started thinking on a lie but he seen it weren't no use. So he grins a kind of big slow grin, and he says, "Aw,

Tom, you know what it's like. I needed a drink real bad and I didn't have no money at all, and there was all that good whiskey, the best there is."

The trouble with Stevie, he was always grinning and joking and people sort of liked him, no matter what he'd done. Even Papa did. . . .

But not right then. He climbed up there and he knocked Stevie off the porch down in the yard, right in the middle of a bunch of banty chickens that squawked and went ever which a way. Then he got him down and he banged on him some, but he never hurt him much. Like he said, you couldn't do much to somebody that was so sorry, all fat and blubbery and grinning at you. So in a little while Papa he got up and left old Stevie laying there more drunk than hurt, and come on home.

Well, Mrs. Squires she come up from somewhere after the ruckus was over, and she found Stevie in the yard. So she hauled him in the house and propped him on the bed, and when she seen he was going to be all right she commenced to getting mad, because Stevie he never told her what it was all about, just said Papa done it. So she lit out walking for our place. There was more guts to her than there was to Stevie, and not much grinning. Not that she had nothing to grin about, married to Stevie Squires. . . .

The funny thing was Mama had been visiting down on Paluxy, and Mrs. Squires and her they reached White Bluff right together, at that crossing on your place. Same minute. First thing Mama knowed, there was Mrs. Squires hollering at her and calling Papa names, and she'd never heard a thing about what happened. I don't guess you ever knowed Mama before she died. Quiet and polite and went to church a lot, and back in those days she'd walk ten miles to help somebody that was sick or had a trouble. Anybody. But she could tell you what, and she could back it up, if she got to feeling like it. Well, she listened to old Mrs. Squires hollering for a while and then she got tired of it. So she picked up a big old cedar stave that was laying there and she started in to swinging it. Mrs. Squires she squalled and she started to backing off, and she backed off some more, and the first thing you know she had done backed right off the bank in a big hole of water. Stayed there too, hair all draggly and wet, just standing in the water up to her waist and looking up at Mama with that cedar stave, and not calling no more names. . . .

Mama she used to laugh about that sometimes up till she died, and she said she knowed she ought not to of run that woman in that creek. Wasn't Christian. But it made her mad, old Stevie Squires's wife calling Papa names. . . .

The Calhouns they might near shot old Stevie later on, up Paluxy. Kept on missing whiskey where they stashed it, so they tied them a twelve-gauge to a tree with a wire hooked on the trigger. And the next time Stevie come easing along there to pick him up a jug, he hit that wire and boom, and it missed him about an inch. Told it around himself. . . . The Calhouns they claimed it cured him of stealing whiskey, but Papa he just laughed. He said, Shoot, the Calhouns was lucky not to have lost that shotgun too.

I reckon it's a long time gone, all that. I'm fifty years old this spring and the old folks are mostly dead. And maybe it never amounted to a hell of a much, what happened around these hills. But it happened to us. Here.

7 ≋ *A Rooted Population* ≋≋≋≋≋≋≋≋≋

Even now, after much bulldozing has been done, the main timber on the place is cedar. Precisionist types point out that this is really juniper, and scholarly squabbles exist, I am told, over whether there are two species of it in the region, or only one. Locals are sure there are two. The one they call white cedar for the pale splotches on its bark—redberry juniper in government bulletins—is despised by just about everyone. Its spindling boughs usually spread out from its root crown at ground level and it is fit for very little in human utilitarian terms except to take up space and soil moisture and to smother grass. When chopped off to spiky nubs— excellent devices for puncturing tractor and pickup tires—it sprouts again with new and vengeful vigor. A few years back, its control in even limited patches of land was a continuing fight, and people had favorite recipes for killing it down for good, few of which actually worked. Old crankcase oil was one.

The other sort is known locally as red cedar and generally has a central trunk that makes a good post, as do its larger branches. Often small red cedars are symmetrical enough to use for Christmas trees, and though the species is just about as hoggish of water and as unfriendly to grass as its white-splotched relative, it is a somewhat more likable plant. In more or less virgin stands it can grow fairly large, up to thirty or forty feet high and a foot and a half or more in diameter at the base of the tapering trunk. A grove of such trees on level land is a pleasant place when you find one— quiet and windless, the ground shaded and fairly free of undergrowth and carpeted with brown cast needles, the air full of the cedar's clean perfume, which is intensified if you are cutting posts and freeing the aromatic sap. Hoops and jars and firestones often turn up underfoot, for the big cedar with its privacy was favored by the old moonshiners, as it is by wild things.

Few such groves are left except in occasional niches that have been hard for post-cutters to reach with wagons and pickups over the years—you can't drag out that big stuff by hand—and have been sheltered somehow from the summer fires that used to tongue occasionally through the oily cedar like a blowtorch when things were very dry, and at times still do. Post-harvesting in the area dating back to Buck Barry's time over a century ago has undoubtedly reduced the proportion of red cedar, of whatever size, and swung the balance in favor of its useless hardy cousin, though it is not possible to know just what the balance used to be, any more than it is possible to know exactly where the brakes extended in the old natural condition worked out through ages of botanical competition and adjustment.

However much of the place may originally have been grassland, all of it but some shrunken fragments of the old fields was cedar and scrub when I first saw it, after the wearing out, after the long exhaustion. Much of the Booker was dozed clear not long before I bought it, but being under lease it was almost immediately overstocked with cows. They ate the reviving grass cover off just about as fast as it could sprout, and it was possible to watch there an eclipsed version of the thing that had happened long before. The brush began coming back, and today the Booker's cleared part, except for fields that are being worked from year to year, is speckled with new cedars up to head height and with all sorts of other scrub. Within a few more years, unless the cedars are somehow grubbed out, much of the pasture will be a sorry brake again. Within fifteen or twenty years you would be able to cut some fair posts from it, though the best of the brakes in the heyday of post-cutting had probably grown for at least thirty or forty.

A friend of mine from that background says that in his prime he could cut a hundred straight main-trunk posts a day in a good brake, felling and topping and trimming and letting his wife and kids drag them to the wagon. He would do it in five hours of steady work, starting at dawn in the hot months and later in wintertime. "Then you was through," he said. "Wasn't nobody could chop for more than five hours, hot or cold. Even if you wasn't all wore out, you still had to haul them in and sort them for size and stack them."

That means a post every three minutes, with time sandwiched in somehow to breathe, to have a drink of water and renew your dip of snuff, to swat horseflies, maybe to kill a rattlesnake. It is seldom possible nowadays, not even for the few younger natives still possessed of that harsh pride in toil and still hanging on in the hills against the lure of city wages. Not even with the raucous chainsaws that are largely replacing axes. In the twenties and thirties a man could still find some virgin cedar, and a great deal more that had been undisturbed since it had begun taking over from the grass long before. Now most brakes that the dozers have not yet reached have been picked over time and again by cutters, and a man has to spend more time looking for posts than cutting them, and even then finding most often skinny "stays" or crooked

73

things of the sort the dealers call "wire posts," which means that by rotating one in the hole you can find one side vertical enough to fit into the plane of your fence.

For a long time the country had a little cedar-oil mill that would pay by weight for whatever contorted stuff people hauled in, and some were able to make a few dollars a day out of that. But the mill has closed down now, and good posts themselves have not gone up in value to match the price of beans and bacon and TV dinners. Migrant cutters compete with locals for what good cedar there is to be had. Steel posts and creosoted pine, mass-produced elsewhere, are queering the market too. For landowners short of help, or for fencing contractors dealing mainly with absentee proprietors, they are easier to handle and install.

All of this militates against the old way, as do the great yellow Cats that growl across the hills, charging the cedars with a raised bright blade to bash them down, then backing off and dropping the blade to catch beneath their roots and shove them to a pile or windrow. There, almost baled together if the operator is good, they cure for a few weeks or months depending on the weather until the needles are brown and crisp and the wood has lost its sap. And then some day when a light wind is right to keep sparks from drifting into places where you don't want them to go, and maybe there is a mist of beginning rain for added safety, you set off a firestorm with a single match, and up with the high oily flames and the soaring big sparks and the unbelievable heat and roar and pistol-shot snapping, goes eighty years or more of something, of the old way, the cedar way. . . .

(Beyond the edges of fields and along the banks of ravines and in other such out-of-the-way places you may, if you care about wild things, leave a few piles unburned to sit there and molder and furnish generations of creatures with shelter and concealment. But their liking for such tangles can populate some of the piles you do have to burn, during the time of curing. Though conscience usually keeps me from burning much in the spring and early summer when birds are nesting and animals are likely to have young, even at other seasons a burn involving more than two or three brushpiles usually offers glimpses of some frantic and perhaps slightly singed rabbits streaking for nearby woods, and maybe a fox or a humped and angry coon. At such times I always hope the piles don't have other residents too daylight-shy to come out even to save themselves from broiling, but the fact is they probably do. . . .)

Up it goes, in sparks and flames and roar. . . . Therefore hail and farewell, old way, cedar way? More or less, I suppose, though there is no forgetting the old way when you are dealing with the Tonk Nation. Even if there were not a good many vigorous representatives of it still around, the country itself would remind you of their forebears every day. Bulldozing does not remove the feel of them. For the country shaped them and they in turn shaped the country too, and though in both shapings there may have been more of destruction than of loving response, the relationship between those people and this land had a kind of rightness to it that we who possess it later stand little chance of attaining, even if we handle it better than they did. For one thing, many of us were not born out of generations of intimacy with this specific land —bitter intimacy maybe, ignorant intimacy often, but intimacy nevertheless. For another, few of us whether born here or not are any longer so desperately dependent on its grudging yield of crops and meat and timber, and it was largely out of such dependence and intimacy that the old rightness derived. Rightness may not be the word, but whatever you call it, the cedar hills and the cedar people were fitted to each other. . . .

The cedar has a rightness of its own, partly through association with those old human ways, partly immemorial. It exists in the groves of big cedar when you happen onto them

75

wandering, and in pronged ancient stumps of trees cut down for posts in another age, stripped and silvered and edge-rounded by weather, the departed and probably dead post-cutters' limb-slash a brittle mulch about them. It exists too in the cedared darkness of distant hillsides nosing out into White Bluff's narrow valley or the Paluxy's, and in the way that birds and deer and other creatures flee to cedar when you flush them in the open. After you have fought cedar in this country for a while, you are not likely to be very sentimental about it, but you can like it where it belongs. On a hundred or so steep acres of Hard Scrabble, clearing away the cedar would accomplish little beyond the destruction of some good wildlife cover and a great deal of mystery and rightness. Those sharp slopes were not meant for grass, and during my time here they will stay as they are.

There is a cleanliness about cedar, an aromatic naturally antiseptic quality allied to the thing that makes a good thick cedar fencepost last in the ground till the galvanized wire stapled to it is rotten with rust. The needles when they break off in your hands, too deep sometimes for tweezers, hardly ever fester as splinters and thorns are likely to do. . . . When you run short of sawed oak cordwood, you can knock over one of the old gray stumps with the bumper of a pickup or a few blows with the poll of an axe. A big one will burn for hours in your fireplace, flavoring the woods and fields down-wind with its smoke. In that smell, which the Bookers and the Kyles knew and all the old moonshiners, and intrepid Indian-battling Buck Barry camping in the Paluxy country while he split his wagonloads of posts and rails, and the Comanches and the Tonks and the nameless peoples in this place in the centuries that went before, is all of cedar's cleanness and all its rightness too.

Despite cedar's long dominion, there is and always has been a big variety of other vegetation on the place. Liveoak and elm—the small-leafed species called cedar elm, though why I have never known—are the most numerous trees of any considerable size. Elm likes good deep soil, but liveoak—more Texan than any other tree to me, even than mesquite—does well all over the place. In the middle of thick cedarbrakes, clumps and mottes and individual big gnarled specimens dome gray-green above the junipers as they stood above the tallgrass prairies in the old days. None are as big as the mossy liveoaks of the warm wet Gulf Coast country, but many have enough size for dignity, and ample years, some probably antedating the cedar that surrounds them by a century or more. They shed their leaves in spring to grow new ones, fight drouth by jamming their roots back into the tight clay or shale between limestone ledges, have a greater talent than any other tree for yanking your hat off your head as you walk or ride beneath them, and with their long twisting horizontal branches furnish fine climbing for children and sometimes goats. In September the little bitter acorns come rattling down, choice fodder for goats and deer and quail and squirrels and other epicures, though a herd of cows that have too freely indulged is a miserable hunchbacked sight.

We have hardly any postoaks, which in some other parts of the county where Cross Timbers sandy land prevails are the dominant trees. Nor is there much mesquite—that thorny, twisted, thirsty, pestiferous, and lacily beautiful legume which in areas a few miles away from this place in almost any direction is a curse in pastures. Spanish oak abounds, sometimes called Texas red oak, never very big and occurring mainly on rocky hillsides where in autumn it frosts crimson and sparkles as the wind stirs it in the sunlight, and hence is praised by all esthetes who view it, even if in other seasons hardly anyone looks at it twice. Redbuds elicit a like response in spring. . . . Texas ash is unspectacular but present. Lone hackberries turn up here and there, brittle and weedy and much afflicted with mistletoe, but sought out by birds for the tiny hard rather sweet fruits that stay on their twigs all winter; Indians liked them too, or at any rate used them for food. . . .

Close beside the creek in places where they can find a little soil, and sometimes sprouting out of the shallow gravel in its bed, are sycamores and cottonwoods and willows, few above medium size, for the creek's usual low-water course over impermeable rock denies them the moisture they need for full growth. Those that root themselves in the midstream gravel-bars seldom reach more than three or four inches in thickness, scarred and leaning and decked with highwater debris, before a big intolerant rise sweeps through and breaks them off or cleans them out, gravel and roots and all. In deeper soil near branches and the creek are walnut, pecan, bur oak, hawthorn, and other deciduous bottomland trees common in the region. And all about the place, but especially on land lately cleared of cedar and fields left fallow for more than a year or so, are seedling and shrubby forms of most of the trees I have mentioned, and a large number of lesser woody plants that rarely reach more than bush size.

Shin oak, usually called shinnery and beloved of rattlesnakes in summer, forms waist-high thickets back in the cedarbrakes and in sandy places, which latter spots also foster greenbriar to rip the rambler's breeches and saw bloody furrows in his flesh. Sumac—locally pronounced shoemake or sometimes shoemate—proliferates, happiest in the mounds of ashy, rich, rooty, loose earth that remain when dozed brushpiles are burned. Flameleaf is the main species; in fall, thickets and whole hillsides of it patch the view with melancholy scarlet as far as you can see from a high place. It can choke a pasture, but bees make a good red-amber honey from its August bloom, wildlife likes the berries, and goats in winter derive much nourishment from gnawing its bark as high as they can reach, which is rough of course on the sumac itself. Its misanthropic cousin poison ivy does well in the shade of other plants and along the banks of branches, as does the privet-like forestiera known sometimes as elbow-brush, for its habit of arching down to earth to sink another root before leaping outward again, and sometimes as tanglefoot, for reasons it will explain to you on introduction. In open pastures too, these and other shrubby plants thrive mightily, stationing themselves according to the soils and minerals and sun and moisture conditions they prefer, and where their seeds have fallen or blown or been carried or excreted. Seep willow (*Baccharis*) that nearly always tells you where there is a wet place; skunkbrush whose bruised leaves for some reason stink less in our region than elsewhere; bumelia called buckthorn or sometimes chittamwood (the Biblical spelling and pronunciation, I suppose, having rung too harshly for nineteenth-century ears); wild china that the wetbacks know as *jaboncillo* because it makes good soap where they come from; prickly ash that has a fine citrus smell but tingles the tongue strangely and taints honey in the hive; hog plum, good for jelly; catclaw; agarita; dogwood; mustang grape; prickly pear; Mexican buckeye; and more . . .

Lore attaches to most of these trees and bushes, not that I know much of it, or that anyone else knows all the rest, nowadays. A wealth of pragmatic and mystical botany must have perished, God knows, when the old pre-horseback hunters and gatherers attuned to these limestone hills by centuries of living in them, were destroyed or driven away. Not only what was edible by a stretch of the hungry imagination and when and where, but also what would ease a toothache or a swollen belly or a festered wound, and what would help you see visions or stave off fanged fantasmal spirits, and what twigs made good baskets for what specific purposes, and what juice would start a woman quivering for you, and all the rest . . . A little of what was left of this primal lore the

Tonks passed on to early whites, but even most of that is lost now too.

It is hard to believe the loss is really counterbalanced by an upsurge of exact scientific knowledge, though I have done my share of poring over books. They are different things. . . . Once a few years ago I went on a rather formal long hike in the West Virginia highlands with some people who knew the names of trees and flowers and birds. One among them, an earnest muscular professor from Pittsburgh in lederhosen and rucksack, knew more names of things than anyone else and pronounced them in a sort of loud litany as we walked. It was a fine, cool, rim-of-the-world sort of place where you could look down on clouds, and it would have been immensely silent except for him. We came across some natives picking blueberries with graceful hand-whittled combs. The professor said they kept the region's ecology upset by burning off the blueberry flats from time to time to get rid of other vegetation. The natives kept combing blueberries and watching us from under the brims of hats and bonnets, with maybe a nudge or two among them, and all of a sudden I wished I were squatting there picking berries with the unecological Appalachians rather than hiking with that fellow in his lederhosen, and learning what they knew rather than listening to him. I admit it was an unscholarly sort of response, and the cast of mind it reflects may have cost me some knowledge in my time.

On a place like Hard Scrabble, which has been undergoing a lot of scraping and plowing and other earth-disturbance in the process of restoration or rescue or subjugation or whatever you want to call it, a slew too much of such hardwood brush springs up and it turns into a problem, as do so many other natural things when the Ownership Syndrome gets one in its clutches. It blocks vision and passage and, like cedar if a bit less seriously, competes with grass for sun and water and nutrients, and on a stock farm grass is more or less the point. In the old virgin days occasional natural fires kept it from taking over, but fire gets out of hand and burns down people's fences and barns and houses, and is no longer viewed with much favor as a tool. On field land you can plow and mow the scrub out of existence in three or four years or so, but not on the rough hills. Hand grubbing is hopeless except in a yard or garden, and bulldozing the stuff just stimulates further growth. Potent modern herbicides, misted over broad areas on the bigger ranches by helicopter, generally do a fair job of eradicating such broad-leafed plants. But they eradicate also a lot of good broad-leafed trees that a smaller and less fiercely economic landowner may want to preserve, and sometimes raise hell with neighbors' vegetable gardens and orchards and shade trees for miles downwind. . . .

To the archaic and musing eye of one who leans, sometimes despite himself, toward the Old Fart school of land use, the best answer to the problem of controlling hardwood brush looks to be goats. They are pleasant animals to have around, and feed by preference on the leaves and sometimes the bark of such plants, concentrating on different species in different seasons. Tumbling along with frequent bleatings behind their billy and a couple of senior does, snatching mouthfuls of leaves as they go, often pausing as an entire flock to concentrate on one bush and strip it, they work hard and daily on your problem, providing also a bonus of plump young wether kids to barbecue and perhaps mohair, if you run Angoras. After a few years of fairly heavy browsing most of the hardwood scrub will be gone.

Such at least is the theory of goats versus brush, which sometimes works and sometimes doesn't. On cleared ground laboriously and expensively reseeded to grass, for instance, your goats are likely to show a quirkish and infuriating predilection for the young grass shoots and to scorn new brush coming up all around. And despite their charms and their appropriateness in the Tonk country they make other problems too, being horribly vulnerable to various sorts of predators. Therefore the goat-owner girds for war with nature in yet another form. . . . The Syndrome is inexorable in this respect.

On the subject of grass, which as we have observed is more or less the point, I would as soon not reveal the far crannies of my ignorance, for it is something that a lot of people know something about and a lot of other people think they do, with resultant strong opinions and disagreements that have been around my part of the world for a century and more. In the West grass looms big in men's interest, of course, being the land's main crop now as it always was, though marketed mainly in the form of meat. Hence the many species that make up the millions of square miles of ground cover we lump under that one term, grass, are viewed by Western human beings in general as "good" or "bad" according to whether or not they make useful grazing.

Rainfall and soil and climate put the Grand Prairie and related regions in the category of "tall-grass country," where under virgin conditions lofty range species lorded it over shorter stuff, and so impressed newcomers that they were forever writing home about grass shoulder-high to a horse. Nowadays a good native stand knee-high to the same beast is fairly rare and flamboyant. . . . Granted, horses are a bit bigger than in mustang days, but the grass is shorter too. Big bluestem and indiangrass and switchgrass, formerly abundant but too palatable as forage for their own good, usually occur only as isolated plants and clumps in most of the region now. Relatively lower, hardier species like little bluestem and the gramas hold on better, coming back well in any pasture where they are given half a chance through brush control and unabusive grazing, and there is undoubtedly a higher proportion of buffalo grass and curly mesquite and other ground-hugging species, characteristic of the semi-arid shortgrass country farther west, than there was in the beginning. There are also a lot more of the less palatable grasses like feather bluestem and *Stipa* needlegrass and the three-awns, for they were attacked less vigorously over the years of heavy grazing, and more too of the forbs known generally as weeds, though some of these latter are good forage for cattle, and some that cowmen detest are appetizing to sheep, just as the hardwood scrub is fine for browsing goats.

Mainly the wildflowers that in the Texas spring and often in early fall make prairie country vivid, and were noted by all the early passers-through, belong to this weed category, while some like plum blossoms and redbud appear on woody plants. Daisies of a couple of dozen kinds, yucca, mountain pinks, asters, prairie clover, goldenrod, the lupine called bluebonnet that Texans especially revere, Apache plume or standing cypress, foxgloves, winecups, various mints and milkweeds, sunflowers, and a host of others that local ladies of naturalistic bent can point out to you. Differing patterns of rain and cold and heat favor differing species from year to year, so that one spring a pasture may be aflame with the red-and-yellow gaillardia daisy known as firewheel or Indian-blanket too, or sometimes chiggerweed for the itching, burrowing mites it harbors, but for years following may have only scattered specimens of that plant.

Within the gross and dependable changes of each year, different grasses and forbs tend to mature or to reach prime usefulness—if they are "useful" species—at varying times, some even in winter like filaree and bur clover and the gratefully named rescuegrass. Collectively they are the thing that makes rangeland worth owning, and the anxiety with which they are watched and nursed along by many people these days can be extreme. One friend of mine when walking through pastures spends about half his time dragging pieces of dead brush around and draping them over clumps of big blue and indiangrass and such plants, to protect them against grazing and let them make seed and spread. . . .

Not that anyone, as we have noted, is going to be able to reconstitute the tall-grass prairies in their primal glory. Hell was played, and so the land will never again be quite what it used to be, except perhaps in geological time, which is slightly beyond the scope of concern for most of us. Hence for a good many years there has been sharp interest in introduced grasses that may adapt themselves better to what the land is now than do the native Texas species. In fields—old cropland that still has a workable pad of soil on top—the choice is fairly wide and includes legumes suited for this rainfall belt as well as a good many grasses so tailored by plant geneticists for nutritiousness and response to fertilization and such qualities that in reality they are domesticated crops—things like coastal bermudagrass, kleingrass, the improved lovegrasses and hardinggrass and others.

Perhaps my own pet cropland exotic, though, is a grass traditionally viewed as a pest. Hated and feared by generations of row-crop farmers and vegetable gardeners (including me when I'm enacting that role) because of its plebeian greed for food and water and the fact that when hacked off it quickly sends up new stalks from fleshy perennial roots, it is the lowly johnsongrass. This unfavored poor relation of the useful sorghums is one of the most thoroughly successful importations of live matter from the Old World to the New, rivaling even English sparrows and white men in this respect. Arriving from Turkey around 1835 and named shortly thereafter for an Alabamian who sowed it and sang its praises as hay, it soon became the chief and most pernicious weed in cottonfields throughout the Kingdom. Many men still alive remember, with ruefulness or disgust or sometimes perverse pride, hoeing it out from between and in the rows day after long hot day. It spread west through Texas not only with cotton but with the railroads, whose thousands of construction mules were fueled with great shipments of johnsongrass hay, full of viable seed.

All it needs to establish a good stand is reasonable soil fertility and disturbance of the earth from time to time with plow or disk or chisel. Unlike the sudans and sorghums and the costly hybrids thereof, it does not have to be reseeded year after year; once the fat perennial roots are well developed it comes back vigorously each warm season on its own. Unlike coastal and klein and other prized exotic perennials it does not uselessly preempt field land during winter months unless you let it; you can work it under in August or September and later sow small grain or legumes for winter grazing, and the johnsongrass is there waiting, ready to take over again thickly in the spring. It mingles well with pleasant summer legumes like sweetclover. Cut and cured right it makes fine hay, or grazed where it grows it will carry cows through the warm months fat and happy. I sense waves of ghostly dismay among cotton-minded ancestors when I set this down, but johnsongrass in the right places is a first-rate forage plant.

On eroded soils and hills the region's most successful introduced grass thus far has been an *Andropogon* that the books sometimes call yellow or Turkestan bluestem but Texans know mainly as K. R., for the King Ranch down on the coast where some of the first American stands were grown. It must have come from an Asian upland just about as battered and tired as the Tonk Nation and with some similarities in climate and soil. The usual practice for establishing it is to dribble its tiny seed, sometimes mixed with seed of native species, onto ground torn up by bulldozers in clearing cedar, though if you have a taste for tooth-jolting activity you can rip up the rough hillsides with some such indestructible implement as a spring-loaded chisel tool and sow the seed with a fertilizer spreader. If rains come when they are supposed to, within a season or so the grass seizes the ground where you have planted it, produces multiple seed crops each year that blow widely roundabout on the wind and sprout wherever they find bare earth, spreading the stand. Drouth and winter cold seldom kill any of it. Livestock like it and do well on it, but it survives even hard grazing by goats who have run out of brush, nursing life in its roots and its gnaweddown squatty crown and shooting up new leaves and long yellow seedstems whenever it gets half a chance. I do not know what secret magic allows K. R. to suck nourishment from gullied subsoil and shallow rocky dirt that other good grasses abhor. But in the Nation it is a useful plant to have around, making turf where bare ground lay before, hazy with purple seedheads in September, its pale stems rippling under winter winds.

Whatever its grazing capacity may once have been, decently restored and maintained range grassland in Somervell County these days is thought by experts to be able to support domestic herbivores at the approximate rate of one animal unit per twenty acres, without much supplemental feeding except in an especially icy winter or dried-out summer. An animal unit being a hypothetical appetite generally though not always defined as one grown cow with or without a calf, or one bull, or three quarters of a horse, or seven goats or sheep . . . You can juggle the rate a bit by balancing the numbers of different sorts of animals you keep, by buying feed, by new techniques of high-intensity rotated grazing, and by the amount of time and money you decide to invest in whatever arable field land you happen to own—clearing and plowing and harrowing and chiseling and fertilizing and sowing to high-yield forage crops to be either grazed or else harvested as hay or grain and fed out in lean seasons. But whatever your place's real capacity may be, you can't strain it much without repeating history and playing hell.

Such abuse can still be seen around, often on the places of people so wedded to old views that earth does not "look right" to them when it is shaggy with grass. But maybe it is perpetrated most generally by renters, who like migratory frontiersmen are not going to have to live with the results. I remember one place up in the roughest fastnesses of the Nation near the Chalk Mountain ridge, which was bought fifteen or twenty years ago by a middle-aged city couple in the expectation of spending their retirement there. Not rich, they labored hugely on weekends and vacations and ended up with some cleared fields among the cedarbrakes, some good fences, a barn with pens, and a neat hilltop house of edgelaid flagstone, looking out northeastward on thirty or forty miles of the Brazos valley.

Following old custom that dies hard (it used to be pleasant, I guess, to wave to the three or four wagons and horsemen that would pass in a day), they built the house slap on a graveled public road. Within a few months of the time when the owner was going to retire and move down there to live— or so the story is told—a roving carload of jolly youths happened along one night, broke in, stole all the guns and tools and appliances they could find, and in departing playfully applied kerosene and a match to the house, which burned entire except for the peanut-brittle stone veneer of its walls. Disheartened, the owners leased the place to a man who must have bitterly regretted being born too late for the frontier. Within two or three years the quantities of cows and goats he shoved inside its fences had eaten it down to bare dirt and rocks. Even the cedars, which ordinarily goats will not touch except for flavor from time to time when the quirk invades them, were browsed up as far as a famished Angora could reach by standing on his hind legs and stretching his neck three or four inches farther than God had intended for it to go.

Then all the animals began to starve, and people say that when what was left of the man's cows were hauled to Hico for sale, they had to be fed in the commission company's lot for three weeks before they were strong enough to be run through the auction ring. The hero of this saga lost heavily on the venture, which might make a good moral except that the place lost more heavily still. It is part of a larger ranch now, but despite recent fair treatment most parts of it still stand out in desolate contrast to other segments of the Nation round-about.

By one yardstick, that of soil conservation, there is no such thing as really "bad" vegetation. All plants are preferable to bare ground because all to some extent tie soil in place and shield it from wind and rain and scouring runoff. In fact, the wider your rural interests grow—economic or otherwise—the harder it is to get indignant toward any of the greenery that lays itself so variously athwart the limestone hills and valleys. A good many species you may not want all over your prop-erty in unlimited numbers, but sooner or later you can find some reason to appreciate most of them, especially if you stay out of the modern trap of superspecialization in cows or a single row crop or whatever. Not that it is hard to stay out of that trap in the Nation, whose uneven surface obstinately re-sists any uniform use. . . .

Thus he who runs a few sheep and goats along with his Herefords or Angus tends to be mellower in his view of weeds and brush than is a strict cow rancher, and he who keeps some hives of bees is mellower still, finding joy in mes-quite and sumac and horehound and broomweed and other abominations. And he who cares about wildlife, as either a pleasure or a source of meat or a crop to be harvested by pay-ing hunters, may be the mellowest of all if he gazes a bit into the intricacies of things. For the cover and shelter that grasses and forbs and trees and brush give are essential to most wild things, nor is there any plant so noxious or prickly that it does not furnish gourmet fare for at least a few members of the meshed hierarchy of creatures large and small that inhabit the region and belong there. All things natural and rural being etcetera . . .

Not that the Syndrome usually lets you enjoy them all with equal gusto. . . .

8 ≋ *An Irrelevance* ≋≋≋≋≋

Maybe this has nothing to do with Hard Scrabble. But it comes to me recurringly here, generally outdoors—seated slanchwise on the tractor and looking back as the tandem disk slices mellow trashy earth in autumn, or crumbling a clod of garden dirt between my thumb and fingers, or laying stone, or clambering on boulders up the creek. Among, of course, the many other past things that come to one recurringly as the years advance . . . Before I had the land, I did not use to think of it much. It is not just a war memory; those are plentiful and cheap enough, God knows, in a time when three or four successive generations of us have seen war. I suppose perhaps what it has to do with is place, and kind, and belonging. . . .

One evening in the summer of 1944 I was deposited on a mosquito-netted cot in a tent in a little Army field hospital at the south end of the island of Saipan. My head and eyes were wrapped in gauze and I lay on billows of morphine, and slept and woke alternately for a while without being much

aware of the difference between the two states. At some point
they brought another man in and, murmuring to one another,
laid him on a cot beside mine; there was a harsh rale in his
breathing and I listened to it and went back to sleep.

Much later when I came awake again the air had the dank
coolness that it has in those islands after midnight and the
sounds were those of the dead hours too—strange bugs and
birds and amphibians calling, distant interdictory barrages
prowling the flanks of Tapotchau, and occasionally a rattle of
nervous small-arms fire. There was a stink of coconut palms
and dead bodies, or maybe it was only in my nose from two
weeks of smelling it. The other man was still breathing loudly
near me and I spoke. His answering voice was labored and
very young, but glad to know that I was there and conscious.
The name he gave was Italian; the accent was deep South.
We talked, with gaps when one or both would drift away.
Mainly he talked, though painfully. He had heard the medics
say that we were to be flown off the island in the morning.
He had been hit in the guts and chest, machine-gunned. He
was glad I was a Southerner and a marine, not a soldier. Did
not know what he would have done if I had turned out to be
a dogface and a Yankee. . . .

It did not seem to have to make much sense. He came
from a place in south Alabama not far from Mobile where a
lot of people were Italian, the grandfathers having come there
many years since. They grew truck stuff mainly, and kept
some animals. I would not believe, he said, the watermelons
his uncle could raise. It was sandy land but rich because it had
been manured and handled well. In Mobile Bay sometimes in
summer fish would gather strangely in the shallows in solid
lethargic clumps maybe a half-acre big, and people would
wade out towing boats and with pitchforks or shovels would
load them full of fish and crabs. He had seen it, done it. They
would discard the trash fish on the beach, and his father and
uncles would go there and bring home truckloads of them,

for the land. Stingarees and things like that . . . Kids had teased him in school about it. . . .

There was more talk, and silence, and after a while the boy said, "Listen. Hold my hand, do you mind?"

I reached out under the mosquito net and found it, a thin dry rifleman's hand that clenched mine hard. The boy said, "You want somebody that knows what you're talking about."

I said, "That's right."

"Thanks, mac," the boy said, and clenched my hand harder still, and died.

9 ≈ Hoof and Paw, Tooth and Claw, Little Creatures Everywhere ≈≈≈≈≈≈≈≈≈≈

Most of the place's wild residents are of species that were here in virgin days, though there have been some notable subtractions and a few additions and some great shifts, not altogether knowable, in the balances that exist between the different kinds of them and between them and the vegetation and the land—shifts sponsored by man and man's own creatures. Some of the changes came about long ago in frontier times, some have occurred gradually since, and still others are taking place today, as the region fitfully awakes from its long and needful time of economic drowsing.

Buffalo and antelope went early, unadaptable to white human ways and appetites, as were the wild mustangs—these last not "native" in a longterm sense but well enough established here by the time the frontier came that they were a solid part of things. The big original predators did not last much longer—the bears and cougars and lobo wolves that kept wild ruminants wary and fleet of foot by erasing those who were not. Anglo-Hibernian owners of unwary, unfleet, tame ruminants failed to appreciate this service of selection, and erased the predators. In a perverse and ironic and very human way, something in most people seems to miss them sorely—we *want* to be able to believe in big violent creatures roundabout, which is of course what most science fiction and most horror movies are about. . . . Hence romantic rumors get started every once in a while about the appearance of an individual or a family of these fanged and hungry carnivores, and more rifles than usual show up on racks in the back windows of pickup trucks. Most of the rumors are apparently based on someone's yen to be his own frontier grandfather— not that anyone with a country bias is entirely immune to that disease. No bears or lobos have showed up in the Nation in modern times, nor are any likely to, but it seems possible that an occasional cougar has. I have heard people whom I believe tell of seeing them in the region. And a few years ago someone found cat tracks bigger than any believable bobcat's on a ranch next to Hard Scrabble, which may well have belonged to a wandering panther with a yen to be *his* own frontier grandfather. The rancher, no crabbed economic utilitarian, believed they did and was delighted, forbidding hunting for a while despite a possible threat to his calves and goats. But that animal was never seen nor were any more of the tracks.

Lesser predators still inhabit the varied, crannied, alternately open and wooded terrain that characterizes most of the area. The most impressive of them is a fellow regarding whom I know very little, nor do authorities agree about him, nor does the usual country alarmism about beasts of prey help much to clarify matters. *The Mammals of Texas*, a state publication, indicates that he is the red wolf, which once ranged the whole American Southeast from Texas to Pennsylvania, a smaller relative of the great gray lobo. But some wildlife men I have read and talked with, specialists in the subject, say the red wolf (*Canis rufus,* sometimes called *C. niger*) is now as a pure species restricted to a couple of handfuls of beleaguered animals in woodlands of southeastern Texas and in upper Louisiana, southern Arkansas, and Mississippi. Other so-called red wolves, they say, are the result of interbreeding between *C. rufus* and coyotes and runaway domestic dogs, a "hybrid swarm" that flourishes on land cleared of woods and brush, more or less created by the times. Nor have they homogenized as yet, for though most look quite wolfish, there is great variation in their size and conformation and skull shape and such things, and even in the way they howl.

Whatever they are, they can run from the size of ordinary coyotes up to eighty pounds or more, and wolf is probably as good a name as any to use for them. Even discounting alarmism, they are not agreeable neighbors to have around if you own goats or sheep or even young calves. They have been growing in numbers in the past few years, mainly in more open country near the Nation. Sometimes you see their carcasses displayed on fenceposts in Bosque and other prairie counties or sight them crossing a road at night, looking somewhat like hairy German shepherds. Evidently they have been moving in to fill the long-vacant carnivorous niche once occupied by the lobo, lured on perhaps by an increase, during and after the Big Drouth years of the fifties, in small livestock like goats and possibly by increasing populations of deer. Lured too, I suspect, by shrinking numbers of people and wider spaces between them as little places are consolidated into bigger ones and cleared of brush—a process that has been more emphatic in the gentler country west and south of the Chalk Mountain ridge than in the Nation itself.

So far I have seen none on Hard Scrabble nor have I heard their howls at night here, though the threat of them hangs close. Others do claim to have heard them, and a neighbor says he has sighted them in his pasture. In places only a few miles away they exist in strength, and goats and sheep are sore beset.

Though the wolves appear to have been favored by new human ways of doing things in the region, our second most considerable predator, the bobcat, probably liked things better the old way, his conservative preference running toward rocky places with brush close by. Likely it will be a long time, though, before the Tonk hills run out of such places and run permanently short of bobcats. They seem to wax and wane in response to fluctuations in rodent numbers, chiefly cottontail rabbits, and are rather scarce just now. But there are generally some around even though their secret and mainly nocturnal ways may keep them from your ken. During "up" periods, their rounded unclawed padmarks show up on creekside sandbars and along dusty goat trails on the hills, and sometimes with luck you flush one from a tangle in the cedar or see a long-bounding feline streak at the far limits of your headlights on a road.

Once years ago I brought sixteen or eighteen tough young bantam roosters to the place and turned them loose by the well on the hill behind the house. I had little stake in their survival, wanting mainly to see if they could last; they were the surplus of a hobby, too small and stringy to eat and productive only of combat and uproar among their parents and sisters in the little flock we kept where we lived then, on a leased exurban farm forty miles northeast of the Nation. I checked them on my visits, once or twice a week. It was summer, with plenty of bugs and seeds, and for a while they did all right, and I thought of bringing some hens down too. Then they started dwindling at a rate of one every day or so. Toward the end, when there were only half a dozen left, I was easing through a thicket at dusk one evening toward the liveoak where I knew they roosted. My foot crunched gravel, and three paces ahead a big bobcat whirled from his stalking

96

crouch and tore out of the thicket past me, pausing at its edge to glare back and then leaping on. . . .

(The absolute last of those bantams, I swear, took up with a wild rabbit. I saw them together at least three times in clearings or along old post-cutters' roads on that same hill, the little cock scratching away in the dust and chuckling with the fervid sexual madness of all roosters, the cottontail quiet nearby. Then they too vanished, the shadow that hung over them having descended. . . .)

But the time when you are most likely to be aware of bobcats, whether or not you see them, is when your goats begin to drop their tiny and tender young all over the wrinkled hills, a subject to be pondered somewhat further along. . . .

Most goat men also have tremors at that same time about the wily and handsome red fox, another rodent-and-poultry gourmet whose larger specimens are generally believed to be as capable as man of enjoying kid flesh, though without benefit of grilling and basting. Like the "red wolves," these red foxes are outlanders in the Nation, but longer and better established. Many years ago the fox-hunters—non-pinkcoated variety—who form so sturdy an element of the old way throughout the southeastern reaches of the United States, brought them to Texas and turned them loose to compete with and sometimes supplant the smaller native gray foxes. They range more widely from their dens than the latter do, and when chased by hounds at night tend to make a long hard jinking run to get away rather than holing up or treeing. Few are caught compared to the grays, but the Tonk Nation's handful of foxhunters are less interested in kills than in getting a full demonstration of their dogs' voices and scenting powers.

Standing in a creekbed or along an edge of woods and listening to the searching pack, they can tell you within a minute or so after a trail is struck what kind of fox made it.

If a gray, the hubbub often ends shortly with a squabble and a few high death-yipes from the quarry. But a satisfactory red may lead dogs on for hours and roundabout miles, the hunters following on foot if necessary across fences and through streams and brakes and shin-oak thickets, and in the end most usually he loses them and the hounds thrash scattered around an area of country for a while with occasional confused bellows. Then the hunters call them in by blasts on the big mellow cows' horns they carry, a sound that stirs me as few other human noises do, and everyone goes home well pleased to sleep maybe an hour or two or three till dawn and then rise to a full day's work, except the dogs who doze around their pens till another hunt.

Foxes survive well even where the more destructive sport of luring them into rifle range with seductive calls prevails, though the balance does seem to be tipping in favor of the astute and vigorous reds. You see them only now and then (birdwatching at dawn with a fieldglass I have sat downwind from one as he waited in tall grass for mice and jumping high pounced down on them). But at times in late winter and spring and in the summer they talk at night to one another around the hills with hollow coughing barks, and at any season their fresh red droppings, full of berry seeds, are clear on stones and hummocks and stumps along pasture roads and trails.

A different breed of hunters and hounds chase coons, and lying in bed at night and hearing them run you can usually tell the difference. Foxhounds are "short-voiced," resonant at times but falling often into yelping and barks. Thoughtful, deep, vibrant bell-voices belong to the bigger, slower, longer-eared dogs whose instinct sends them on the trail of coon and cat. Of bobcats they tree few, of coons a good many. But there is less addiction to these dogs in the region than to foxhounds, and coons abound, as they seem to just about everywhere else—far more than in bygone days when their pelts were in demand and people were hard up and a couple of dollars or so was worth a bit of effort. They dabble in the creeks and branches for minnows and crawfish and such tidbits, leaving a crisscross of handprints in mud and sand, stage great squalling mating orgies in February and March in the woods, and though unsociable regard omnivorous mankind as a generous provider for omnivorous coonkind, through gardens and orchards and garbage cans and sheds full of succulent fowl. Even kittens can be a treat for some old gourmet coons. . . . Of all the Nation's raiders I like coons best, I think, and hence am queasiest on those occasions when the Ownership Syndrome brings me in conflict with them rather than with less anthropoid species.

Among other beasts the Syndrome lumps as "varmints," we have some ring-tailed cats, which are not cats at all but cacomixtles, close kin to coons. They have flat skulls and flattenable bodies that let them fit into cracks in rocks and trees and buildings, and their habits are so shy that you can live a life among them without ever knowing it, unless your dogs happen to run one up a tree near the chickenhouse in cold December moonlight. And possums, though not often many, for they like the more heavily wooded bottoms along the Paluxy and the Brazos better than the creeks and hills. And plenty of skunks of course, and undoubtedly other predatory fellows whose range includes the county but who have never let me see them—things like mink and weasels.

Of nonvarmints whose chief role in the chain of things is to be chased and slaughtered by us varmints—or who, if they eat flesh, eat quite small flesh or eat it in peculiar ways—there are swarms, from deer on down through birds and mice and shrews and reptiles to the vast kingdoms of bugs and microbes. Considering their numbers, I know the names of only a few species and have seen fewer with my eyes. But without even the most insignificant or disagreeable of them Hard Scrabble would be a different place, just as it is different now, diminished, from what it was in tall-grass times when bison and antelope and mustangs grazed here instead of cows and goats, and lobos and panthers and bears and wild red men engaged in natural selection. If there is anything left here of a golden age, varmints and nonvarmints and trees and shrubs and grasses and waters and soils and rocks have everything to do with it. They make the place work, sometimes for me but mainly for its own sake and the world's. They were here before me and they will be here when I'm gone. There is a fair chance that even if technological bad luck hits them, as it likely will, many will still be here when man himself is gone. If you tend toward bastard pantheism, as I do, that can sometimes be a cheering sort of thought.

Deer, large and edible and traditionally a fit quarry for man the intrepid hunter, have a rather central place in most people's view of wildlife. Ours are whitetails. They had been just about wiped out in the Nation when I first knew it, having been regarded since frontier days as free meat on the hoof at any time of year, though some big ranches not far away sheltered populations of them. At present, though, they are thriving better than they did before white men. Several things have helped bring about this change—the waning of the old way and old views, new ownership of land and a jealousy about hunting rights, increased areas of hardwood scrub in the period after cedar-clearing, an absence of the old big carnivores, wide plantings of lush forage crops, and so on. Like coons, deer when not overhunted take kindly enough to human ways, at least in lightly peopled country.

The biggest reason they are doing well, however, seems to be the virtual elimination of a humble yet influential member of the Texas ecosystem called the screw-worm. This spiral maggot hatches with swarms of siblings from the eggs a specific blowfly lays in scratches and wounds on animals, and feeds on the host's living flesh, creating a still bigger wound for more eggs to be laid in, with ultimate mortal results for said host unless he has an owner and the owner sees the trouble and doctors it in time. Screw-worms not long ago were one of the uglier facts of stock raising anywhere in the belt of country, several hundred miles wide, through which the flies fanned out northward in the spring from the subtropical frost-free areas where they lived through winter. Like all agents of death they had a useful role in the natural scheme of things. But few men, nature-minded or not, who ever saw a cow with a nose or an ear turned into a deep pink-drooling pit lined with gnawing larvae, are likely to bewail their current scarcity, even if it has a lot of implications.

Control, as many people know by now, is a shrewd matter of lowering the creatures' birthrate. Along the Mexican border each spring large numbers of sterilized male flies are released from airplanes, enough to upset the breeding balance and prevent the annual northward spread. Most of the time it works, but occasionally a mild winter queers its mathematics and brings a summer infestation, never yet as bad as before, so that everybody has to start rooting around in vet cabinets for disused bottles of screw-worm dope and tools like Burdizzo emasculators, which alter bull calves without breaking the skin.

Control has helped the deer, which have never learned to live easily with barbed wire (panicked, they often charge a fence head-on instead of jumping it as usual) and thus are subject to many cuts and scratches. During my time around these parts they have increased dramatically enough to turn into agricultural pests in some sections of the county. Hard Scrabble is too small to have a population of them that can be called its own; they range through the neighborhood at will. But their tracks are usually thick along the creek and in the fields, and you often see the deer themselves in winter oats or wheat or while wandering quietly with a dog in the brush. Oddly, though more numerous, they seem in general shyer now than when I was first squireen and two or three at once would sometimes ghost silently out of a thicket to watch me at my digging and carpentry. The thinning of the cedar may have something to do with this, and maybe I myself am more absorbed in one project or another and hence am less observant, which is a thing the Syndrome does to you. . . .

Perhaps along with deer should go a mention of certain exotics that tread our cedarbrakes and pastures. They include such species as Asian blackbucks, Mediterranean moufflons, and English fallow deer, but they do not date from ancient days nor do I believe they are destined to survive for long. Four or five years ago one of the Nation's city ranchers got tired of patching the high expensive fence around the pasture he had stocked with them—the moufflons especially, it seems, being inclined just to charge on through heavy net wire whenever they wanted to get to the other side of it. So he fenced the escaped moufflons out, whereupon they charged back in again. Whereupon the owner in disgust opened the gates and let the whole zoo out. For a time I would occasionally see the compact herd of fallow deer grazing specter-pale along back roads at night, but so did some local midnight sporting types with spotlights, and I don't think many have lasted through.

Once riding around the high Booker pasture in a pickup, I stopped to talk with a couple of men digging post holes for a neighbor, a pair of the peripatetic Mexican nationals who show up in the region now and then, and departing leave behind them stout fences and corrals and sometimes pretty stonework. The burlier of them observed that our deer were indeed different from theirs at home, a specimen having just passed by that morning.

They had said they came from the state of Durango. Probably, I thought, their pueblo was in a part that had mule deer. I said, "Well, a little different. Maybe yours have black tails instead of white."

He looked tolerantly at me through liquid shrewd Indian eyes, leaning on his crowbar. "Tails, *chihuahua,*" he said. "A little different, no, señor. Much. *Mucho muy diferentes.*" And went on to describe what he had seen that morning— something big with humpy shoulders and long back-curving horns like swords. . . .

(Another sidelight on exotic-game preserves in the county—there have been three or four such ventures—occurred one evening when a truckdriver stopped at one of the highway filling stations in Glen Rose to ask directions to a certain ranch. He had a small covered cattle truck full of foreign antelopes and things, but attached to its rear was a trailer with two loud hungry full-grown African lions inside. The driver got his directions and the filling-station people got on the phone, and considerable angry turmoil got a toehold in the community before it was determined that the lions were bound for a municipal zoo somewhere and not for a roving life in the cedar hills.)

Lesser mammals on Hard Scrabble, as just about everywhere else on earth, are chiefly rodents. Fox squirrels sustain themselves on acorns and seeds and fruits and birds' eggs and such things, usually beating me to the fall harvest of nuts from the native pecans scattered through the bottomlands. Jack-rabbits on occasion lope jitterily away from my approach on the high Booker, but the place is too brushy to suit them well and they are few, preferring wide uncluttered grass. Cottontails thrive everywhere some years but at other times, beset by disease or an upflux in the raptorial beasts and birds that prize their tender flesh, they are very hard to find.

Of rats and voles and mice and such small deer we have legions, of a number of species all subject to the same sort of cyclical waxings and wanings as rabbits. For a year or two after the Big Drouth ended with gushing rains in 1957, there was a nuclear explosion of little rodents in the region. Granaries and grass and field crops suffered heavy damage; the root zones of cactus and yucca and other protective plants were riddled with holes; and almost any broad piece of junk or lumber lying on the ground had a half dozen or more underneath it. A dachshund I had then never quite got over that era of plentiful rats and was obsessed for the rest of his life with sheets of old roof-tin and plywood, snarling and yapping and tugging at their edges until his mouth would bleed. I knew a buzzard too, broken-winged from someone's casual shot, that lived fatly on a grassy hillside where I sometimes hunted, hopping about like something out of a cartoon and catching rats alive. . . . Then in response to all that wealth of rodent-meat, bobcats and foxes and hawks and snakes and such things burgeoned, and the small deer vanished or at least diminished hugely. It was a good textbook demonstration of the prime function and value of predators—though lost, I fear, on most of those who witnessed it.

A separate sort of mammal is the nine-banded armadillo, another range-expander that was scarce in North Texas in my childhood but is found all over the region now, a special frequenter of patches of deep soil like Hard Scrabble's little fields, which make good burrowing ground. Encased in jointed flexible armor, they grub noisily around in grass and surface litter for bugs and worms and larvae—generally at night in summer, but in winter mainly during the warm hours of warm days, shell armor not being a very good overcoat. Like most animals equipped by evolution with extra protection, they seem to have rather dim brains and their eyes and ears are not alert to danger. With a small amount of stealth you can sneak up on one where he roots and grab him. He will then give one huge vertical leap designed to tear himself loose from your grip, which it most often does (it is rough on armadillos, that habit, when cars pass over them on roads), and will bound away grotesquely toward his nearest hole or a brushpile, uttering as he goes a long complaining growl that is one of nature's most peevish and disgruntled sounds.

Armadillos are not revered by vegetable gardeners and people with pretty lawns, but except for sometimes rooting in such spots they are not a major menace to man's interests. They are bedeviled by small boys and all dogs, but only an occasional big dog learns the trick of crunching them or getting at their soft underparts before they reach a burrow, and I suspect the same thing is true of wild would-be armadillo-eaters. Once underground, even in a hole they are digging as you watch, they are just about impossible to extract without a spade. You can seize one's scaly tapering tail and pull with all your strength, and as the little shovel feet keep digging your arm will go right on down the hole with him.

In Mexico and among South Texas Latins they are traditionally good table fare. The wetbacks—at least those from armadillo regions—club one and gut it when they find it, out working, and bring it in at night to cook with beans and peppers. *Chacun à son goût.* . . . I have eaten young ones that were excellent, broiled and basted over mesquite coals, tender and porkishly flavored. But an encounter with the flesh of an old tough specimen, insufficiently parboiled, may dull your taste for 'dillo for a good long while. A chewed hunk of it gets bigger and bigger and bigger in the mouth. . . .

In birdlife we are relatively rich; the cedar hills along the Paluxy have some fame among nature-minded folks throughout North Texas as a sort of crossroads birding area. Eastern and western species often overlap—you used to need both of Peterson's *Field Guides* here, before he wrote a strictly Texas one. Vegetation and terrain lure in some types not usually seen north of the Hill Country down by Austin and San Antonio—things like vermilion flycatchers and golden-cheeked warblers and house finches. And the wintering population of northern birds is dense.

Bird lists are nice if you like birds, but I think this is not the place for one, nor could I present mine with much pride. I am not adept at birding, being too often preoccupied with other things and inclined to get impatient with minor specific distinctions, like that Englishman who complained that one small brown bird was very much like another small brown bird. But birds have always mattered to me, and over a period of time I have more or less casually noted the presence of well over a hundred species in the country here along White Bluff, from a stray golden eagle on down. A good dedicated Audubonite could easily have found two or maybe three times as many.

At daybreak in a moist green spring, even I can lie in bed on the screen porch and know the waking songs and calls of twelve or fifteen different familiar kinds—quail, doves, redbirds, mockers, tanagers, orioles, gnatcatchers, titmice, chickadees, woodpeckers and wrens and flycatchers of various sorts, lark sparrows, towhees, and the like. Plus, nearly always, two or three or more unknowns . . . Then the chorus swells till individual songs are lost in it. Nor have I in an often rootless life found many seasons and places so pleasant for coming awake. Maybe the nearest thing to it in my memory would be a room I had in Santa Cruz on Tenerife one very good year long ago, where I could roll up on the pillows and look out across the ocean at huge red thunderstorms on the mountains of Grand Canary, against the dawn. Birds sang outside there too, but I did not know their names. That being a long long way from the Tonk Nation . . .

The changes the Syndrome has sponsored in the past few years have altered the numbers and kinds of birds we have, though I know I have seen only the most obvious of such shifts. Before, for instance, there were few mockingbirds, but plenty sing and scold here now in the oaks left when the cedar was cleared; they dislike brush and require an ample view. Mixed big flocks of wintering finches hang around the brushpiles that result from clearing. Open-country species such as scissortailed flycatchers and paisano roadrunners and some hawks like us better now also. But the two or three wild turkeys I used to see have left for parts unknown, and other birds that crave the cedar's privacy have moved to the remaining patches of it or onto uncleared neighboring places. You have to walk a way now to find the great barking winter congregations of robins and the high-voiced flocks of waxwings, and I hear fewer screech owls' bubbling wails at night close by the house, and regret the loss. Nevertheless, a lot of cedar is left and will be while I'm here. The biggest piece of it, the steep rough Kyle hillside east of the creek, remains as it was, nearly impenetrable, ready each March for the golden-cheeked warblers that fly up from Guatemala to nest there, as do a wealth of other less vivid avian types.

Buzzards wheel in our sky throughout the year, two species, and have a roost behind the Booker bluff where dozens drop down at sunset. You have to be a real whole-nature pantheist to find much to like about them, but their function is a strong one in the frame of things. Thin-skinned carrion they rend and gobble in short order—quick service, though it can be an annoyance when you're trying to find out from signs what beast if any it was that killed a goat or kid. But their consumption of a dead cow is a drawn-out obscene conviviality perhaps best left undescribed, much of it dependent on decay and the avenues opened by stronger-jawed scavengers. The end result is a pile of stomach herbiage and a strew of stinking bones and rawhide, which mice and other things gnaw away in time, for phosphorus. Yet a vulture is beauty in the sky. . . .

And like all people who look around where they live, we have a collection of known bird personalities, not so often individuals as flocklets and families for whom the place has become a habit, and whose nestings and conflicts and appetites and tragedies and triumphs come under our eyes.

Some migrate in seasonally; others stay. A pair of phoebes preempts our eave-lights or the kitchen window's drip cap for a nest platform each spring, and for me the place's single most distinctive summer sound is the querulous squeaking of a family of blue-gray gnatcatchers that come back year after year to dwell in the good liveoaks by the house. To watch one on a twig with his beak held proudly high and that monotonous mew emerging, high music to him and his, can be a study in the relativity of esthetics. A horned owl on Snipers' Hill will answer if you hoot back at him on winter nights. The recently finished barn, a truss-roofed semi-open structure, attracts all sorts of small birds, to whom it seems perhaps a big shady tree or maybe an airy cave; trim canyon wrens in particular favor it, flitting about the rafters and rasping at the cat. Bewick's wrens and Carolina wrens are everywhere, building nests in spring under tractor hoods or among your tools and bins of nails and bolts, even if you have put up gourds and boxes for their use. Cardinals, jays, painted buntings, the garden's hummingbirds . . . But I seem to have promised there would be no lists. They belong on the place, the birds. They will be here when I'm gone. . . .

Yet the birds that move me most belong not to the place but to the air—the spacious passersby, the big migrant geese and cranes and things that pattern the sky in spring and fall, trumpeting their indifference to patches of wrinkled hard-used earth that lie between where they've been and where they're bound, whether to coast or northern nesting ground. More vulnerable to man's changes than most small species— maybe doomed—they yet have more of eternity in them too. . . . And one October morning years ago, before I owned the place, I was on White Bluff alone when the hawks came through. There was a new norther, as there often is when birds move over us in fall. They came in towering whirlpools, three in all with a thousand hawks or more in each and clots and flocks elsewhere, some quite low—all buteos as far as I could tell, redtails and Swainsons and other broad-winged soaring types. The whirlpools moved with the north wind across the silent land and the hawks circled in them, silent, each somehow alone as we are used to thinking of them and yet part of a big whole too. By the time the third tall spiral flight passed over, the first was on the south horizon, invisible except through a glass. I had not heard of such flights before, nor have I seen them since except in minor form. Afterward a neighbor told me that as a boy in Oklahoma he had once seen hawks fly through like that, and people called it a "hawk storm." After fifty years he remembered it well. So will I mine if I last that long.

By testimony of the oldest part of the Old Word, God laid a curse upon the serpent and put enmity between him and the woman, and between his seed and her seed, and in Somervell County as elsewhere on the globe few people have doubts concerning the correctness of this state of affairs. Mainly in these quarters when anyone says "snake" without a descriptive prefix he means a rattlesnake, and usually when he says it he has a tale to tell, for rattlesnakes are much more productive of narrative than of hurt, hurtful though they can be on occasion.

We have enough to keep us conscious of them, if un-doubtedly fewer than there were in Indian days or in the time of cedar's reign or even when I first came on the place. Dogs and livestock get bitten by them and for the most part survive. Once one struck me on the boot from underneath a piece of ledge stone I was lifting to carry away, and the pos-sibility of them at certain times and places gives life a little piquancy. In recent years, without especially looking for them, I have come across six or eight a year, usually in fields when plowing or mowing but sometimes too in unbeseeming spots like woodpiles or front yards.

By cocking an ear to stories that come your way you can get descriptions of some gargantuan Somervell County rattlers. One man told me as a Gospel certitude that in moonshining days he met one on a dirt road in the cedar so large that when it coiled and raised its head it was glaring him in the eye across the radiator cap of his Model T; he said he backed up and drove out as he had come rather than dispute the right of way. . . . But legends proliferate in rattler country anywhere, whether based on fact or whiskey or creative fantasy. The biggest one I have seen on Hard Scrabble was only about four and a half feet long before being draped dead over a fence (where they stretch, after which process most big-snake measurements are taken . . .), though he was fat and ugly enough to satisfy my own modest aspirations in terms of sizable serpents.

During the cool months rattlesnakes foregather in torpid tangles in dens beneath hillside ledges or occasionally under old houses and other structures. Certain enthusiasts sometimes spy them out and with squirted gasoline fume the whole lot into the open, there to kill them or occasionally to stuff them into towsacks and bear them off alive. I have found no dens on Hard Scrabble, though there could be some. Out of a hole on a neighbor's place one March, such hunters took over seventy in an afternoon.

If there are fewer in our neighborhood now than there were not many years ago, the hunters may have had something to do with it—but not so much perhaps as cedar-clearing and possibly goats, which have a reputation for driving them out. This in turn may have less connection with active goatish hostility toward snakes (you can hear some fine wild tales about that also) than with the fact that goats gnaw down the shinnery and other underbrush in whose thick moist shade rattlers love to harbor on hot days, for they move around only at night in summer, and are abroad in daylight usually for just a month or so in spring and another short time in fall. One July midnight two or three years ago my sheep-dog Blue, who once nearly died from a bite and hates rattlers above all living things, bayed one beside the house. When I flicked on an eave-light and went out, eight feet from the coiled and buzzing viper lay interested but unperturbed the children's pet Nubian milk goat Door Bell and her twin kids, cudding placidly. No active hostility there . . .

My bastard and inconsistent pantheism, I confess, breaks down a bit in relation to rattlesnakes and copperheads, of which latter we have also a few. I kill them when they turn up, but without the vengeful satisfaction that attaches to the slaughter of such things as horseflies and squash bugs and out-law dogs. I suspect that if I were living on the place all by myself, a cranky hermit without children or pets or stock to worry about, along with most other living things I would let the poisonous snakes pretty much alone also, leaving them to the slithering thermosensitive pursuit of rodents that is their main absorption. Though I am of Eve's own distant get and lack special affection toward legless fanged reptiles and have a wary respect for their powers, I lack also the loathing some people feel for them. I have seen a tough brown bulldozer man who would take on three beered-up opponents in any tavern fracas, having uncovered with his blade a thick writh-ing rattler beneath a cedar's roots and having seen it bashed dead with a stick by someone else, namely me, get down off his yellow tractor and vomit long and hard. . . . The fact is that few people get bitten by them, and very few of those few die, and when we have succeeded in exterminating them, as probably we will, something in us may then begin to miss them, as something in us misses bears and panthers. For they too are a part of the way things work, they and their very fearsomeness. Despite Mother Eve and all that.

In fact, this unprepossessing spread of dirt and rocks and

brush has on it enough creatures, those we have glanced at and others, who are all a part of the way things work, that it would take a set of volumes for a knowledgeable man to tell about them right, and a book at least for a mere resident peasant like me to put down what he observes more or less ignorantly from year to year. Harmless snakes of varying lengths and habits and shapes and colors, toads and frogs and lizards and terrapins and turtles, the little bass and bream and minnows that valiantly repopulate White Bluff from the Paluxy when storms set it flowing again after drouth—swimming up the waterfall's spout like miniature salmon and taking possession of the renewed pools, sometimes to grow there during years to angling size before low water lets coons and herons and other native fish-fanciers get at them and clean them out. . . .

And bugs, some obscure and some legendary and all with specific ways of being whose study would reward a lifetime's work if a man were built that way . . . Tarantulas and scorpions and centipedes and other southwestern uglies that become merely factual and rather interesting after you've lived with them for a while. Garden beetles and weevils and aphids and moths and caterpillars, the focus of much grumbling Old Fart activity with potions and discouragements, and on the other hand earthworms, the ancient earth's real plowmen, which the O. F. prizes and seeks to foster . . . Mud-daubers, specialists in adobe construction and the collection of paralyzed spiders. Leaf-cutter bees, plugging bolt holes and tubing and any other small cylindrical cavities you would rather have unobstructed. Black polistes wasps that rain fire-hot on your head when you chop at the wrong cedar tree and shake their nest, and red ones that build beneath crumpled tin and beehives and other things on or near the ground. Big biting red ants, and the smaller varieties that countrymen lump as "piss ants" and use for rustic metaphor ("He wouldn't pay a nickel to see a piss ant eat a bale of hay," etcetera). Tumblebugs, born to roll big balls of poot along rough ground, in poetic simulation of much human effort. Cicadas, the Texas "locusts" without whose high pervading rasp there could be no July afternoons. Ticks and chiggers and mosquitoes, and flies of half a dozen sorts to plague your stock and you—somewhere, maybe later, there has to be room to set down a diatribe on horseflies, concerning whose noxious ways a Tonkish peasant becomes unwillingly an expert. . . .

All a part of it, they and the rest on down to the microorganisms of the soil. Teeming around you seen or unseen, going their separate forceful driven ways that add up somehow to a whole and single Way whose intricacies no man truly knows. Making the place work, sometimes for man the Head Varmint and sometimes not, sometimes for themselves and sometimes not, but always for the sake of the Way, and for the world's own sake.

10 ⪨⪨ *His Chapter* ⪢⪢⪢⪢⪢⪢

As always, after rising and turning on the coffee he went to stand spraddle-legged in shorts on the little concrete-floored side porch, facing the eastern horizon's pale blushful smudge of foretold daybreak. Stars still hung above it and he could see no clouds about, though wishing for them. Between him and the predawn were a honeysuckled fence that shielded the house a little from the highway, the highway itself with honkytonks and welding shops and repair garages and quick-food stands all silent now, their neon mainly dead, and then prairies dropping to a far-off wooded riverbottom and rising beyond it, specked here and there with random lighted windows in creepingjesus suburbs that had not been there three years before. At a distance to his left were the night lights of the city that had spawned the suburbs. Puked them, the Old Fart put it to himself when pondering such matters, but he was not pondering suburbs now. He was watching the promise of day, and waking up, and relieving himself on vocal absorbent flowerbed soil.

With shudderings he finished, felt suddenly the windless

morning cold of March, and went inside. Beneath blankets Samantha stirred and spoke from a mouth stiff with sleep, concerning her spirea. He shoved down a flick of rage not only at what she was mumbling but at the fact of her being awake. On Sundays, when he did not work his half-day at the station out the highway, he counted on two or three hours of quiet and solitude to muse and putter before she got up for church.

"Nitrogen," he said. "Potash. Good for them bushes. I hit a different one every day."

Muffled and descending, her reply sank back into sleep. Relieved and a bit guilty because of it, he eased into pants and flannel shirt and blue peaked cap and went out to the kitchen. Into a glass of cold milk he crumbled wedges of last night's cornbread and fished them out with a spoon and ate them, then poured and sipped black coffee with honey in it. Considering the silent radio, he decided to leave it silent, not caring about the news and knowing already what the weather reports would say, weather being something he did care about and always had. Had had to care about . . .

Southwest dry winds off the Old Mexico desert, or maybe a dry norther with no Gulf moisture in the air for it to loose. Clear skies, as there had been mainly since early January, the autumn's rain sunk two feet deep or more by now. A winter drouth was harder to take somehow than summer ones were, unreasonable. . . . A hell of an electric bill there would be this month, for pumping from the well to the garden. She would have some things to say. Let her. . . . It cost less than the new city water, to which so far he had refused to be connected, though they came and threatened him into hooking up to the sewer they had finally pushed out that far, despite a good septic tank that sub-irrigated his fruit trees. Creeping, crawling, surrounding-him bastards . . .

Nursing his coffee cup between big-knuckled hands warmed by it, the O. F. cursed creepers and crawlers and rainlessness. He was not, however, very angry. The city would come and eat him up if it wanted to, and of drouth he had a lifetime's knowledge and could accept it when it came. Nor was there any longer a problem, for him, of wide pastures needing rain. Just a vegetable garden, and it could be watered, if expensively. And a piece of bermudagrass front lawn and flowerbeds too, hers, but the longer the lawn waited for rain the less it would need to be mowed when warm weather came; the O. F., though tolerant of such foibles in others, lacked enthusiasm for lawns and flowers and other tame, growing, troublesome, pretty things that demanded water and care but couldn't be eaten or fed to animals. Wild growing pretty things, he conceded, were something else and he liked them. Besides, some of them furnished honey and others grazing and they all helped hold dirt where it belonged. . . .

It would be time to milk if he still had a cow but he didn't. When the old one had died the females, Samantha and their married older daughter Kate who lived in the creeping city, had kicked up such a fog about his getting another that for once he had gone along with them. In secret he had not much minded, being a little tired of seeing milk go to waste or to chickens because he and Samantha could use only a little and Kate had decided raw milk was unsanitary. But for livestock now he was down to hens and bees and he missed having animals around, to worry over their quirks and needs. During practically all of his life there had been animals to think about and care for, sometimes hundreds of them. . . .

For the O. F. had been a cowboy once, of sorts. Not born to it, but a fair enough hand nonetheless. He had not especially intended all that, but when he thought about such things he had not intended a hell of a lot of what had happened in his life. Except leaving Oklahoma . . . He had grown up in the southeastern corner of that state, the Little Dixie part along the Red, good farming country in its flatter parts, mild green country with most years plenty of rain. But its people had been around there for a good long while, and their ways tended to hem you in, if you were restless and ready for work that went somewhere, and part Choctaw and the part that wasn't came out of a family that had been share-croppers since who throwed the chunk. Hemmed you in especially during a Depression that started just after you got married, having waited till things looked right . . . He made up his mind finally to quit being hemmed in, and afterward he supposed that had been the same thing as making up his mind to leave, though to begin with, leaving had not been what he had in mind. One afternoon he cornered his boss at the barn mule pen, a man of about thirty who was also his landlord.

"I need a little more money, Josh," said the O. F., then a Y. F., twenty-seven. "Me and Laurie we're scraping bottom. You ain't paying me no more than you pay them darky mule-drivers, and me doing a good part of their work."

"But they ain't got no eighty acres to share-farm like you do," the landlord said. Country neighbors all their lives and remote kinsmen of some sort, they were easy enough with each other, the main difference between them being that he had hold of a thousand acres or so of land, most of it his wife's, and the Y. F. had hold of nothing much but a girl wife and a baby boy, and his wife had nothing but a daddy with a grocery store from whom the Y. F. would accept no help. The best land the landlord had he farmed for himself with hired labor, and the Y. F.'s job in that operation was taking care of the mules, nearly sixty of them. What he got from the sharecrop place, if anything, was extra.

"Eighty acres," he said. "We been over that. Them clay hills is plumb wore out, like they was when your papa got through with them. It takes about ten roosters to fertilize one egg, up there."

The landlord grinned and said, "Didn't I use to farm it too? I told you, whenever old Haskins makes up his mind to go ahead and die, I'll let you have that place he's got."

"Haskins is good for another twenty years," the Y. F. said. "Anybody that talks that much about how he hurts . . . All I want is five dollars more a month, Josh. Thirty-five measly bucks."

"Ain't nothing measly about a buck right now," the landlord said. "I can't see it."

"Well, I ain't staying."

"Sure you are," said Josh. "No place else to go, these days. Loan me a bite off your Tinsley, if you got some that ain't sweated up."

"No, I ain't staying," the Y. F. repeated without anger, fishing for his tobacco and pondering the fact that after all that was what it came to, not staying. Leaving Little Dixie . . . Well, by God, that was what it came to, then. . . .

The old Chalmers touring car, shot when he bought it and not much improved since, carried them as far as Sweetwater, Texas, before it blew up for good. An aging bachelor with a filling station watched it die with them, continuing to squirt his hose into the radiator even after it was clear that whatever water went in was coming right back out again through a big crack in the engine block, not that the tires would have gone much farther anyhow or the gasoline money either. Then he put them in a lean-to room back of the station and fed them pinto beans and biscuits until the Y. F. got a job carrying water in buckets to workers on a pipeline, kid work at kid pay.

Still and all, he believed it was going to work out. But then one night the baby died with a quick fever before they were even certain he was sick, and her family sent her a train ticket so she could come back home and eat groceries out of the store with them, and she left alone because he would not go with her.

"Not won't, honey," he said. "Can't. It's like I'd done swore to it. I left out for good. You go ahead if you want to, and I'll send for you later when you got your feelings straightened out."

"I don't promise nothing," Laurie said. "I just want my mama. I want to sit down and look at some trees and not think about nothing at all."

Later, divorce papers caught up with him somewhere and he signed them. . . . He was still twenty-seven, having been doing man's labor since fourteen when his parents and sister died of the World War flu and he quit school to drive pipe-wagons in the oilfields for a while. He had now no people anywhere closer than an aunt or two and some cousins. He could not think at all about the baby for a long long time, and he felt guilty about Laurie too, all the rest of his life. But she had known about the leaving for good. . . .

Josh wrote him also and said a lot of the mules were sick and soremouthed and he had not really known the Y. F. wanted a pay raise all that bad, and as the Y. F. read that part he grinned a little bit sourly. He wasn't going back. He might be good and messed up, but he wasn't hemmed in any more.

He did miss mules and cows and things, though, and missed farming talk and country talk, there among the rootless hard oilfield workers. They worked through country—mesquite country and grass country, sandy and rocky, rough and smooth—but they paid it no mind at all. By now he had followed work a hundred miles south, into the rolling limestone Edwards Plateau region, a full pipeliner himself with fair wages for those times. But one Saturday when he heard a dried-up old rancher talking in a café with someone about trying to hire a fence crew, he sidled three stools over and asked about it. And though the pay, besides food, was not much more than tobacco and shoeleather money he took a job, riding out the next day on the back end of a flatbed truck with fifty sacks of cottonseed cake and three Mexicans and two bleary pale winos while the rancher and a couple of slobbering border collies sat in front. He knew about post holes and barbed wire and all that tedium, but it would be country work anyhow. He had had enough of long straight ditches and of threading big pieces of iron pipe into one another, and of listening to his fellows' talk of intermeshed weekend beer and fights and poontang. People were the different ways they were and he had known about that for a long time and it was all right with him. But a couple of his mother's half-Indian brothers had been mean, troublesome, hard-case drunks and as a kid he had seen enough of that. It was not a way of life he hankered toward. . . .

Nine months later when the fencing was all done the Y. F., having outlasted a succession of Anglo drifters whose thirst that limestone vastness enhanced, and several wetbacks whose homesickness finally won out over the lure that even Depression gringo wages held, went to the ranch house to draw his pay, which he had let ride till then. It was a two-story, wooden-galleried cube of limestone slabs put up in a liveoak grove by the rancher's grandfather in the late 1860's, when he had brought his clan there from the Fredericksburg German country, with Comanches still around. It sat in a pretty valley, and the barn and other outbuildings were of stone too, with hewn timbers, more solid by far than any country structures the Y. F. had ever seen before. The rancher, a widower in his late fifties named Schraeder, lived in the house with eleven border collies, sipped bootleg *sotol* through the day without ever getting drunk, was attended by an aged scolding Mexican cook who had her own stone cabin nearby, and for help kept a couple of married vaqueros whose children were shouting this evening down at the springfed cypress-bordered creek below the house where they swam.

He had a big nose and small sharp dark eyes and spoke

nasal West Texas English tinged by the separate facts that he had grown up speaking German at home, and that during the several years since his wife had died he had had little occasion to speak anything but Tex-Mex Spanish except on visits to town. There was windmill grease on his shirt. He said, shoving a sheaf of bills toward the Y. F. across the table, in his office by the living room, "I stuck in a little extra. Shame it ain't more, the way you worked."

"I only done what there was," the Y. F. said.

"I watched you," old Schraeder said. "Getting ten hours a day out of them old rummies without even making them mad. Treating them Meskins like they was people and learning some of their talk."

"Nothing hard about that. They're pretty good folks."

"Damn right they are," said Schraeder. "One of my grandmamas was a Meskin."

"One of mine was an Indian."

"You like this country?"

"I guess I do," the Y. F. said. "It ain't what I'm used to, but a man feels like he amounts to something, sort of."

"The way you handle them wagon mules, I bet you could make out with cows and horses and goats and stuff."

"I reckon I could."

"Well, God damn, I guess we'll keep you," old Schraeder said without the subject's having been mentioned before, and kicked at a dog beneath the table that had just horribly broken wind. He said, "She always feeds them frijoles. . . . You'll have to take orders from Domingo for a while, but I don't guess you'll mind that. He knows more about the place than anybody, maybe including me."

"You got some farming that needs doing," the Y. F. said.

"*Farming?*"

"You got some flat bottomland here in this valley that ain't never been turned," the Y. F. said. "Deep black dirt, two or three hundred acres anyhow, maybe more. It don't need nothing but a little brush cleared off. You could run water on it out of that creek and raise plenty of winter oats and hay and stuff. Or anything else."

"*Chingar,*" old Schraeder said. "All we needed around here was somebody else trying to run things. It was one reason my grandpapa moved out on them other Dutchmen way back yonder, to get away from dirt farming. . . . That and a Meskin wife that didn't like Dutchmen and they didn't like her."

"Just the same, it makes sense. Ain't no point in buying all that hay and feed you use."

"We'll see," the rancher said. "You'll be staying here at the house; there's a room old Juana can fix up for you."

Which was the start of that . . .

He added hot coffee to his cup without sweetening it further, and carried it out the back door into the little patio space there, under a big hackberry. Gray cold dawn light had come on, with no wind still, and somewhere a redbird throated chew, chew, tentatively and did not finish the song. The space was paved with old street bricks he had hauled in from a dumpground, and had flowerbeds and chairs and a table and a grill, also made of street bricks, where sometimes he cooked meat. It was enclosed all about with fences and hedges and had evolved in the past few years as a refuge against the increasing stir of people as the neighborhood built up around them. The O. F. liked its privacy though without usually admitting that he did, it having been Samantha's idea in the beginning.

Beyond the gate in the wood fence that walled the patio to the rear, in the bare-dirt chicken and laundry yard outside his garden, he paused to look at his bees, three trim white hives that he had broken down and rummaged through a few days before, to find that they had wintered well and were rearing young for spring. One solitary worker trundled out onto a hive porch in a little semicircle, found the air still too cool for bees, and without stopping went back inside to spread that news. Later in the day, though, they would be working oaks and things for pollen. The O. F. while sipping coffee and watching the hives reached up with his free hand and felt along a hackberry branch that dipped down across the fence, and thumbed the green flex of emerging buds. He would have to move the hives soon, probably to the orchard now that no cow grazed there to nose them over. Samantha claimed they soiled her sheets on the line and the O. F. knew it was true; a bee with a load of poot was too neat ever to drop it in the hive but even in winter would fly straight out and cut loose in the air. He liked bees and had been around them forever. At Schraeder's he had kept fifty-odd colonies, a few in good frame hives like these and the rest in tall boxes of the sort his father had once used. . . . Here near the city they were less pleasure than they had been at first, with people planting ligustrum hedges that queered honey and spraying poisons that killed bees.

The thermometer bee, or another like it, came out and looked around again. "You better go back in there and holler up a rain dance," the O. F. told it. "Ain't going to be much flowers, the way things are."

Setting his empty cup on one of the hives, he dipped milo maize from a can in a shed and scattered it, then let the hens out of their house. They filed through the little flap-doored entrance and down the cleated board in order of their known precedence, fat big Orpingtons certain of their dignity and in no hurry, each with one wing clipped to keep her from flying over fences. He wanted to hatch some eggs this spring, and needed a rooster soon. . . .

Beside the henhouse on the alley side his eye sensed pale movement, and when he turned and looked, it was a little red-

eyed, bench-legged, white feist dog standing with some sur-
prised belligerence not far from the hole through which he
had just come under the heavy net fence, and which the O. F.
had been intending for weeks now to stop up.

"Dog, what you got in mind?" the O. F. asked.

The feist replied with a low-muttered insolent growl
whose purport was clearly that it was none of the O. F.'s business. But it was. The O. F. knew, from out of his long
countryman's experience with wandering canines, just about
what the feist had in mind, or what if not now he would soon
have in mind.

Nothing having happened, the dog tried a somewhat
more confident growl almost edging into a bark. The O. F.,
raising one shoulder and lowering the other and waggling
loose hands at his sides, leered grotesquely and lurched toward
him. The half-bark became a squall and the feist turned and
ran for the hole under the fence, bumping his head three times
against the thick bottom wire before he got it through and
fled off down the alley.

You could practically always do that with little red-
eyed dogs. . . .

"That ain't a very nice way to act," someone said, and
the O. F. swung guiltily toward the voice and saw a dark lean
tousled girl in green standing in the alley, smiling slightly. A
part of his mind recalled hearing a car door slam on the highway and then an engine's surge; someone had let her out.

"I got chickens," he said—unnecessarily, for the big hens
were chortling and scratching among the feed he had strewn
for them.

"We lived in a country kind of a place when I was
little," the girl said. "And we had us some big white turkeys
and a dog got in and killed twelve of them one night. Not
even to eat, just to kill."

"Uh-huh," said the O. F., relieved to find comprehension.
"Did your daddy get the dog?"

"I never had no daddy," the girl said shortly. "At least that I remember. He hauled out."

The O. F. grunted and studied her. The long black hair needed a hard combing and there were smudged pouches beneath the dark eyes, but it was a shapely enough lean face with maybe a little Indian in it, or something like that. And a lot of tiredness, years of that . . . Not over twenty-five or twenty-six, maybe less. The green dress was rumpled and into his head came suddenly an old jukebox tune, with fiddles. Coreen, Coreena, it said. . . .

Coreen, Coreena-a-a-ah,
Where'd you stay last night? . . .

He said, "I got a girl that looks a little bit like you."

"I bet she looks better than me right now," the girl said. "I bet she ain't sneaking home to her kids up no damn alley at six thirty on Sunday morning."

"She could be, honey," the O. F. said. "I don't know where to God she is."

"You run her off."

"No," he said. "No, I don't think so. Maybe I ought to have known more than I did, to help her some."

The girl looked at him gently but with dismissal; she had enough troubles of her own, the look said. . . . "Anyhow, your girl had a daddy," she said. "Good-bye, old man." And went on along the alley, teetering a little on high heels in its dry rough-rutted ground. . . .

You're all mussed up,
And your clothes don't fit you right.

Feeling older than he had before, the O. F. brought salvaged bricks from a pile in the corner of the chicken yard and laid them in the hole beneath the fence, stamping them firm with his heel. He was not ready to think about Midge yet, Midge being one trouble with Sundays, when you did tend to think. Midge who had come to see him six months before, for the first time in nine years, and had gone away into nowhere again . . . He passed through the garden gate and closing it behind him squatted at the end of a row of young potato plants to survey the lines of early things, frost-safe or nearly so, that he had been putting in since January, each in its proper time. English peas grasping upward blindly for the fencewire trellis he had erected for them. Radishes and lettuce, already usable. Chard and beets and carrots and cabbage and collards and onions, some almost mature and others just thin green lines of recent sprouts, and in between the rows the nearly weedless, cultivated prairie earth, blacker now than when he had first turned it up from sod nine years before, mellow and sooty with humus from the manure and hay and compost he had fed it season by season, year by year. Ritually and almost without knowledge that he did it, he reached down and grasped a light clod, and felt it collapse flakily between his fingers.

By God, he might not know all he needed to know about people, and he was fairly certain now that he never would. But he knew dirt, and dirt knew him, and dirt mattered. The feel of it light and right in his hand or the smell and look of it turning up and over from a plow or slicing beneath a hoe or churning under the tines of a tiller took away from feeling old and set worry to one side. He knew it was not so for everyone. . . . Of boys he had known in childhood, raised on the same tired red hill land his father and he had had to work and live from, many had taken off for towns and factories and filling stations and railroad jobs as soon as they were big enough, bitter against the soil for the rest of their lives. Others less rebellious had stayed on to hate it and fight it where they were, as their fathers had done, maybe with tractors now, maybe forcing a little more production from the sour clay with what bagged fertilizer they could afford or their landlords were willing to furnish. Or maybe doing it better now; he did not know. He had not gone back to see, ever. Nor felt the need to go.

There were bound to have been some, he knew, who like himself knew about good dirt from seeing it in the bottoms that richer farmers owned, and on the high hillsides too steep to plow, where trees grew from it and grasses held it firm. Some even who understood that by caring and by work you could make sorry tired old dirt over again into good, if you had time and the stuff to do it with. His mother had shown him that in the little garden she kept, red rain-eaten clay in the beginning, with a little sand to it, like everything else around that farm. He had watched and helped from babyhood as she hauled to it pitiful interminable buckets and barrows full of chicken and mule and milk cow poot and forest leaves and pea hulls and hogpen muck and dead dogs and snakes and poultry-plant guts and heads and feathers and anything else she could get hold of, and dug them all in with a hoe, and sowed year after year in the darkening loosening soil her queer Choctaw jumbles of corn and tomatoes and beans and squash and things not even in proper rows, but always lush.

You could only own land in your head, his mother said, the way she owned that garden. They had never had title to it or to anything else worth having, but they had eaten well just about always. It was God that did it, she said, God in the dirt. You fed God and He fed you. He supposed she had been about half-crazy, his mother, raised among the sad, beaten, uprooted, preacher-hating Indians that were her own mother's people, with a white sot father who showed up from time to time to make another baby. Other people had thought her crazy. He did not even know how she had worked out that business about God, or where the seed of it had come from; some full-Indian farmers he had known had been as ironheaded and brutal toward the land as anyone else.

But he was glad enough to have had her for a mother, crazy or not, for what she had shown him about dirt. Dirt was, if truth were told, a big part of his own religion too.

And despite old Schraeder's voiced distaste for farming, he had had a streak of that religion inside him. It was the damned Dutch blood, he said. Mainly he had it in terms of grass and rain and animals, and keeping cows off a hilly range that was starting to wash, and refusing to put out poison bait for coyotes till they had eaten up two or three dozen goats, and things like that. But long before the Y. F. turned up at the ranch, Schraeder had been aware of that good bottomland and had thought over its possible use. Now, with someone else who cared, he found a contractor with a big crew of wetbacks and set them to grubbing out mesquite and pear, and months later when they were through they had uncovered nearly four hundred acres of flat plowland in six fields along the creek.

It was too much farming for mules and a man or two or three, though the Y. F. said it wasn't, not if they concentrated on getting one or two of the fields in shape each year. He started in stubbornly with a team and a rusty double sulky plow traded from a neighboring ranch, but a couple of Saturdays later old Schraeder rattled home from town with a new green tractor and a one-way disk plow chained down to the big bed of his truck, and told the Y. F. to go in and charge any other implements he needed.

"A field a year ain't enough," he said. "I want to get a look at the whole shittaroo all green and pretty before I die."

The climate with its long dry spells and its searing winds and its short wet stormy times whose moisture you had to save and use just right was new to the Y. F., and Schraeder knew nothing about farming at all. Their first winter oats were sparse and nearly worthless for grazing because the Y. F. had not allowed for moisture and time enough to rot the turned-under sod before he sowed. But a wet spring followed and in the summer they made enough sudan hay that Schraeder sold five thousand bales over and above what his animals could possibly eat in the four dead months of the winter to come. In time they got the feel of it, aided by the virgin land. . . . The fifth year, the Y. F. ditched and bordered for irrigation in two of the flattest, largest fields and sowed them to permanent alfalfa, and before long the farming and the haying were an easy part of the ranch's functioning, along with calf work in spring and fall, and doctoring through the year, and shearing mohair goats, and fencing and fixing windmills, and the other things there were to do on eleven thousand rough acres with three hundred cows and six to eight hundred goats and assorted horses and mules and machines. By then the little colony of ranch Mexicans saw him as a part of things, and liked him. He was into his thirties and therefore, I suppose, no longer a Y. F. but just a lean tough-fibered F. The hard, dusty, pleasant work suited him well, even horses, for he had always been quick with his hands and with beasts. And if he remained clumsy with a lariat rope, a tool you needed to come to young, the fact was that with Domingo and Tomás around, nobody else got to do much roping anyhow. . . .

In the town he found a library with a section of farming and livestock books, and he took to deviling old Schraeder about new and better ways to do things, sometimes with success. They built working chutes and headgates in the corrals, which disgusted Domingo and Tomás but got cow work done faster and less roughly, and cross-fenced some of the pastures to manage the grass better, and rotated crops on the farmland, and began to put bulls with the cows for only a couple of months a year, to make calves drop together in the spring before screw-worms made a start. From books, most of it . . . Sometimes, though, Schraeder balked.

"I don't want no part of it," he said of a hog-raising scheme the F. proposed. "No more than I did with them snotty-nosed sheep I finally got shut of. If you like hogs, you build you a pen out of sight down the creek somewhere so they can't get in my water or eat my grass or stink up my air, and I'll sell you grain and hay for what it costs to raise, and you sell them fat nasty bastards for what you can get, and keep it. I ain't no hog man."

Later on, out of hogs and other things that Schraeder didn't mind his doing but wanted no part of, the F. made some years as much as four thousand dollars besides his pay, but that too suited the old man fine. If you did your work for him he was for your getting whatever else you could, and for that matter some of the F.'s random projects, like the bees and the big vegetable patch by the creek, had side benefits for everyone. . . .

At thirty-six he married the librarian in the town, a spinster of thirty-three. It was perhaps inevitable, since she was one of the only unmarried women he ever saw, and Samantha saw few men who cared for books. The ones he liked were only one kind of books and no Hawthorne or Poe, but books. . . . It was his energy too, she said later when things had gone a bit sour and she was wondering aloud what had inflicted them on each other, a habit perhaps developed by reading Poe, or someone. "Like something was about to break out through your skin," she said. "Like you were going to start running, or jump up in the air and yell."

"I still got it," the F. said. "You just don't like where it goes to any more."

"I don't care where it goes," she said. "I just want a house in a town and some neighbors the girls can learn to talk to in English. . . . What you like is doing things. What I want is to be somebody."

Though without saying so, the F. could not see the difference. What you did you were.

Of the way he was in those early years at Schraeder's, he later remembered mainly a feeling like leaning forward on his toes, straining to get on into what came next to do. All the hemmed-in Little Dixie thing was gone, along with red clay and Laurie and Josh and the rest. So God-awful many things to do now, good things worth doing, and the days and years so short . . . After they married they lived in a rock house by the creek where one of Schraeder's uncles had once lived, and a baby came, Kate, and a war too but they did not want him at his age with a mule-kicked knee, and still there was more to do than there were days. When Midge was born in the last year of the war and Samantha started tugging toward the town, he was forty-two and had been at Schraeder's, he counted up without believing it, for fourteen years. He wished to hell the young bad years had gone that fast, and the good ones had slowed down.

Not that they were finished, just changed a little . . . He did not have the habit of introspection, but he knew he was not built for fighting with a woman. As far as he knew, she was right, and that possibility made him guilty. Women, he recognized by now, made him guilty. . . . With money he had saved from pay and hogs and things he bought a little white frame house in the town an hour away from the ranch, and she moved there with the girls. The arrangement had worked as well as anything could have worked for them, he guessed. He stayed there in town sometimes, driving out to work, but less and less with the years. Mainly he used his old room at Schraeder's house and moved out to the cottage by the creek when Samantha brought the kids down for weekends, and always for the summer. Summers were good, the girls at the creek or on ponies, yelling Spanish with Tomás's kids, Samantha soft and easy with him now that she could get away when she wanted.

Old Schraeder said little about other people's business, but observed one winter night at supper, "A man like you and me, he don't want to expect too much of a woman and kids. It's like he ain't got room to give them what they want."

He had two children in their forties, the F. knew, neither of whom ever came to the ranch. The daughter was a hard drinker working on a fourth rich husband in San Antonio and the son was an executive of some sort. . . .

He said, "I reckon you're right. The trouble is, there's Midge."

"Midge," Schraeder said, and grinned. Kate at fifteen was the head of her class at the town's high school, but Midge at ten was another thing. "The trouble ain't Midge," he said. "The trouble is you and the way you're so damn crazy on her. Why don't you bring her on out here and make a tomboy Meskin cowgirl out of her, like you want to? She could ride the bus to school."

The F. shook his head. "Samantha don't like that notion," he said. "And I guess she's right. They fight all the time, but a little girl needs her mother."

(He had told Midge that too, after she had brought up the same idea one evening and there had been loudness and Samantha had left the room about to cry. Midge looked at him with hazel eyes out of a dark Indian-jawed face in which he could see his own. "I don't need her," she said. "I don't need her ever. I need you and Concepción and Paint and the creek."

"Honey, it won't work," he said. "We got to think about your mama." And she had turned and run out of the house, after which he had been obliged to feel guilty about her and her mother both. . . .)

Schraeder said, "Uh-huh. Did you all bring in that old cancer-eye cow this morning?"

He died that year at eighty, not frailly diseased but hacked up in a wreck of the new car he drove between the ranch and town with the pedal on the floor. He lived through whatever they did to him at the hospital, and the F. with Domingo and Tomás was let in to see him. Old Schraeder with tubes running in and out of him breathed hard and looked at the F. through half-closed small dark eyes and blinked in recognition.

The F. said, "We're here."

"*Hola*, Don Gus," said Domingo softly. "Man, horses are not that bad."

Schraeder blinked again, then closed his eyes. They went out and sat in the corridor with a priest whom Schraeder, a thoroughly apostate Catholic, had refused even to look at, until a nurse came to say that the old man was dead, and the F. felt somehow that it had not ended right. They had been together for twenty-four years, he and Schraeder, and there were things he would have liked to say, though he did not have the words and perhaps they hadn't needed saying. . . .

He stayed on at the ranch as manager for seven years after that, hardly ever seeing Schraeder's son to whom he sent accounts, running things as they had been run, though without any longer the push to find new things to do and new ways to do the old ones. Then in 1962, with Kate through nurse training and married to a young intern in Dallas and Midge just finishing high school God knew how, the ranch was sold to an Abilene oilman who had ideas of his own about how to run it and a manager of his own to carry them through. Domingo and Tomás stayed on with their wives and what children were still there, but the F. moved out with little regret except over leaving them; he was fifty-nine and had money saved besides a lump that Schraeder had willed to him. He walked down and kicked at the dark moist earth of one of the alfalfa fields, and that was good-bye enough between him and the place. He would own it in his head, if he never saw it again. Schraeder had understood about that. He had owned the ranch himself, in his head and on paper both, but he had known that the F. and Domingo and

133

Tomás owned some of it too. The F. guessed the oilman and his manager would own it that way in their turn. He hoped for the sake of the land that they would.

Midge was supposed to go to college that fall and Samantha said she wanted to, beneath the sullen silence that had come to be her way toward them. In between spells of running off to New Mexico with a girl friend and getting expelled from school for smoking or squabbling with teachers or something else, she had always been good with English and math and things she cared about. But one Saturday night in August she went out to a movie with a local good-looking dreamer who had had a couple of years at the University, and on Monday she telephoned from Austin to say that they were married.

"That's what you want, is it?" the O. F. said against Samantha's sobbing from the sofa. For an O. F. he felt himself to be by now . . .

"I guess so, Papa," she said. "It's time I did something on my own."

"Well, see if you can do it right."

"I will," she said. "Tell Mama . . ."

"What?"

"Nothing," Midge said. "Don't tell her anything. I love you." And hung up, having said that last thing for the first time in years . . . The trouble was, he saw, that she was the way he had been, dark and quick and restless and hemmed in, and he had not been able to help. There had been a time when he might have helped, but he hadn't.

He made a try, too late. She wrote them once and then no more, and after four months he drove to Austin to look for her. The address was in an old unpainted district near the river, with used-car lots, and there was a hard fat woman who said yes, they had lived over her garage for a time and had left owing rent. "He growed a big mustache," she said. "All he done was monkey with that God damn motorsackle

he traded his car in on. Took it apart and putt it back together. They come to repossess it but he had done lit a shuck
out of here."

"Midge said he was writing on a book."

"Some book," the fat woman said. "All them God damn
gears and wheels and nuts and bolts and things drooling
grease on my driveway. I think she was pregnant when they
left. In fact, I ain't real sure they left together; he might of
took out first. . . ."

After that, the O. F. considered, things had mainly just
happened to him, more or less hemming him in again, though
it did not matter as it had when he was young. Old, having
known something different for a while, you went ahead and
let things happen and said the hell with them. Most
things . . .

Anyhow he had put this place together; whatever it
was was mainly his doing. When Kate had had her first baby
in the city where her husband was a resident surgeon and
was going to practice later, there had been no good reason to
resist moving there as Samantha wanted to do, to be near. Not
into the city itself—he had had the sense to balk at that. But
onto a bought half-acre of nearly open prairie by the highway
well outside of town, with some hackberry trees and a little
house that he braced and re-sided and re-roofed and added
onto that first year, besides starting his garden and orchard.
Scrawny though it was, in shaping it up with fences and pens
and sheds, in turning new earth and nurturing trees, there
was some of the feeling he remembered from the good years
with old Schraeder. Sometimes in his mind as he worked he
talked to Schraeder, arguing with him usually as they had so
often argued, for Schraeder even dead was very stubborn,
and so was the live O. F. Their worst disagreement had been

over whether or not to stretch expensive nonclimbable Ellwood V-mesh fencing around the rear of the place, Schraeder saying it was a waste of money. But the O. F., who won the argument, was proved right later on when the neighborhood grew and small boys proliferated. . . .

She had showed up at the filling station one day in early fall, having found out somehow that he worked there. It was a big messy friendly station and garage with a café next to it, out beyond the edge of things, and was much favored by truckers and by countrymen hauling trailerloads of animals to or from the city's auction yards, and people like that. They were one reason the O. F. had taken part-time work there five years before—they and the fact, which he cited obdurately to Samantha and Kate, that he had always earned some sort of a living and wasn't going to stop doing so till he had to. He understood their objections, as mother-in-law and wife of a sharp young doctor on his way up, to greasy-handed garage work and banter with the profane owners of small ranches two counties out from the city; he was even willing to feel a little guilty about it. But the people Kate and the doctor knew did not hang around that station, and the O. F. kept on with his work.

He was at the grease rack that morning when the station's owner, a hardworking nervous man of fifty, came to get him. "You got a personal customer," he said.

"Quit it," said the O. F. "I ain't got time to kid. That fellow wants this pickup by eleven."

"I'll finish it," the owner said. "She wants you, asked for you. Wish some that looked like that would come around asking for me."

She was parked beside the station in a big maroon hardtop, and the O. F. when he saw her said, "Lord God."

"Hey, Papa," she said, a woman, with made-up eyes and lips and tended dark hair and a yellow open-throated dress that looked expensive. She said, "I wanted to say hello."

"Get out of the car," the O. F. said. "No, wait. I'll tell them I'm leaving and we can go someplace and talk."

"I don't want to talk," she said. "I'm not going to stay. I just wanted to get a look at you."

"Something to look at, ain't I?" the O. F. said, seeing through her eyes old peaked cap, stained green khaki uniform, seamed sagging bespectacled face, calloused grease-marked hands, all. . . .

"Damn right," said Midge. "You're beautiful."

"You won't . . ." he said, and stopped, knowing her as stubborn as himself, and no longer a child. He said, "What are you doing, honey?"

"Dancing," she said.

"I'm talking about every day. What do you *do?*"

"I dance," Midge said, and grinned. "They call it exotic. . . . I make out all right, I guess."

"Here? This town?"

"No. I move around. Papa, don't ask questions."

"Still married?"

"Just don't," Midge said. "Some of the answers you might like all right, and some of the others you wouldn't, and there isn't any point."

"All right," he said, for she had always been able to make sense to him when she wanted to. . . . "I missed you."

"God, I missed you too," she said, and looked down at her lap. When she looked back up again her eyes were shiny but she said, "Good-bye. Tell Mama and Kate I said hello, if you want to."

"I probably won't," the O. F. said. "Could you send a postcard once a year? It'd help."

"Maybe. There isn't much point, though. I left, Papa."

"Yes, you did," he said. "I guess you had to."

"Good-bye," Midge said.

"Don't let them get you down," said the O. F.

"They already did," Midge said, and started the big

137

engine, and drove out into traffic, not looking back. . . .

He supposed it was something just to have seen her, to know she had survived. Even if it did wake the whole thing up again, inside you . . . It *was* going to rain, some time soon. Rising from his squat at the end of the potato row, he felt it in his mule-kicked left knee, and gripped the kneecap with his hand as he straightened up. Toward the southeast when he looked, a long dome of misty cloud showed above the horizon, blowing in fast from the faraway sea and obscuring the risen sun. With certainty he knew that the land would get rain out of this one, and high time, too. . . .

"Hello, Grummer," the boy said behind him.

"Don't let them chickens in," said the O. F., shooing with his hand. The big yellow hen squawked and ran back out through the garden's gate, and the boy in Sunday clothes and tie closed it behind him. "Hello, boy," the O. F. said. "You and your mother come to get Grummy for early church?"

"Yeah, but she's not ready. What you doing out here?"

"Watching things grow," said the O. F. "If you lean down and listen right close, you can hear them squeak, coming up out of the ground."

"Go on," the boy said. "Mama says it's nasty, that junk you put in the garden. All that ganure and stuff I helped you with."

"The nastier the better," his grandfather told him, bending to yank at an early sprig of johnsongrass. "And after you feed it to the dirt and the dirt eats it up, it ain't nasty any more. It's beans and potatoes and such."

The boy looked dubious, but he would think it over; he had that kind of mind. They got along well enough, he and the boy, considering that they only saw each other once a week or so these days. But the rest of the time it was Kate and her ideas about how things were or ought to be, and the doctor father, and school, and TV, and God knew what all else, and before very long there wouldn't be much he'd want to hear from a beat-up sort of country grandfather that chewed Tinsley Natural Leaf. There were signs already. It was all right; the boy would have to live in that city world of which the O. F. stubbornly knew as little as he could manage to know. . . . He wondered for maybe the thousandth time if Midge had had a child or children, and if so what they were like. He saw them as like her. Briefly and with a foreknown ache of longing, he indulged in a vision of himself in a rock house in a creek-watered green valley like Schraeder's, but his own, with dark and quick and restless grandchildren all around, learning country things. . . . At night sometimes he went to sleep with that vision in his mind.

The boy said, "Man, those Lions really clobbered them last night."

"Did they?" said the O. F., and tousled the boy's combed head, feeling it lean gladly into his touch.

"Grummer," the boy said frowning.

"Ho," the O. F. said.

"Grummer, say you had like a dog and he died, and you buried him in the ground. . . . And then something green grows up there and you eat it. Would you be eating that dog?"

"In a way you would," the O. F. said. "I reckon we eat just about everything that ever lived, every time we eat."

After thought, the boy looked up. "I don't care," he said. "It's not nasty. It's like eating Jesus in church."

"Maybe it is, at that," said his grandfather, nudging dark loose earth with his toe and feeling in old hurts the certainty of rain. "We feed the dirt, and the dirt feeds us."

11 ≋≋ *Helpers* ≋≋≋≋≋≋≋≋≋≋

I have only scant understanding of the quirk that has made me need to find out so many things in life the hardest way, by doing them or being done to by them, myself alone. Wherever it came from, in terms of Hard Scrabble this attitude has meant making a lot of mistakes, for I grew up only a part-time country boy and much nonrural life had intervened since then, so that there was much to learn. It has also meant long days and weeks and even months together of working hard by myself, and thus of squandering time. For it is an axiom that two men teamed on country tasks do not just halve the time one man requires, but divide it by four or six or so.

Notwithstanding these things, though, I doubt if I had another chance to start work on the place that I would much change the way I went about it. The learning was needful, and if the manner of it led to some errors and wasted some time, it also kept me in fair health through my forties and gave me an intimacy with the land that no other approach would have afforded. And, as all us Old Farts know, it is only through intimacy that you can own a thing. Because ownership dwells not in courthouse files but inside the stubborn, hard-way human head.

Nevertheless, there do come times when you see things slightly otherwise. Times when having learned what there is to know about a given kind of work you would just as soon be able to get through a piece of it faster. Times when country things need doing and noncountry things have a prior claim on you and need doing worse. Times when your aging joints and muscles—which improve not at all in the forties but do well to hold their own—stage a mutiny at such prospects as tangling with three or four miles of new fence all by themselves. And times also, if you are of that ilk for whom understanding or the effort toward it is a main point in life, when you wish desolately that there were more leisure in which to squat down in the shade and hear birds sing and ponder what a country place and your work on it may mean. And it is at such times as all these that you begin to think of Help.

Through most of history, nearly all men who have interested themselves thoughtfully in country life—the improvers of tools or techniques or livestock or plants, the pleasant long line of writers on nature and the soil and the soil's people, the pleasant longer line of contemplative dwellers on the land—have had a comfortable toehold on one of the middle or upper ledges of a stratified society and have not had to strain their sweat glands much. Thus Vergil and Columella, thus those sturdy and obsessed eighteenth-century squires like Bakewell and Tull and Lord Charles "Turnip" Townshend, and their American disciples like Washington and Jefferson. Thus even, say, that eloquent stormy yeoman Cobbett, and Albert Howard, a patron saint of O. F.s everywhere, concocting lovely fecal compost at Indore with coolies who worked for thirty cents a day. . . . You mastered your subject and your hands knew the wherefore of harness and plowshare and fork and hoe and scythe and hive and breeding rack, but mainly you stood back and told peasants or slaves or hired men whether *their* hard hands were using those tools badly or well. It was a long enduring state of things, of which ironic Fielding wrote, from his own upper ledge: "Those members of society who are born to furnish the blessings of life now began to light their candles, in order to pursue their daily labors for the use of those who are born to enjoy these blessings."

It would take a somewhat redder-eyed egalitarian than I to maintain that it would not be fulfilling to own or control a large hunk of usable land intelligently, while having access to the cheap services of subordinates to carry out maintenance and production and improvement, as well as to underpin one's own gentility. In personal terms, I doubt I would have much liked the need to fret paternally over the feuds and foibles and health of numbers of other people, or having very many of them between me and the land. . . . But, good or bad, such times are abruptly gone. I know millionaire oilmen, country-quirked like me but on a grander scale, who cannot find and keep the help they need to make their places function right, while still showing the paper profit the IRS requires. Most of us have to be our own peasants now, or maybe owning land we are yeomen or kulaks or something on that order. Rural gentility subsisting on the land is a phenomenon discerned as a fading part of the scene in backward regions and countries or glimpsed while reading in old books, and thoughtful contemplation of country things comes hard on time stolen away from sweaty needful work.

In our wonder world, of course, machines are supposed to make the difference, and to some extent they do. I lack the general faith in technology whose most poignant recent manifestation has been the statement, oft repeated, that if we can reach the moon we can surely cope with earthly problems. Such contemporary fondness as I have for machines—a little,

I admit—is cooled by the fact that they war almost totally with the Thoreauvian ideal of simplicity to which I subscribe without ever having practiced it very purely. Besides being dirty and noisy and coming from somewhere else, they break down from time to time and require dirty repair, and the parts all come from somewhere else too if you can find them and if they even fit in place when you finally get them home. . . . But not having found any way around it, I own a fairly adequate complement of farming stuff acquired through the years, much of it second- or third-hand, and of other tools which, self-powered or hitched to the Ford tractor, can do jobs men used to have to do with hand tools or with animals. When these won't suffice for the work at hand and I have the money to spare, I don't mind hiring in bigger machines.

But machines have their limitations, especially in country like ours. The post-hole auger that fits the Ford, for instance, is a handy tool in dirt, but dirt two feet deep (or three or four, for corner holes) is rather rare where most of Hard Scrabble's fences run, being confined mainly to the fields, and the auger won't dig stone. Core drills will, but you have to have a good jag of work laid out before they will come to you at fifteen bucks or more an hour, and even then if they encounter what the operators call "tombstone rock"— hard crystalline ledge stuff—fence costs can zoom clear out of possibility.

Nor can bulldozer men bring in their behemoths for small jobs. Since the early fifties, the heyday of the independent machine operator around here, the price of a new D-6 Cat with blade has risen from around $12,000 to the neighborhood of $41,000, with some notable improvements in design and function but not all that many. Faced with the payments due on such amounts and with big occasional repair bills, the men who like to run them have been turned into harried moderns, eaten on by economics and forced, by the time and money required merely to move the mighty tractors, to prefer big jobs even if two or three counties away. So a small landowner saves up a growing list of bulldozer things to be done, and after a year or so when the list gets long enough he calls one in. But some things on the list may have to be done when they have to be done, and thus may have to be done by hand—by said small landowner, or by the landowner with helpers, species human.

Most of the time this state of things bothers me less than it does some other landed types. Once you have found that you can do almost any of the work yourself, even if slowly, you are less nudely vulnerable to the need for help and you can be more choosy about such help as you do occasionally hire, eschewing brash or surly characters and seeking people alongside whom it is good to work, talkatively or in silence, people whose feel is right. Given the limited sources of country labor these days, sources which like White Bluff's springs in summer are often weak or dry, you sometimes have to wait a while. But good people do turn up.

Suppose we describe this next segment of our book as fictional. It concerns a twilit legal zone and some helpful criminals I have known, and fiction appears to be the usual and perhaps best form to use when writing of such matters, as witness our recent rash of Mafia novels. Not that the criminals here in question come near the *mafiosi* in glamour or success-fulness. They are humble Mexican citizens who flow up into Texas and indeed the whole Southwest from below the border, looking for work, and their crime is being here and working, and the twilight zone of legality is the rather fuzzy and varyingly enforced set of rules applied to them and their gringo employers by that arm of the U. S. State Department known as the Immigration and Naturalization Service, re-

ferred to familiarly if not fondly among many of them as
La Migra.

In my scant experience, the Migra and its enforcement
branch, the Border Patrol, have some excellent people in
them, tending toward good-humored tough efficiency much
like the men they chiefly pursue. I have no large quarrels
with them or even with the higher policy-makers whose
hammerhead they are. What I do have is a longstanding affection for wetbacks, having been working with and around
them, not at all steadily but from time to time, since I was
about fifteen and spent a Depression summer on a cousin's
ranch where a crew of Mexicans, mainly spare dry men from
the spare dry Pancho Villa country of Chihuahua, were
cutting timber with axes and crosscut saws in the bottomland.

Their leader and dominant personality was a rugged
gentle rather professorial sort of man called Pete, reputedly a
bloodspattered cavalry colonel during one of the post-
revolutionary Mexican political spasms of the twenties, but on
a losing side. Most of them had drifted up through Texas laying ties and driving spikes for the railroad, a main employer
of alien labor in that era. By the very foreignness of those
hard and humorous men, and their acceptance of what life
sent in the way of pleasure and passion and deprivation, and
the mystery of how they had come to be there, and the
profanities and rudimentary words and phrases and songs
they taught me in their slurred and lilting dialect, there was
seeded in me a lifelong fascination with Latin people and
ways and a perception of romance as still a possibility rather
than something that had been grapeshotted to death with
Great-uncle Willie Harkness at the battle of Fredericksburg,
Virginia, or had gone up the trail with the last herds of
longhorns.

That is not a small gift to receive when you are young.
Therefore, gentle reader, do not look here for solemn discussion of large issues labeled Exploitation and Labor Compe-

tition and Living Conditions among Migrant Workers and César Chávez and things like that. Look rather for a confessedly unimpartial view of what are, in general, some of the most pleasant of earth's many lawbreakers.

The average number of sons of bitches, a Spanish friend of mine used to say in Catholic acceptance of human imperfection, is just about the same no matter where you go. Most wetbacks Hispanically share his opinion, and exemplify it too. By no means are they a uniformly delightful category of our species, for you can easily find among them individuals who are morose, lazy, conniving, murderous, quarrelsome, drunken, thieving, or otherwise quite human. Coming from a hard-scrabble old-style rural background, within the framework of their Indian-Latin ways they tend like the vanishing Somervellian cedar folk to be what they are all the way and the hell with bland dull sameness. By and large, though, the bulk of objectionable *mojados*—wetted ones—seem to gravitate toward urban places, where there may be more scope for their propensities. Those who reach us on the land are most often simple tough peasant villagers used to hard labor and austere living, and willing to work for a time in womanless exile for wages which, though usually scrawny by gringo standards, can add up to a wad of cash to carry home to wife and children, or to parents, or to the affable whores and hawklike con men awaiting their return in Mexican border towns.

Being outside the law, they are vulnerable to cheating and brutal employers here in the States, and gringos being human too you can hear some sorry tales. In most of rural Texas, though, wetbacks are hired singly or in pairs or trios by relatively unprosperous and inconspicuous small-ranchers and farmers, hard workers themselves and honest, who have a job to do that needs some extra hands. Despite a language gap precariously bridged by pidgin Tex-Mex and gesticulation, they are glad to get such help for a couple of simple reasons.

In a day when country labor is scarce, wet Mexicans can and will undertake the hard hand work involved in fencing, grubbing out prickly pear and resprouted brush, and other more or less unmechanizable rural tasks, and most do it well and willingly, which makes them pleasant to have around. Furthermore the pay they ask for it, while amounting to a good bit more than they can make at home, is within the limit of what small farmers and ranchers can spend for such badly needed occasional labor and still maintain an illusion of solvency. Small farming and ranching in general being something of an economic disaster area these days, on which subject perhaps more later on, in its place . . .

(Readers staunchly conservative in bent may take off here with their own dissertations on the theme that Americans no longer like hard work, and that they can indeed do better than the wetbacks simply by sitting around on their fat duffs in cities collecting unemployment compensation and food stamps, a situation which has already progressed a dire long way toward wrecking the scheme of things entire and is certain to finish the job if it remains dominant, etcetera. In rebuttal, liberal humanitarians may well declaim that if country jobs were decently rewarded plenty of country workers would turn up, that to pay even dirt-poor aliens less than standard American hourly wages is exploitation, that if small-ranchers and farmers cannot survive while paying such standard wages then they richly deserve to go under, etcetera. Let both factions and any others in view feel free to expatiate thus, with gestures ad infinitum, etcetera. My own concern is with what is, insofar as I can make it out. . . .)

In pairs and threes and fours most usually they come, following various underground-railway routes they know or have been told of, or cast up in our hills by some concatenation of accidents. South Texas close to Mexico has far more than does our neighborhood, but the wages they get there are lower too and there is always among them a sort of hydraulic pressure northward, Chicago being for some reason a legendary El Dorado, seldom reached. . . . At times the cedar hills hold a fair number, at others very few. During one period some years back when evidently the Migra was under little pressure from above concerning them—it was the era of legal *bracero* importation, for one thing—Somervell County sheltered a large enough colony, many with wives and children, that they held Saturday night dances outside of Glen Rose. But at one such gathering a humanly frail *mojado* got overly beered and knifed another one dead, and the Migra at the sheriff's request came down like a minnow seine, and for a good while thereafter fence crews and goatshearers and such folks were very hard to find.

I and the place and other places where I have lived have known—hypothetically, fictionally, at any rate—a spotty succession of wet ones, though not very many in all and none for long at a time. Few with family ties want to stay more than three or four or at the most six months, nor is there often even that much essential work stacked up and ready for them to do. All but one or two have left agreeable memories of themselves when they went, and have left good work well finished, and have left also bits of worthwhile knowledge I did not have before. For most of them know a lot of fine country things, though generally here in the States, daunted by our machines and other wonders, they are uncertain that these things are worth knowing and keep quiet about them unless asked.

They know, for instance, more about the unrefrigerated preservation of food in a hot climate than any USDA scientist will ever know. A surprising number can lay stones skillfully in the old flat-bedded honest way, or hew handsome square timbers out of logs, or plaster walls, or finish concrete. And many carry around in their heads a pharmacopoeia of simple natural medicines and cures for human and animal ills. One mustached lame Tamaulipan of fifty-five or so, a quiet and rather formal man who said he had once owned a little ranch but had gambled it away while drinking mescal, showed me the surest treatment for ivy poisoning I have ever tried, maybe worth sharing here even if it does demand a certain Spartan frame of mind in the one being treated.

Together we were patching fences on an old place I had rented, clearing brush from the line and restapling and in places restretching the wire. Along one wooded creekbottom section the poison ivy was lush and belt-high. Antonio started snicking in it with the honed Collins machete he carried. I stopped him and said we had better get a tractor mower or something; these bushes were bad stuff.

"I know," he said. "It's *hiedra mala*. Some call it *hincha-huevos*."

"Egg-sweller?"

"You know, if one should squat down in it without pants . . ."

"You don't catch it?"

"*Sí, señor*," he said, and went on slashing. He was a politely stubborn fellow and had some ideas about corner-post assemblies, for instance, that I never did manage to eradicate. . . . That night I gave him laundry soap to wash with, but by the next afternoon he had tiny taut pink blisters all over his hands and forearms. Heating water nearly to a boil on the stove that evening, he dipped a towel in it, slapped it as a poultice on the rash with only a slight ridging of his jaw muscles to show how it felt, and repeated this operation each time the towel cooled until he had covered all the affected parts. Next morning the rash was gone. It works for me, sometimes requiring two or three applications on successive days. You can hold the poisoned portion of yourself under a bathtub tap and make the water gradually hotter till you howl, or want to, then make it a little hotter still. How feasible it would be with swelled eggs I can't say, that contingency not having arisen. . . . Lame formal Antonio stayed

149

with me, doing corner posts still in his own private way, only until we started fixing a final stretch of fence that ran along a public road and unknown people would slow their cars to watch, making him nervous. He liked me and liked the work, he said when quitting, but the Migra had caught him once that way, and this time he was not yet ready to be sent back home again. I found him another job in remoter surroundings, and still remember him with gratitude each time the ivy gets me, as it usually does two or three times a year.

As a functional stock farm, insofar as it is one, Hard Scrabble was given perhaps its most notable boost out of economic extinction, aside from the clearing and shaping done by bulldozers, by a pair of fictional wetbacks named Cuco and Rubén. Cuco is short for Refugio; do not ask me why. Rubén is not short for anything, though he was the shorter of the two, trim and Andalusian in appearance, with large liquid untrustful eyes and a mustache and small feet and hands and clean neat ways. He was around thirty, had a wife and young daughters in the Durango village he came from, and in the way of work liked best those tasks where order and precision matter—things like getting fences arrow-straight, and making tight wire splices, and laying stone, and painting, and troweling concrete or wallboard joint cement—though for his size he had good shoulders and could hold up his end of any job.

Cuco, very much on the other hand, was darkly Indian and slabsided and high-shouldered and brute-powerful, but not large. His face was pitted and his teeth, when they showed in a ready ironic grin, were strong and white and aimed in about twelve diverse directions. He was twenty years old and single, and liked violent smashing work with sledgehammers and axes and crowbars, possessing a greater aptitude for breaking tool handles than anyone I have ever known. Like Rubén he spoke the rapid rhythmic dialect of Durango, pleasant to hear and hard to seize. But he came from a different village—an *ejido*, a government-sponsored co-operative farm on which, however, his family had no patch to till and therefore had to work for other people.

Women in Spanish countries keep their maiden surnames when they marry, and children take the father's but with the mother's tacked after for formal use, to the eternal confusion of social relations with Anglo-Saxon types. Cuco's main surname, however—Carvajal—was the same as his mother's, as I learned when he wanted to send her some money and I was getting data from him to use in routing a cashier's check. I commented idly on that fact while scribbling.

"*No tengo papá,*" he said. "I don't have a father."

Something in his voice was taut and I looked up to see on that usually sardonic, tough, don't-give-a-God-damn dark face an almost girlish vulnerability. "He died," I said. "I'm sorry."

"I was born without a father," Cuco said insistently. "Later my *mamá* married another man."

I started to say it didn't matter to me, which was true enough, but it had clearly mattered so painfully to him somehow in a small cruel village world, and mattered so much still, that I did not. In lieu of speech I jogged him on the shoulder with the heel of my fist, and he grinned, and that was that. I knew his secret burden now, and he could live around me. . . .

They had fallen in together at Ojinaga across from Presidio in the Big Bend, where Cuco had come with a younger boy from his pueblo for the purpose of crossing and heading for golden Chicago, and Rubén had come alone with much the same thing in mind. They hung around for a week or so and listened to loafers in cantinas and to smugglers and other experts, learning what to do. Once across in Presidio, if possible, you got rid of your round-crowned Mexican straw hat and bought a cheap gringo one, hats and huaraches being a chief means by which the Migra spotted you. If you had fifty gringo dollars each—some said more—you could put yourself in the hands of a *pasador* who would smuggle you in a car-trunk or a van or under feed sacks or somehow up the one highway to Alpine and then maybe to Fort Stockton, putting you in touch if you wanted with a boss contractor who could find you a job somewhere.

But if you were as broke as these three, you shunned the highway with its Migra checkpoints and struck out on foot northeast through rough desert mountain country, equipped with food and water. Someone had an old dirty marked-up Texaco map and showed it to them. A windmill was somewhere in here, and a spring just about there up a blind box canyon, and a sparse few other watering places elsewhere. Missing them, you could die, as many had. . . . At some of the ranches along the way, not all, you could count on beans and information. It was best to move at night, but easier to get lost then too. . . . They furnished themselves with plastic Purex bottles for canteens and one midnight waded the shallow river and entered a sewer main (*"Qué peste había!"* said neat Rubén of it. "What a stink there was!") that led them into the heart of metropolitan Presidio, population one thousand. Emerging through a manhole they were collared by the waiting law, subjected to formalities including fingerprinting, celled overnight, and the next day given a compulsory free ride to Ciudad Chihuahua in a baggage car of the scenic Chihuahua-al-Pacífico line.

Juárez was better when they managed to get there. They learned of some famous boxcars which, if you boarded them in the Juárez yards and sat very tight and had luck, often passed the border without trouble and went straight to golden Chicago. It worked, except that golden Chicago two days later turned out to be the T. & P. yards in Fort Worth, Texas. There their car was shunted onto a siding and when all human noise outside had ceased they emerged blinking and hungry into hard August sunlight, dangling their Purex bottles, to take a stroll down West Vickery Boulevard, known in my childhood there more colorfully as the Stove Foundry Road, the site of jungles where hoboes camped between journeys on the freights.

A decent rather sentimental man I know who ran a boarding stable passed by, knew from their hats and clothes and air what they were and how fast the law would grab them, put them in his pickup, fed them large quantities of hamburgers and beans and pie and coffee at a counter joint, let them go to sleep swollen-bellied under a mesquite beside his stable, and called me to come act as interpreter. In the end he kept the young boy Raúl to work at the stable (later when Raúl went back to Mexico, he and my friend and the friend's wife and children all wept long and soggily . . .), and I carried Cuco and Rubén down to the wilds of the Tonk Nation, where I was ready to get moving with the main part of my fencing. This fifty-mile trip, which conceivably falls within the purview of one of the Migra's less fuzzy rules labeled Illegal Transport of Aliens, is by far the most fictional part of my tale. . . .

Much of that fall I had to be away from the place and often away from Texas. I spent the first two weeks down at the place with them, and together we built forms along a rear strip of the still skeletal but roofed pole-frame barn, had a slab poured and troweled it smooth, and enclosed a room for them that was later to be my office—where, in fact, I write these words. After that I had to go about my own affairs, showing up periodically with quantities of food and fence materials and laying out new projects for them if they had finished the ones laid out before.

Unsupervised, they did some dull work indifferently, such as grubbing out young cedar on the Booker hill—this being one of the continuing jobs that they went back to if I was not around when they finished a piece of fencing. But they liked building fences and took pride in the way they came out, pondering and wrangling over the best way to keep all wires taut in difficult places where the land ran up and down, moving posts an inch or two to insure straightness in the line, tamping and bracing their corners to withstand a Brahman bull's charge.

The hardest stretch to build was on the east, where a three-quarter mile piece of boundary runs along a humpy ridge with ledge rock in many places only inches below the surface of the ground, if below it at all. For reasons all too clear, no decent fence had ever been put up there; to chisel out with crowbars the foot-and-a-half or two-foot holes required to set cedar posts right would have taken just short of forever. I hired a core drill in to bore holes for corner posts and anchor points, then brought a load of expensive T-rail steel posts. With a sledgehammer and a short chisel bar made from an automobile drive shaft, Cuco and Rubén drove holes every fifteen feet along the line, knocked the bar loose and pulled it out, and rammed a steel post down where it had been.

It was mean jolting work, as anyone who has ever swung a ten-pound sledge for long at a time can testify, and that September was unrelievedly hot. Yet the ching-ching-ching of the big hammer and the bell-note of the sleeve post-driver hardly ever stopped during the day, pausing only as they moved on to set another post—or occasionally when training helicopters from Fort Wolters up by Mineral Wells came over low and my employees hit the brush, not having swallowed my statement that these planes had nothing to do with the Migra. . . . If there is anything beautiful about any wire fence—a doubtful esthetic question, I admit—that is a beautiful fence today, fit to grace a roadside rather than a lonesome ridge, as resilient as when they stretched it except where bulls on either side have disagreed or a scared deer has sailed into it full tilt or the foxhound folks have clambered over a bit roughly in the heat of a midnight chase, at which points it sometimes needs a little patching and tightening, like all other wire fences in existence.

By late November, besides cutting posts and grubbing cedar and helping me with odd construction and farming projects, they had built enough new fences and refurbished enough old ones to turn Hard Scrabble from a semiwilderness, encroached on frequently by neighbors' livestock and incapable of holding my own animals except in a couple of restricted pastures, into something that was beginning to resemble a stock farm. And Lord Hard Scrabble himself, the stock farm's high squireen-yeoman-kulak, began to weave sweet visions of fat cows, sheep, and goats in balanced numbers complementarily chomping away on the varying types of herbiage that each species prefers, and being rotated seasonally to different secure pastures. Which was, of course, before the question of predators and outlaw dogs, among other questions, obtruded in all its clarity . . .

They were on each other's nerves by then, as they likely would have been even had they differed less. It is a sort of prison existence for unsophisticated people used to village stir and rub and jangle and gossip and teeming family life—stuck out on a patch of unpopulated alien land where even the winds and night sounds have a gringo strangeness, cooking your own meat and beans and scouring your own plates and pots, your only relaxations sleep and talk with someone you are tired of talking to and a little beer brought out by the *patrón* and some Mexican movie magazines and a radio to catch the high-watt all-night border stations, making you more homesick still. And without women.

(Once in October some friends of ours camped on the Kyle hill behind the house for a weekend in a trailer and a fancy tent, bringing their baby and a Spanish nursemaid, a pretty Pamplona girl with a pleasant twitch in her walk who was living and working with them while she took some college courses. She viewed work-stained Cuco and Rubén with

Basque hauteur and dodged all but the briefest conversation with them. But at precisely five thirty-five the next morning Cuco, who loved my screaming chainsaw and took pride in his talent with it, tuned it up in the cedar as close as he could get to their encampment—about thirty feet away—not even watching as it howled and gnawed its way through limbs and trunks but grinning with his big mouthful of crooked white teeth at the wide-eyed sleep-tousled heads popping into view, especially at hers. . . .)

Cuco developed a way of looking sidewise at Rubén when the latter said something to me, and giving a short coarse nasty laugh. Rubén in turn began to sulk some days and to refuse to talk to him even about details of their work. Once before, I had told them I would take them to Fort Worth and turn them loose in the North Side Latin section there for a weekend any time they wanted, but they had heard of the network of informers in such places and said they would rather not risk it. (Relations between *mojados* and their American cousins, despite current enthusiasm about a United Race, are a tangled subject, perhaps best bypassed here. . . .) I made the offer now again, going over to their room one evening after supper. The radio was blaring border mariachi, and in the air there lingered the smell of some piquant mess they had cooked up out of the meat of an Angora wether we had slaughtered two days before.

Rubén said, "I don't need to go. This one, yes." A nudge of contemptuous shoulder upward toward where Cuco sat hunched on the edge of the top bunk, his large dirty bare feet hanging almost in Rubén's face. "He thinks he needs a girl."

Cuco gave his special short coarse laugh, reflected for a moment, and then said stubbornly that no, by God, he didn't. . . . They lasted till a wet snow blew in with a norther in early December; I shall not soon forget their faces as they stood and watched the alien hostile soft white ice slanting from cold clouds. That afternoon, agreed again for once, they announced an invincible need to light out for Durango. We made a shopping expedition to Fort Worth where they bought high-heeled sharp-toed boots and big rodeo hats and leather jackets and other items with which to wow their respective pueblos, and then I put them on an El Paso bus, not without twinges of the sort that increasingly with age the sight of guts and innocence and honor and other such curious antique attributes arouse in me. . . . Within a month or so, each had written separately from his home saying that if only I would drive down and meet him on the border, he would come back and work some more. I answered explaining that that would be Illegal Transport of Etcetera, and besides at the moment not much more work was laid out to do. They wrote again, more urgently, Rubén offering to bring his wife and daughters and work for six months free, Cuco averring he would constitute himself my *peón de confianza*, a bull-fighting term meaning roughly right-hand man. In time the correspondence developed a ping-pong quality and I fear that I quit answering. But I wish them good things wherever they are, fictional fence-building Cuco and Rubén. Although I never told them so, they own a piece of the place.

End of this particular fictional section . . .

Other such part-owners, none of whose contributions have been quite as large as that, have included some local men, especially in the early days when more of them could be hired to fence and chop and build and dig. Even then there were not many available, for the bad drouth years of the fifties had chewed away at the numbers of cedar-hill folks, often small landowners themselves, who were around to take wage work. Of those who did some work for me the chief perhaps was (call him) Ansel McDowell, who with such help as he could find fenced the boundary between me and an absentee neighbor, an Abilene dentist who agreed to share costs if I, being somewhat less absentee than he, would see it through. (And if at this point the nonrural reader begins to formulate the notion that fences take unreasonable amounts of time and trouble, he will be flatly right.)

Anse with his wife Sadie, childless, lived frugally on a hundred acres of steep Nation cedar land with one small field. Sadie was large and had Women's Lib a good many years before it came on the general market; one neighbor of theirs said that from a half-mile away with a fair south wind blowing he could hear every word she shouted at Anse, usually instructions. Anse viewed his cedars not as pests but as a crop and over the years had spent much time in his brake, cutting out scrub white stuff and trimming lower limbs from the red cedars to make their trunks grow into straight prime posts. In places the effect was almost topiary, the rounded dark-green crowns set on long clean stems rising from rock-strewn white caliche soil. . . . When he needed cash he would chop a few posts for sale from this well-tended forest, selecting his victims carefully. Though his origins and his manner were intensely local, he was really a European, Anse—meticulous, making do not just adequately but proudly with what there was at hand.

Like many another native he was hooked on Levi Garrett's salty snuff, and was never without a wad of it tucked into his lower lip, which he replenished occasionally from a square brown bottle carried in a pocket of his baggy bib overalls. Being myself often a tobacco-chewer when outdoors, I have no quarrel with snuff-lovers, except in one respect. Once when young I worked for a couple of weeks in a dry hot June shocking bound sheaves of wheat—an itchy monotonous task since erased by machines—with a wiry old snuff-dipper named Dunnington. He was a good companion, quietly wry and untiring, but we had only one water bottle between us, a glass gallon jug stashed beneath a tree or a tent-like shock of wheat and wrapped in a layer of dirty white cloth that we dampened from time to time to keep it cool. Drinking from it, when you looked down through the jug-mouth into the liquid depths you could see thousands of flecks of golden tobacco drifting about, washed from Dunnington's crusty lips. There was not any question of rejecting it; the weather was much too hot, and I was too young to get brash about an adult comrade's ways. You shut your eyes and drank, or occasionally when you were near the creek you sneaked down there for a more esthetic draught.

Thus when I worked with Anse I took my own canteen along. . . . Mainly he had to make do with random other locals hired for a few days each till they decided that Unemployment Comp was preferable to Anse's reactionary disgust. The fenceline passed through thick cedar and they cut posts for it as they went. Anse had two axes, one heavy and the other a superb little double-bitted thing he used for trimming, honed like a knife, its twenty-seven-inch handle shaved down so that when you swung it it had almost a golf-club whip, though if Anse saw you pick it up and swing it he would look dark till you put it down again, axes being private things like briar pipes and dogs.

One day when I climbed the hill to see how Anse and his current aide were coming, I found the little axe under a tree with its tailored handle split and repaired with spiraled friction tape. I remarked on this to Anse. He glowered down the line to where his large fat helper, without enthusiasm, was whanging in a hole with a crowbar.

"*He* busted it," Anse said with the jaw-wagging articulation to which snuff-dippers are prone, since the stiffness of their lip's burden keeps it from shaping consonants by itself. He spat thinly at a stone. "Sade is sure going to be hard to get along with," he said. "She had it fixed just like she wanted it. That's her axe."

Kids are a sometime, summer source of help and a rather

pleasant one too if you have the time to stay on top of them. I have no sons to harry about the place, but adolescent relatives and the sons of friends occasionally fill in. It is best to have them in pairs, but usually unwise to turn the pairs loose to labor without supervision for very long at a time, an approach that can lead to botched projects and large quantities of what the Marine Corps used to call "grab-ass," as well as to a life-long misconception on the kids' part (I admit to a sort of square-jawed tutelary impulse here) in regard to what work is. Working with you and under your eye they can be good help, especially at less brutal jobs like carpentry, though heavy digging and pounding such as the wetbacks glory in can strain young muscles and bring them in at night hollow-eyed and disheartened. Nor does the fact that they have to work during summer vacations, in the worst of the Texas heat, help their confidence at first. Some stay on and some soon depart, immunized for life against agricultural and blue-collar enthusiasms. Not being very jockish about such things or insistent that people fit in with my own perhaps skewed ways, I have liked one or two of those who quit as well as any who stayed.

But if they stick, as most at Hard Scrabble have, they are likely to get a second wind and to end out the summer strong and brown, hard-handed and hard-bellied, slogging into anything that presents itself with joy in their own new power and in the scorching, glaring, insect-singing August days. And watching, you are seized by pride and envy and remember when you felt that way too. . . . Among those who have stayed out their time at the place and put their mark on it are big Royce who dreamed of his love while heaving five-gallon buckets of mortar and concrete to me on a scaffold; Mark and Bobby, Yankee and Texan, whose rivalry with each other led to a slew of fenceposts in the ground and to friendship between them; Charlie who in another month or so would have been a better carpenter than I, for whatever that is worth; Suter, slight and lean, who would not admit that a wheelbarrow full of concrete was too much for him to handle and by God in the end it wasn't. . . . Part-owners, like me and the Mexicans and the folks who were here before.

There is another category of country help to which I have never had access, feeling sometimes jealous of those who do. This is the aging bachelor or widower, often but not always a relative of the owner, who is weary of striving and is looking for a quiet place to live and pecking useful work to finish out his days. Many such men have been drifters, good with their hands at a number of things, and I have cottoned to most I have known, perhaps because during parts of my own life I have tended toward lone drifting too and with a little less luck, early and along the way, could have ended up something like them myself. In fact, I can imagine not minding it much. . . .

A friend of mine who lived on a country place outside of Nashville, where I used to visit him on trips to Texas from the East, had a long-lost uncle like that who showed up one day to check on his dead sister's son, my friend, and stayed nine years till he died. He had been a lumberjack and a cowboy and an electrician and some other things but had remained at bottom a Tennessee mountain man, ripe with knowledge of hickory splits and herbal teas and hog slaughter and buckskin and vegetables and other old Appalachian basics. You couldn't be sure he was going to do anything you wanted done, his nephew said wryly, but he stayed busy all the time, up before dawn and puttering dexterously at whatever he had decided his hands would do that day. With children he was a sort of white Uncle Remus, full of tales and lore, and every six or eight months he would go off to Memphis or Atlanta or somewhere, not inflicting it on the family, and get hog Skid-Row drunk for a couple of weeks or so, showing up afterward smelly and tremulous but purged at his cabin on the hill, to take up country life again. . . .

Not that all such resident helpers are of a comfortable folksy stripe. A year or so since, on a trip to the south, I went with a ranching friend in the hills west of Austin to carry his eighty mohair goats to another place where a big shearing crew was at work. While they finished with the goats that belonged to the place itself, we left ours in the trailer to avoid mixing and talked with the place's doctor-owner against the ordered exuberant uproar in the corral. There some of the Mexican crew, with clattering shaft-powered shears, were peeling the hair off scared Angoras held between their legs and others were dragging unsheared squalling goats to them and dust swirled and small shouting dark boys chased newly naked beasts into another pen.

My eye kept coming back to one of the goat-draggers, a fleshy sweating Anglo, short but awkwardly powerful, who brought the big struggling wethers to the shearers with ease, but often missed while grabbing for their hind legs and then stumbled or fell down or caromed off the corral's fence-boards. He said nothing as he worked, but his eyes went constantly around among us and the crew, who watched him nervously sidewise and did not laugh at his floundering. The puff-crowned railroader's cap he wore was queerly set, too big and pulled squarely down against the roots of his ears, its striped bill sticking out straight and flat in front, worn childishly somehow rather than humorously as people often wear such things.

During a lull while the shearers drank water and talked and smoked, the fleshy man came over and stared hard and brightly at me, not listening to the talk between my friend and the doctor. He said very loudly, "I was a-riding that *big old Tom horse* down by the creek this morning and what do you think I *seen?*"

"What?" I said.

"A great big old damn *squirrel!*" he shouted, picking up tempo. "He run up in one of them *pecan trees,* and I got down off that *horse*, and I throwed a big old *rock*, and that son of a bitch run *right smack in a HOLE!*"

It was the sum of what he had to say, and he turned and left. He was not drunk but something else that went with the set of the railroad cap and with the restless eyes. Later on my friend said he had gone to pieces in Korea, during the retreat from that disastrous reservoir in the north, and when the Army had finally turned him loose with a pension the doctor, his cousin, had set him up there and came weekly to lay out things for him to do. My friend said he bothered no one, and worked mule-hard twelve and thirteen hours a day. . . .

I seem to have wandered a bit afield. But if you have come this far with me, maybe you're used to it.

12 ≋ 2 x 4 ≈≈≈≈≈≈≈≈≈≈

I placed a jar in Tennessee,
And round it was, upon a hill.
It made the slovenly wilderness
Surround that hill.

WALLACE STEVENS,
"Anecdote of the Jar"

The notion of making Hard Scrabble "useful" was something that crept in on me slowly with time, like arthritis—nor at some discouraged times have I been sure it was any less noxious than such more physical afflictions. In the beginning I saw the place as a refuge, a scrap of the golden interim spell to which I could get back from time to time, and ramble and hunt and ponder and read. A bit later, when Madame began to view it as something besides a steaming cedarbrake full of horseflies and both of us were thinking in terms of how to help children touch reality—and were assuming we had some inkling of what reality was in times like these—I came to consider it a refuge for us all, as a family, a small shift certainly but one wherein lies perhaps some hint of the delayed domestication to which I was yielding in those years.

Even a refuge, though, needs to be habitable. And habitability involves, among other things, shelter. And shelter involves usually, among other things, construction. And construction is, among other things, what this chapter is about. . . .

Probably the order in which my different attitudes toward the place occurred was lucky. On a patch of land like this one—reverted to scrubby wilderness through years of abandonment, its "improvements," such as they had been, destroyed by time and by nature's eternal push to smudge out the spoor of men—there is inevitable conflict between on the one hand revival and use of the land, and on the other the arrangements that have to do with being there more or less comfortably, for a weekend or a summer or for good. Time and money and thought and energy all come into the problem, and with a wife and two female children whose idea of simple living is much less stark than your own, the conflict on occasion can be fierce. . . . In real wilderness in the old times, where survival too was a factor and simplicity was a norm, more solid agricultural settlers like the South Texas Germans sometimes solved that question by first raising a good barn, moving family and workstock into it, shaping up the farm, and finally at some later time getting around to building a house in which to live. Not for us, though, such sturdy hardheaded directness. Not for us, in fact, any real awareness of conflict until later. At first the idea was some sort of house, with a well and a few other things to help it function.

As with many country things, happenstance and whim had much to do with the house being placed just where it is, on the lower south slope of the hill—a gentle nose, really—on which the Kyle shack once stood, and then in fact still did. The Booker with its higher oak-motted hills and ample views was not yet part of the property, and getting to the steep Kyle land across the creek was hard, as it likely will always be. One or two possible locations on the creek lacked oaks. For scope of view and for airiness—especially then, with cedar all around—the Kyle shack's own site farther up the nose was the best accessible building site with good trees, as the old sites often are. But there was at the time in my mind a notion that has not survived—that perhaps some day we would build a bigger house there, letting the first small structure then turn into a guest cottage. Therefore it should not take up that spot, but should be somewhere nearby.

In such odd time as I had then, I crawled about in the nearly solid brake on the hillside and chose a site above an outcropping ledge stout enough to underpin the stone cabin I envisioned, half-ringed by good liveoaks and with elms in the flat and the branch below. I chopped down a number of cedars and piecemeal demolished the most satisfactory car I ever owned, an old Studebaker of the Loewy design, by using it as a tractor to snake out felled timber and to yank stumps, before giving that up and calling a dozer in. Meanwhile I had a new well drilled on the hill not far from the Kyle house, and that first summer, with occasional help from a teaching colleague and small relatives, I built a rock pumphouse around it, trying out there in miniature, before confronting the house itself, the modified Flagg system of masonry I had dreamed up from reading books and from looking over other people's stone triumphs and disasters.

If this were a how-to book, honor would here require a discussion of Mr. Flagg and a detailing of the advantages and shortcomings of his system as I see them. But it isn't, and the gentleman's books, or someone else's books about them, in all likelihood repose in your local library for handy consultation. (I note that the Nearings, in their *Living the Good Life*, are detailed in their description of this method, which they employed.) In essence my own adaptation consists of laying up a shell of stone in the style one favors, leaving it knobby and rough on the inside, and then pouring and tamping juicy

rich concrete between the shell and an inner form to bring
the wall to full strength and thickness. At first blush it looks
to be another modern easy-way corruption of traditional
techniques, and it does in fact absolve the workman from
the need to master some few tough essentials of the old way,
such as laying bond stones clear through the wall to tie it
together. But it is not veneer, and its results come out tighter
and much stouter than old walls of equal thickness no matter
how expert the hands that laid them up, particularly if like
me the mason gets so fussy about strength that he goes to
poking steel bars and such things in the concrete too. Nor, as
I found out later with some pleasure, does the method lack
the glow of age. The shrewd ancient Romans themselves
employed a like approach, using pozzolana cement as the filler
substance.

About midway along in any sizable project, a muttering
sort of question begins to eat at the amateur stonemason's
mind. It comes in various and sometimes obscene phrasings,
but basically it says: Why in God's name stone? What got
me into this? And basically it is, at least in pragmatic American terms, unanswerable.

If it asks itself too early along, the mason may lose heart
and quit the job, as hundreds of unfinished stone projects up
and down the countryside inform a knowing eye. The most
notable of these that I have seen in our region is a small two-
story frame farmhouse, occupied till not long ago by an
elderly pair, with a gaudy tricolor flagstone veneer that
reaches almost to the second story before jaggedly petering
out. It has an arch-built rock porch that displays the same
mingling of chocolate and red Palo Pinto County sandstone
with white local limestone, all laid on edge, and around the
unroofed flat top of the porch is a spiky parapet of rufous
and yellow petrified wood. The tale behind this uncompleted
wonder, whose truth I cannot vouch for, is that when the
elderly couple were young, back in the 1920's or '30's, the

husband undertook in his spare time to transform their wooden house to stone and the wife, in the manner of wives, was wont to stand in the yard and analyze his efforts. One hot Saturday afternoon she caviled at his placement of a certain piece of rock, preferring perhaps a red over a brown, or maybe a white for a change. He said the rock he had already hammered into shape for the spot was all right, in fact perfect. Her objections grew loud. . . .

Without ever having known him except by sight, I am certain it was a day on which the muttering question had been maggoting in his head. For what he did at this point was to lay the stone in question on his scaffold where he stood, clamber down into the yard, and say quite matter-of-factly to his spouse, "All right. If you know so damn much about it, let's see you finish the job."

Even the scaffold, warped and broken and grayed, still stood there to a time within my own awareness of the place. . . .

Why stone, indeed? As a people, we generally lack the sense of *being* somewhere that has long made natives of the Old World build homes with generations of blood descendants in mind. In my own direct paternal line, a relatively staid succession of Southerners who drifted during three centuries from the Virginia Tidewater down through the Virginia and Carolina Piedmont and the cotton states to Texas, not my father nor his father nor his grandfather nor his great-grandfather eventually settled and died where he had been born. Having drifted a good bit myself, I am not at all certain I am now finally glued in place for good, and even if it turns out that I am, my children may well not want to stick forever in the Tonk Nation, despite its many blessings. The sensible thing, in truth, would be to build as the Kyles built on their hill, for quick abandonment, and in a way their old shack finds a parallel in the houses of most current suburbs, which are not built for staying either.

Unanswerable in any practical way . . . I guess the Three Little Pigs come into it from far back, with their propaganda in favor of solid structures, and half-recollected pictures in childhood books of crooked gabled rock cottages in oak forests with witches or fat housewives peering out their doors, and a deep irrational seated preference for limestone country and for the types of trees and grasses it nourishes and the houses men of former times made grow up out of its own strata of rock. I remember responding with warm recognition to the rubble limestone houses of South Texas and the Edwards Plateau when I first saw them as a boy, most often built by old Germans and nearly always tin-roofed, and to the ones in Mexico and up along the Shenandoah. And later there was Europe with wide limestone valleys inhabited for millennia, and the whole blue Mediterranean ringed with limestone towns and forts and farms and ruins, and people, including me at times, still living in houses built five hundred or a thousand years before, sometimes whitewashed or plastered over, sometimes with the old rough-squared pale rubble or cut stone showing bare in its weathered strength and honesty. People in such places do not find it hard to believe that we have racial memory of a time when layered crevices and caves and overhangs were European man's main form of shelter. For they live in houses whose textures and feel are an outgrowth of such remembrance.

But let us not try to out-Lloyd Frank Lloyd Wright, the late revered. . . . In Somervell County and most of the rest of the Texas limestone country there was a good bit of such racial remembrance, or whatever it is, in the old days—if less emphatic here than farther south where European immigrants brought it fresh with their baggage when they came. Even among our Anglo-Celts, at least among those who thought they had come to stay, itinerant stonemasons had steady employment wherever they went. Often European themselves —German or Irish most often—they built chimneys for log

or frame homes, and foundations, and storm cellars, and sometimes whole limestone houses that stand venerably in and
around towns like Glen Rose and are speckled here and there
in our hills and valleys, usually with good farmland nearby,
or what was once good farmland. Some of the prettiest of the
work was not domestic, but shows in the rear ends of old store
buildings on courthouse squares (the fronts being for the most
part faced more formally), or in structures like the fine old
mill Charles Barnard had built on the Paluxy in the 1860's,
which still stands in the town once named for it.

Thus, though irrational, wanting a stone house on one's
fragment of this country was at least not alien or subversive.
There was perhaps a queerness about my wanting to build it
myself, but that was noted more by city friends than by the
county's natives, most of whom understand a need to learn
the hard way and alone, and how you come to own things in
your head by working with them, and other such abstrac-
tions. As for me, once the idea had leaped fishlike into view, I
knew it had been lurking there for a long time, waiting its
moment, the need to build a house. Of stone . . .

The project, for that matter, did not amount to very
much, except in terms of an amateur's need to learn as he
went along. A limestone cabin of a plain old shape, its walls
of rough-squared slabs laid flat as they had lain in the earth,
thick or thin as the spot demanded, gray or cream or white
in the varying shades of the country's strata, just as they came
to hand from the pile. The gables of stone also, and the whole
thing rustic without any artful rusticity such as comes from
deep-raking mortar joints and letting a few stones stick out
from the wall's plane an inch or two and laying a few others
on edge. An old house even when new, made for easy stark
interim-time living and being, more solid by far than the
doomed shacks I used to camp in but with their simplicity
and scale. One good stone room with bookshelves and a fireplace for cooking and heat and staring. Overhangs fore and

aft under a tin roof to resist sparks from brush fires, the front one to be slabbed and screened as a sleeping and eating place, the rear an open woodshed with a sink and a cold-water hydrant for washing up, and with also a hazy future involving its possible enclosure as kitchen and bath. Windows and doors linteled in the old way with big single beams of stone, and the windows tall but only wide enough to let in air when air was what you wanted, without inviting the Texas light and heat inside to kill the shady cool that stone imparts.

In that simple form, the main part of it got built the second summer. After I had dug the footing trenches down to rock and had had a ready-mix truck out to pour them full of concrete and had built the inner wall forms of braced insulating board, I hauled in stone and mixed mortar and laid up the walls by myself till they reached a height that called for a scaffold. At that point, lone hard-way learning being one thing and idiot ironheadedness another, I admitted to myself without fighting it much that I needed help. Stonework done alone at best is slow; the walls rise gradually and at the end of a long good day's laying you are lucky if you can stand off a way (as you always do) and tell much difference in their level from that morning. It is not possible to do what natives call "making a show," as you can with carpentry sometimes, when a whole structure's frame may loom against the evening sky where at dawn there was nothing at all. The solitary mason on a scaffold—I did try it briefly that year—needs to be one of those stubborn few who, if they exist, like to do a thing without ever getting through. Chiefly he clambers up and down with rocks and buckets and mortar troughs and tools—an approach known in the region as "piss-anting," for the endless toting involved—and occasionally he lays a stone. Therefore I hired a big strong local boy, the son of a friend, to run the mixer and shape stones and hand things up as I worked.

The rocks we used came partly off the place, sledged

from exposed strata, and partly from a neighbor's quarry where bulldozers had curled out great flat boulders of hard blue-centered stuff, ideal for shaping into lintels and corners. Some came too from old chimneys on a friend's nearby ranch, a few of them already knocked down by dozers or by time, others awaiting a like fate as they stood forlorn among horehound weeds in uncleared cedar against the ghostly remembrance of a log or plank house burned down long since, their fireplace lintels usually cracked and sagging. In these chimneys' stones squared and faced a century or so ago by masons whose names I never heard, there is a special feel. They are grayed by weather and lichens and starred by the old ones' bush hammers, and they tie the house to the region's past and the human past in a way that the house's shape and texture alone could never do.

Not that I ever got past a bite of guilt at tearing the chimneys down. You worked the chisel point of a crowbar into the joint beside a big corner stone near the base and pried it free, for the old lime mortar was mostly dissolved away and the whole thing was held upright in part by gravity but even more by simple habit, by the mere fact of having been a chimney for so long. Like a chopped tree, the chimney would sway thoughtfully for a moment before falling, giving you time to scuttle back. Then it would lean down on the wounded side and crash flat to earth with a brittle roar and billows of alkaline dust, and what had once been the winter focus of some family's life was abruptly a long disorderly heap of stones on the ground from which men now dead had dug them.

But they were sound shapely stones to build with, after you chipped away the creosote and the pink-burned rotten edges that had bordered the flue. And furthermore (said guilt with a self-righteous air), the chimneys were doomed at any rate, and who knew that some of their stones had not come from earlier structures still, or that some day they might not

be plucked from the ruins of one's own house to suit still
another human use, as Roman stones and even bits of statuary
and fluted columns show up in the rough walls of Levantine
fortresses the hairy Crusaders built, as Babylonian palaces'
glazed bricks form walls of Arab hovels? . . . For any human excresence on the land is brief in the land's own terms,
though it last for thousands of years. Nature and the hands of
later men both push to smudge out our spoor. Look on my
works, ye Mighty, and despair. . . .

It was a good hard-driving summer, and the muttering
question—why stone?—plagued me a little but not as much
as it had with the tiny pump-house a year before. There was
shimmering, locust-singing heat but a little rain also, and I
was still of an age to thin and harden to the work. The walls
and chimney took the two of us six solid weeks beyond the
time I had already put in alone on them. I had built a shack
on skids to stay in, but mainly slept outdoors on a cot with a
mosquito bar, under liveoaks beside my rising structural mar-
vel. After we had quit in the afternoon and big Royce Lee
had cleaned the mixer and barrow and gone home, I would
steel-brush the faces of the stones laid that day to remove the
crisping mortar stains before they set hard, and would stand
back and admire for a while, one with the old itinerant Germans and the slave stonemasons of Greece.

Then I would go bathe at the waterfall and would come
back in twilight to eat crackers with something straight out
of a can or jar, too tired and obsessed for hunger, and would
lie down and sleep, half-waking pleasantly sometimes to a big
wind or a fox's bark or the bumping beneath the cot of an
old armadillo with a stub tail, dog-gnawed, who grubbed in
the oaks' leaf-litter, or to a close chuck-will's-widow or a
screech owl, who like all his tribe did not screech at all but
bubbled and gently wailed. . . . It was my first and perhaps
best summer of real intimacy with the place, and the first
summer I had spent working and living steadily outdoors in

Texas since I had been young. The sounds and the smells and the feel of the weather were known things, but with echoes. The rattle of black wasps flying out at your face to warn you from their nest, the slowing cluck of the rain crow, the chicken cackle of alarmed quail, the steaming southeasterly winds that blew like the sirocco for days without stop, and the clean dry hot ones out of Mexico. The hour of quiet cool just after dawn on a hushed and dewless August morning, birdsong having waned as nesting slowed and the moult began . . . When I was working by myself and more or less quietly—in June, and in early September on the roof and porch, after my helper had left—deer and wild turkey and other participants in the Way would come and watch from the cedar's edge, perusing the shape of change.

Laboring thus alone, the Changer himself grew queer, personalizing tools and materials and sometimes speaking to them and to himself in language unknown to the run of men. I know from talking with others honest enough to admit to such foibles that I am not singular in this, and therefore don't mind recording, though unsure of anyone's interest in it, that a toenailed spike, driven slantingly into a board to fasten its end perpendicularly to another member, is for me in privacy a T. Texas Toenail, after a honkytonk singer who used to call himself T. Texas Tyler and for all I know still does. Or that before grabbing hold of a fat heavy building stone, of the sort that needs a grunt and a blasphemy to lift, I am likely to address it in the words of the song men are said to have sung while marching in against the Mexicans at San Jacinto: "Will you come to the bower I have shaded for you?" Or indeed that—but maybe those examples will suffice. . . . It is in such ways that we Old Farts make long days short and mitigate the years.

Before October came in wet and cool, the strong shell of a little house stood on the ledge where tangled cedar had dozed before. The windows and doors were not yet in, nor was it ceiled inside. But it was roofed all over with tin—aluminum, actually, over good solid sheathing and felt—and the floor slabs were down and the porch balustraded and gabled with rough-sawed cedar planks and their battens. And the fireplace worked, so that with a little scrap plywood tacked over some of the draftier openings it was a snug enough place to camp with a dog and sundry field mice and woodpeckers.

Without having owned a house before or even having wanted to, I owned this one in just about any way you could name. Its shape had come from my hand and pencil. Each stone and board had known my unprofessional touch, and incorporated in the mortar and concrete of the walls were quantities of my dripping sweat and a little even of my blood, from mangled thumbs and things. To this day, there are individual bits and pieces of the house that I cannot see without remembering the building time. Not all its bits and pieces, luckily, for I have found that when work goes well you can usually look at even a recently installed item—some difficult stone or beam or corner assembly—without being able to recall putting it in. . . .

But there are, for instance, some thick, 350-pound, blue-heart lintels over the main door and the windows that even now, eleven years later, bring back to me clearly the frustration of trying to sledge and chisel them into shape where they lay cracked out of their natal ledge on a hilltop (my helper got a steel chip off the hammer's face in his forearm during that), the ease with which they balked homemade engineering measures intended to raise them up where they belonged (we finally brought in the well-driller with his gin-pole truck), and the relief of seeing them mortared firmly into place. There are learner's mistakes also that I remember from having had to live with their effects—such things as a poorly flashed chimney, and mortar that is too gray, and old form lumber left under the main room slab to breed termites, though they have slacked off now, and some slight undulations in the roof where I miscalculated plate heights by three quarters of an inch or so. . . .

Enter Madame, with a liking for cool fall weather and approval of the simple solid result of my summer's work, and also with some unsimple ideas about its future development and a willingness to help with plastering and such things. . . . From that point on, the house has never really quit growing, nor has any segment of it ever really reached completion, though this early part is battered enough by now—upkeep not having been a big activity, with all else there has been to do—that some people take it to be quite old, unrespectably so. I see no point in tracing out the later stages. Suffice it to say that during them I became, among other things, an electrician and a plumber, and that the present structure consists of the main stone room, its porch, a kitchen and bath, and two frame rooms jutting off the right rear end. The whole thing has three separate levels of floor and some varying lines of roof, and without being intentionally quaint is reminiscent of the old helter-skelter tin-roofed houses of stone and vertical boards in the German country of South Texas that were the first rock houses I ever cared anything about, which may give a measure of how far I have progressed in taste since childhood. A proposed and already blueprinted two-story frame bedroom addition off the left rear, if it materializes, will—maybe—complete this ramblingness.

Different visitors respond to it differently. Some see it for what it is, whatever that is, and like it. Others, usually contemporary and urban types, clearly feel and sometimes say that if a man is idiot enough to want to build his own house, then the house ought to end up as a startlingly distinctive and tasteful structure—a rustic geodesic dome, perhaps, or something on the order of Robinson Jeffers's domicile at Big Sur or the Paolo Soleri concrete interminables. Alas, for many reasons, this house though interminable is not of that ilk. . . . Some countrymen, perhaps in similar vein, are apt to be troubled by anyone's having put a lot of work into walls that are just simple and "old-timey," without colored or fancy rocks or other embellishments. One such who came while I was building, a decent and helpful man, said when he saw how pigheaded was my resolve to lay my plain hunks of limestone flat and plain, that he knew of some fine red or green or blue dyes you could mix into your mortar or even paint on mortar already set.

But it is mine, and there by God it is. Inside the chimney's masonry there lies a piece of paper with a scribbled curse on it, directed at the man who tears the house down, as some man likely will in time.

Look on my works, ye Mighty.

Most other construction on the place has connection with the Ownership Syndrome and hence with "usefulness," and like the house it has gone on more or less constantly, with one or two projects usually in flux and none of them ever quite finished. In all they add up to not very much—some goat sheds and a tool house and a "bunk house" (my old shack on skids, furbished) and a fair-sized barn. Most are of pole-frame design, held up by creosoted timbers anchored in concrete, and are sided with vertical rough-cedar one-by-twelves which were widely available during the period when I was doing most of the building, the issue of some vast cut-out-and-git-out operation on the West Coast or in Alaska, but have now grown scarce and costly. Such is my cranky nostalgia that I would have liked to use wide yellow-pine boards such as the old ones used, even though cedar is better, but cut-and-git long since ate up most of the East Texas pines big enough to yield such planks.

Construction grows easier with time and practice, except

insofar as encroaching years make certain heavy tasks harder. You waste fewer motions and you make fewer botches and you know the order of things, without having to study and fret so much. You are less in a hurry than you once were, and if on some day you manage to "make a show," good enough, but you know by now that making a show depends on much preliminary work done right—measuring and laying out and digging and concreting and such things—which cannot be rushed. You know your tools and you pace yourself, and the pace you set you can hold.

The stonework I felt a need to do is done, and I plan to do no more beyond a foundation or so and maybe a garden wall and a couple of chimneys—and those only if I can't find someone else I trust to do them right. Carpentry, though, is lighter and suits an aging type better—but inexplicably I find that the part of it I like best these days is the heaviest part, framing and big rough work. I used to tie trout flies and wind my own rods, and am still capable of spending hours carving a bit of mother-of-pearl to inlay in something useless, and days shaping and fitting and oiling and polishing a walnut mantel board or a gunstock. But there is an exuberance in sawing strong two-by-fours and -eights and -twelves to shape and setting them where they go in a structure's skeleton and clinching them there with thick spikes under the pound of a twenty-two-ounce waffle-faced framing hammer, and then looking afterward at what you have done. Maybe, even if no longer in a hurry, I have succumbed to the country satisfaction in making a show, or maybe hidden aggressions are venting themselves through that brutal hammer's stroke.

During my forty-ninth summer in this vale of human effort, I built most of a sixty-by-forty-six-foot unlofted barn by myself, though I had the sense to buy made trusses and in the end to have the galvanized roofing put on by a couple of men more used than I to that glaring, sizzling, thumb-busting task. Even while I was doing it, I considered that it was fairly ridiculous for a rather bookish man of such years to be scuttling on all-fours around a network of plates and joists and rafters and purlins like a great cautious middle-aged spider on his self-spun web, conscious always of the ground an uncomfortable distance below, especially when he dropped a tool and watched its fall and bounce and knew full well there was no bounce in him, but only thud and crunch. Yet it did not hurt to learn that I had still not quite worn out, and besides it is a rather good barn for our mild climate, and the place had need of it. When fictional Rubén and Cuco showed up the following year they helped me with the workshop and storage and office part along the rear, and the summer after that—or was it two?—I and a couple of hard-slogging teen-aged boys piled in and finished it up. More or less . . .

If you build a thing yourself you are not in much danger of taking it for granted for a good while after completing it. Rather you run an opposite danger of overappreciation, as some passages in this chapter may show more clearly than I might wish. Besides the usual daily process, while building, of standing back and marveling a bit at what your deft hands have wrought, there is a sort of continuing recognition of yourself in the things around you, which can sometimes come out a bit weird. I have caught myself, for instance, twisting the handle of a toilet installed by me, and conjuring up with pride a lyric picture of its erstwhile contents coursing down a sewer line I laid to a septic tank whose setting in place I at least severely supervised. . . . Fortunately, such acute identification with your work does taper off in time, but there remains a day-to-day, semiconscious awareness of what you have built which, together with your sense of the slowly recuperative land around you, can weave a quiet but solid satisfaction, and a perhaps less solid but nonetheless agreeable illusion of independence in a world of intertangled men.

If the work were truly handcraft, of course, that independence might be less illusory, but except for the stonework not very much of it is. Had the building fever touched me earlier in life—and I am glad it didn't, for there were other things that needed learning and doing in those days—I have no doubt that I would have been capable of going to such extremes as burning my own lime for mortar, and hewing out rafters and joists from cedars and oaks and ashes I felled myself, and riving shakes for a roof, and all that. For if you are going back to barehanded basics you might as well go all the way—other things, that is, being equal. . . .

But other things are not equal. One comes to know time as the stubbornest foe, and comes to know too that there are some things he is not going to get around to in life, or comes to know that if he is going to get around to them, he'd better take some shortcuts. Technology being the main repository of shortcuts, he comes then in somewhat gingerly fashion—if he is like me, anyhow—to the idea that he needs technology's help. And technology being also a sort of disease, the help he ends up accepting is one slew of help indeed.

Hence I rip and crosscut and bevel bought boards, ravished mechanically from some far-off unlucky forest and sawed and squared and surfaced in some screaming distant mill, with a toothed and noisy apparatus in whose fabrication I had no part, and through whose nurturing triple-wired cord flows energy derived from the pollutive burning, somewhere, of fossil organic matter built from sun and rain and soil and the holy germ of life a good many millions of years ago, and irreplaceable except on the same scale of time. And I own and use also electric drills, concrete mixers, air compressors, and an array of other ungentle, unsimple, unbasic powered tools and implements. This is because of time, and because human help is scarce and dear, and because too I am willy-nilly a corrupted impure inhabitant of this corrupted impure shortcut world we have built, in which simplicity is much harder to reach and touch than is its opposite, and in which the technology on which we lean may end by erasing us all.

However, like most impure men I am fairly adaptable too, and I will not pretend that I wade through construction projects with grim corded brow and gritted teeth while pondering such sobrieties. Building things for yourself and yours is mainly pleasure, or ought to be. The tools whether powered or not become extensions of you, and the materials whether fabricated elsewhere or not are what you have to work with, so you shape them and put them together in a form you have dreamed up, and in all that there is a measure of simplicity and basicness and even free will, if only relative. And in the world as it is, which is surely far from ideal, the use of such tools and materials is often the only way you can get some things done by yourself—the world as it is having also made it needful that you often do them by yourself, if you are going to do them at all. . . .

There is much to think about, building, besides the building itself. Some of the things you think about are around you and some are far away and some are nowhere at all, being quite abstract. But you have time for them if the work is going smoothly and your hands and tools are functioning of themselves and you are not driving to get the job done by that night, or by the weekend, or by the Fourth of July. Your mind can go its own way.

Once while roofing a tool house I worked out a rather elaborate argument in favor of a general Western reversion to the Roman Catholic faith, but it must have had some holes in it, for I myself never came anywhere near to acting on its conclusions. In general the cast of my thought while building is not heavily theological, but then neither is it at most other times. I do remember one showery day that first summer when my teaching friend and I were working on the pumphouse, and theology or something related seemed to rear its head. Through ignorance, we were using stones that were much too small and laid up very slowly, and at least four times that morning we had had to halt work and spread cement sacks and scrap material on top of our wall, to keep a sudden rain from weakening and washing out fresh mortar.

A new cloud came in low with a heavy wind, and a premonitory bit of thunder whiplashed briefly overhead with the sound of some huge machine's shorting.

"That's right, damn you," I said looking up. "Go ahead and crackle."

"Tell 'em," my colleague said with approval, thrusting his trowel toward the sky like a Roman's short stabbing sword.

It answered. Out of the cloud a thick and crooked jag of lightning reached crashing down, lovingly touched the top of the electric meter pole forty yards down the hill, and lingered there for a second or so with a fearful whispering aftersound as its power rushed down the ground wire to earth. It deafened us and quite literally raised the hair on our heads, and it left a smell behind. I have always liked thunder and natural uproar, but I didn't like them that time. We dismounted from our sawhorse scaffold and covered our work with sacks and sought shelter in a dry corner of the whopper-jawed old Kyle house as the rain began to pelt. Nor did we again address the clouds with flippancy, or at all. . . .

Weather is often a central theme in your thinking when working outdoors. By and large, the sort of dry Texas weather that builders like is the opposite of what farmers and stockmen yearn for. If you are playing both roles you are sometimes in a schizoid bind, though the fact that your preferences don't matter does keep it from getting severe. From another point of view, too, if you are both builder and yeoman farmer you ought to be able to find something to like about almost any kind of weather, except things like tornadoes, and the utter hostile hatefulness of big hail.

But one does have sometimes unreasonable vagaries and quirks concerning weather. Except for the first few clean northers that slam down at us in the fall, killing summer's hold, I dislike big shoving continuing winds, which make all wild things nervous and grab at boards in your hands and set your dogs to barking moronically at nothing at all. East winds, heavy or light, rub me wrong also, seeming nearly always to have a sort of malarial feel in them. Of the individual months, I have least fondness for February and August, with their dogged lingering insistence on what they are, even if they do have the function of preceding our fine, long, usually mild springs and falls and of making them more welcome when they get here.

If you like the year's changes, you tend often to think of seasonal weather in its most classic form, which is to say the form that you yourself prefer. Hence summer around Hard Scrabble—the time of year when I have done most work here, from circumstance—appears to my imagination in other seasons and places as a long succession of bright days with small sheeplike clouds coasting across a pale-blue sky from the south or southwest, impelled by a dry breeze that pleasantly, coolly evaporates your sweat. And every couple of weeks or so, a high anvil-headed thunderstorm shapes up against the horizon and moves its black boiling center straight at you and cracks and roars, and the smell of the first drops pounding down is of wetted dust, of cedar, of manure's ammoniac cleanliness, of all the vegetation that has been waiting for that kiss—a better smell to someone with crops and animals on the land than perfume or beefsteak.

Occasionally it turns out somewhat like that, but more often otherwise. Summer here is just as likely to be a sequence of sultry still days that steam you like a crab, when you work wet to your knees and change shirts three times a day and even breathing gets a little hard. Its rains may not come at all, the few thunderheads that do form moving not straight at you but slantwise away, and everything green dries to death or dormancy. Or it rains too much and swelters in between, and all manner of enemy bugs proliferate and wax fat on you and your cows and your blackeyed peas. Or the Gulf sirocco blows night and day for two or three weeks and maddens everyone. Or the classic southwest Chihuahuan breeze turns into an endless blowtorch blast. All these can be summer too.

Your reaction to weather varies much with your mood, of course, and most of all with your physical tone. If one year you quit smoking and run inexorably toward tallow about the guts and jowls and tail, work during the middle and late summer is going to be harder on you than it ever was before. And if among the rewards you reap from a lifetime's casual contempt for your body's needs and limitations are a few mildly calcified joints, then a damply frigid windy January day spent putting tin on a pasture goatshed is going to show you new possibilities for discomfort. And both cold and heat do seem to get a little fiercer as the years pass by in movement from wherever they are born toward wherever it is they go. For often it seems it is they that move, not we, and they abrade us in their flow. . . .

Yet early or late, fat or skinny, supple or stiff, abrasive or abraded, I tend each year to be grateful for the seasons' iambic rhythm, with a preference toward heat if I were forced to choose an extreme but a gladness always for the big clean cold when November and December bring it down, with geese and cranes, from out of Canada. . . .

Another subject which if neither poetic nor profound is often quite strong in the thoughtful Tonk Nation builder's mind is that of horseflies. (I told you there had to be a place for them; indeed, horsefly thoughts could fill a chapter if one would let them have it.) Not for these large gray *Tabanidae* the tepid blood of shade-tree idlers, poised to swat and gloat. They crave the laboring sunlit yeoman's nobler juice, and it is when his horny hands are filled with tools and nails and boards and kindred items that they love him most of all. I know the attribution of any reasoning power to bugs is a fallacy, but when you are their victim it is hard to avoid sometimes. And for that matter the millions of years of effective conditioned responses built into the Nation's horse-flies by natural selection do come very close to reasoning, and no one who has had intimacy with them has any doubt that they know quite well when a man's hands are occupied and his bent back under a tight-stretched sweat-wet shirt is open to assault.

They like movement in their targets; sitting quietly you will be little bothered. But there is not usually much reason to want to sit quietly in the sort of calm hot places they frequent—back in the cedar, or in the torrid lee of a building, or anywhere outdoors when the sun is strong and there is no breeze, for wind or a touch of cool makes them lie low. The only valid reason for being there is to work, and it is work—activity, motion—that frenzies them and focuses them on you. In their repertory of tactics, the most common is a blundering, buzzing, bumping, seemingly aimless series of collisions with your person, followed—when you have quit paying attention—by a quiet landing in a suitable spot and an insertion of that great soda straw each carries on his nose. It can make a hole as big as a pinhead that will itch for hours, and on stock a few years back these small wounds were occasionally a starting place for screw-worms.

At other times they may buzz you in circles at a distance to gauge your mettle, or sneak in soundlessly for a suck of blood before you know they are there. If there are only two or three or four, you can down tools and wait out their maneuvers and swat them when they land and lower their proboscises, for during one brief moment they concentrate on drilling or on the gourmet delights in prospect, and grow unwary. Well slapped, they crunch and die most gratifyingly. But if there are many, the best you can do is roll down your sleeves and pull out your shirttail to make the cloth as loose as possible on your body, and then just take the bites that come with as good a grace as you can muster, my own grace in this respect being rather poor.

They are hell on horses and cows, the latter being likely

to graze at night during the worst of the horsefly season and to clump during day in thickets where they can rub off such flies as do find them. No chemical repellent or poison seems to have much effect. Goats, which appear to be pestered little if at all, have some sort of answer. But whether it involves a peculiarly goatish scent principle or their furious tail-wagging and ear-flapping and stamping against all insects is information which, in the manner of goats, they keep to themselves. Maybe it is worth noting too at this point that horseflies seem not to like their diet flavored with the strong chili peppers that our visiting wetbacks require in large numbers for contentment. At least I have labored in the cedar with a pair of these gentry and have been eaten up myself, while observing clinically and enviously that such flies as lit on my companions' shirts sat there thoughtfully for a moment, then flew away without making use of that horrid prong. ("What flies?" said Alejandro when I started to slap and curse. . . .)

In a dry summer horseflies last as a prime nuisance for only a month or so, peaking in July, but if you have helpful rains staggered along the way, you have horseflies all summer too, often well into September. The only evident way to cut down on their numbers is to get rid of all the cedar and small brush where they harbor, but in the Tonk Nation, as we have observed, that takes a bit of doing.

Yes, they are part of the Way. I'd just as soon, however, that they were somewhat less a part of my own corner of it.

Ghosts visit you too, while you work. Some of them are the ghosts of old locals whose traces and detritus mellowly litter the place and who once reared their own rough constructions here. Madame insists that a female one of these used to pinch her on the rump, not hard, for a time after we first moved down to stay. . . . Others are exotic in the Nation, ghosts we brought along when we came, in our heads. Of them all I think the one who is most often with me at building work is my father, who died the year I started the house and never saw it or the place.

He was a complex and rather selfless man, so responsible toward others that he spent much of his life in worry, at least after the Depression burned in. Of fulfillment, I think he found a good bit in friends and in his family, though I myself caused him further worry often in my restless years. There was something left over, though, and a part of it came out through his hands with tools, for he cared about building things. A merchant, out of a family of merchants and lawyers and other professional men, he nevertheless would have made a good artisan and might have been happiest being one. What he liked was finish work and cabinetry, carefully fitted things that you could sand and polish for hours after you had put them together. Because he had little spare time and tended to feel out methods for himself, the things he built only occasionally looked professional. But some did, and all were solid and honest, and we eat now on the screen porch in summer from a redwood table he made.

Young, I perversely wanted no part of all that, though he tried to interest me in it, which may have made me back off farther still. . . . He gave up finally, saying that he guessed I was just not manually inclined. For he never shoved at me, having been shoved at a bit too much himself when young.

But I seem to have picked up some things from him regardless, and among them is a sharp, illogical sense of the pathos of cheap and inferior tools. He used hand tools, good ones and not very many of them, succumbing only late in life to the allure of a Black and Decker electric drill and an oscillating sander. They all hung oiled in their places above a work bench, the edged ones always sharp, and he was made queerly nervous by the sort of collection of random screw-drivers and loose-handled dull things that most people ac-cumulate in a kitchen drawer for odd repair work they can't avoid.

And strangely today, despite a rather long and happily slobbish former career of owning loose-handled dull things if any tools at all, I myself am uncomfortable and sad when I watch someone going at a job with a Japanese cast-iron claw-hammer and some odd levels and chisels and drill-bits culled from a "99¢ YOUR CHOICE" table in a chain drugstore, employing them ineptly on work they could not do right even if used with skill. I can't say exactly why I find it sad. In theory I don't mind the worker's ineptitude, for it is often in my mind that building and making things may well be a trap into which I have fallen much deeper than I should have, and that I might waste less time on all that if I were more inept myself. . . . But those cheap tools in someone's hands, for some ingrained reason, give me a feeling very close to the one I get from looking at a specific young sharecropper girl's face in one of the old Walker Evans photos in *Let Us Now Praise Famous Men*, an unfocused, uneasy melancholy. Maybe it has to do with the fact that among the worthwhile things this country of ours still has to offer, decent tools are one, valued through the world, and to be so ignorant of what your hands can do that you do not even know about the im-plements that will help your hands to do it right, is somehow very sad. Or maybe it's something else. . . .

Most of my father's tools are among my own now. I do not keep them nearly as well as he did, though more or less in order. I use them as I work, feeling him in the balance of an old Plumb hammer or a supple Disston handsaw. I suspect or at any rate hope that his ghost gets a smile now and then, watching my obsession with doing things I would not do when young, with him.

13 ≋ *Another Irrelevance* ≋

That last stretch of the island's coastline was mainly tawny stone cliffs rising from blue deep water, with occasional pinnacles jutting up alone from the sea, and here and there a cove with a beach, and few people. We dawdled along it in good weather, Rafael and I, moving on late in the mornings after coffee from the place where we had anchored the night before unless we decided to stay there for another night, stopping at noon or earlier to gather shellfish and to spear seabass or crayfish or whatever else we could find while diving in the restless rocky water along the shore, cooking these things with rice and oil and saffron over an alcohol burner for a midday meal, dozing and swimming and talking through most of the afternoon before cruising on to some other sheltering cove for the night. It was nearly time to sail back to Mallorca; the trip was almost done.

One morning, out of bread, we put into a cove with a tiny beach and no sign of people except someone's old lateen-rigged fishing boat pulled up on the sand and a path ascending to the top of the cliffs. Climbing it, we came up into a little valley of baked pale earth. On its slopes goats were browsing scrub under the eye of a taciturn mongoloid boy, and in cloddy dry ground on the valley floor there was a scrawny stand of American corn and farther up among almonds, healthier strips of wheat or rye.

At the head of the valley was a low house of yellow stone belonging to a short scar-nosed man whose family, when he came out to talk with us, peeked one-eyed from around the jambs of doors and narrow windows, except for two little mongoloid girls, less shy, who came and stood at his elbow. He had bread, yes, plenty of it, the hard dark island sort that kept forever. They had baked three days before for the month. . . . He did not often see strangers here. It was his boat at the beach; his oldest son fished with it, catching sometimes enough to carry to market in town. . . . He sat us down in bright-painted chairs his mother made for sale to tourists in San Antonio Abad, on a stone-floored gallery looking back down the valley at the sea, and made us drink with him, passing the one glass around, a bottle of wine made from his grapes, while we ate hard salty goat cheese and olives his wife and mother brought. Part of the time he spoke in awkward Spanish for courtesy, knowing me to be no islander, but he lapsed often into dialect with Rafael, who translated some of it. As we sat there, pigs and children and poultry came to study us, all shyly, quietly, politely. . . .

Three of his eight children, these two little ones and the boy with the goats, were not normal. He spoke of it calmly, a natural misfortune, and kneaded one's head with affection. Another of the daughters was delicate. . . .

"No, man," he said to a question from Rafael. "It's not a hard life here at all. Work, yes, but for that the Lord made people." He had the valley, with dirt in it, and some others he knew had only rocks and scrub, or no land at all. There were meat and fish and bread and oil and wine and milk, and the other things you could grow. When it rained right . . .

More than enough for a family, and who needed money except a bit for taxes? . . .

He had been off the island only once, when the Nationalists had drafted him and carried him away, reluctant, to soldier at Guadalajara and Madrid and to have his nose slashed by shrapnel. His people had been here always. He would not leave again, not for anyone. . . . In the end Rafael checked over the delicate daughter, a ten-year-old, as best he could without his medical things, finding what he thought might be a heart murmur. When the little mongoloids crowded in jealously he thumped their chests too and laughed with them, and told the father that if he would bring the girl to Palma on the interisland steamer, she could be examined right.

The little man nodded and thanked him gravely, but later when we were walking back toward the cove with the bag of things for which they would take no payment, Rafael said they would never bring the child to see him. "It's all God here," he said. "God does things; man puts up with them. We're still Arabs here in the islands."

"God did quite a bit to him," I said. "Three out of eight."

"Yes," said Rafael. "And do you know a thing?"

"What?"

"He is more man than we are," Rafael said, edging with the heavy sack of bread and red wine and apricots and melons down a twisting path to the sea. "He is entire."

14 ≋ The War
with Mother N. ≋≋≋≋≋≋

*Oh, labor is the curse of the world, and nobody can meddle
with it without becoming proportionately brutified. Is it a
praiseworthy matter that I have spent five golden months in
providing food for cows and horses? It is not so.*

NATHANIEL HAWTHORNE, concerning his
participation at Brook Farm

or, on the other hand:

*Whatsoever thy hand findeth to do, do it with thy might,
for there is no work, nor device, nor knowledge, nor wisdom,
in the grave, whither thou goest.*

ECCLESIASTES 9:10

In the golden time that existed or could or should have
long ago, one speculates, men weighed lightly on the land, for
they were few and undemanding and it was wide and rich.
They did not so much use it as admire it, enjoying the plenty
with which it rewarded nimble hands and brains, knowing
their part in its sacred Way, sensing the spirits that imbued
its trees and beasts and waters and winds (O large and meaty
aurochs, forgive me while I poke this spear in your bowels.

. . .), chomping occasional ears and noses off of fellow-human intruders on their loose nomadic territory or maybe off of one another, for sport.

But if such an age did exist, one knows, it was only a shelf and a resting place, an interim time not meant to last more than enough short millennia to glue itself teasingly in the collective unconscious. For nimble hands and brains were not shaped by golden ease, but by harshness and change and flux. And harshness and change and flux raged in again to smash the golden time with floodings and glaciations and five-thousand-year drouths and drifting, shifting continents and God knows what all else, each event a part of the Way, and out of their pinch and scratch came further shaping of men's lives in the form of herding, and farming, and building, and jealous-boundaried private claims to specific hunks of land, and towns, and nations, and politics, and war, and business, and games played with balls, and other sorts of progress. Some backwatered breeds remembered the Way was sacred (O great Goddess, absolve me for slicing your earth with this plow), but mainly such sacredness choked the path of change and was twisted aside to fit the new scheme of things (Our thanks, Lord Dionysus, for the superior vintage this year, and will you take part in our orgy?), or else was relegated un-derstandably furious to the heavens, Zeus shooting thunder-bolts at people's meter poles.

It was not thus? All right, it probably wasn't. But it was something like that. . . . And even as ontogeny—or so they preached in Biology One—recapitulates phylogeny, so have I as chief resident peasant of my own sacred if tired bit of earth progressed through at least certain early stages of our race's march away from blessedness toward glory. For in my time here at Hard Scrabble I seem to have been impelled not steadily but surely away from an erstwhile hunter-nomad's simple-minded happy admiration of what was left of wildness, after the rub and smudge of history, to a need to shape and fructify—a need in short to use. The end result is a herder and farmer and builder of sorts, if still not quite civilized.

Resentfully sometimes, one keeps seeking reasons why he chose to come this route, trying to see what it was that made him vulnerable to the Ownership Syndrome's sway. . . . In part, I suspect, it has to do simply with being human, and wanting to view from the inside a kind of activity that has helped shape human beings into what they are. Because if I believe that whether it existed or not, the paleolithic golden time with its sense of the wholeness of natural things sank into our genes and memory, I believe also that sowed seeds and tended beasts and tilled dirt and their rhythms did like-wise, for these things grew out of natural wholeness and our attachment to them is very very old. As witness the ancient matriarchates and their ritual murder of kings, and all those old dying and reborn gods serving green fertility's ends.

Other reasons that suggest themselves may be less nobly abstract. Plain moneymaking economics has not been strong among them so far, but there will be a place later on to look at that. . . . A more basic sort of refuge economics, though, has played a certain role. Lacking much faith in the wisdom and durability of current ways, the Syndrome's chosen victim tries to shore up defenses for himself and his in the form of vegetable garden and grain-fields and beehives and domestic animals and the pastures they require, and most of all in the form of knowledge of how to manage and nurture these things. Not that fifteen fertile acres or less, well tended, wouldn't serve that purpose—and the purpose of human un-derstanding too—a good deal less painfully than a piece of mainly rough country the approximate size of the principality of Monaco.

Personal heritage gets into it, certainly. . . . My parents had left behind their own country and small-town back-grounds, but the links and the kinsmen were there, and touch-ing me as I grew up was a continuity of concern with crops

and land, water and livestock, weather and grass. And in the
Texas of my youth, even in its cities, a special aura attached to
ranchers, including small-time unprosperous somewhat
raunchy ones smelling of Smear 62 screw-worm dope. Some
of it lingers today, so that when a man garners from petro-
leum or elsewhere large quantities of cash, he still often
hastens to invest part of it in a ranch, because the respect that
his money alone may not command from the old Establish-
ment can perhaps be lured within his reach by possession and
management of grassed earth and glossy bovines. If this specific form of the regional quirk has had anything to do with
me and Hard Scrabble, though, it hasn't had very much, for
as a ranch—if a ranch at all—the place is smaller than small-
time, and such social aura as it gives might not really be considered desirable. . . .

The Syndrome. It moved in slowly with time, like arthritis. . . . Wherever it came from and whatever it consists of,
it sets you somewhat at war with the Way, or seems to. By
trying to do things right, you may minimize the conflict and
in truth, if you have any benevolence at all toward the land,
hardly anything you might do will be half as destructive as
what men did here before your time, through ignorance and
frontier-mindedness. But the fact remains that when you start
to run livestock and to sow seeds for their benefit, you are in
essence declaring yourself Head Varmint, a substitute cougar
and lobo and screw-worm and bear who aims to ram his own
tame herbivores into the niche the Way once reserved for
wild ones, and to nurture and harvest them for his own ends,
subjugating as best he can various hostile aspects of the natural
order.

My varmintcy first showed its teeth in the mid-sixties
when over a period of a couple of years I had about forty-five
acres of the Kyle place dozed clear of cedar and sowed them
to K. R. grass, patched some old fences and built one or two
new ones by myself, and moved some Angus cows down

from the rented land we lived on then. In the same era I bought a used Ford tractor with implements and began a fight—escalated when we acquired the Booker and lasting to this day—to restore the little fields to productivity. And thus has gone the slow and uncertain push toward usefulness, in a halting rhythm of bulldozings and fencings and plowings and sowings and livestock purchases and births and losses and sales. It has been interrupted often by long or short spells when I could not be here or had other things on my mind, has alternated with obsessed bouts of construction, and has been counterpointed—quite poignantly of late, since we moved down—by female cries for more and better housing. Furthermore it has devoured much time and energy that might (or for that matter might not, and let us save that question) more wisely have been sluiced into other kinds of equally human effort elsewhere. . . .

In these preparatory stages, fences have absorbed more time and work than just about any other of the Syndrome's activities, and there has been no way around that, for little fencing was here before and to manage animals right you need a good bit of it, even on a small place. It keeps them on your own land rather than on someone else's—most of them anyhow, for some individual bulls and goats have disdain for the privacy of property. It protects sowed fields, and lets you rotate grazing on your rangeland, giving gnawed grass a chance to rest and grow again. It guards young heifers' chastity till they are ready for love and its results, and later holds them under your eye for their first problematic calvings. It channels your beasts and tames them, and unless you are addicted to cowboying in all its old violent, horseback, rope-swinging purity and have neighbors all around you who feel the same way, it is altogether indispensable.

It is also a vast how-to subject, with enthusiasts who will vibrate your ear for hours regarding techniques of fence construction, and who wrangle among themselves over such things as deadmen, the length and positioning of brace struts in end and corner assemblies, the right net wire for goats, and the depth of corner holes. The main aim is strength and durability, and the main limitation is how much time and/or money the fence enthusiast wants to pour in. You can often recognize an oilman's ranch by its corners and gateposts of thick heavy oilwell drillstem pipe, painted with aluminum and sometimes topped with knobby cones from old rotary bits; one such gentleman of whom I know bought his own core drill rig for $15,000 or so and set his steel corners nine feet deep in concrete. . . . Even so, nearly any fence is a compromise that falls short of some ideal of sturdiness (say a mortared stone wall ten feet high and three feet thick all around your place, with six-foot ones for cross-fencing), and all are doomed in time to sag and rust and be replaced, as the brittle bits of rusted barbed wire grown into oaks and elms here and there on Hard Scrabble have told me time and again.

Some parts have their own early doom built in, especially the watergap parts where fences cross creeks and branches. Hard Scrabble, though small, is hellishly wrinkled and has about ten of these structures, of which two or three or four are apt to "go out" with any big storm, some just sprung apart and dangling, others washed away whole toward the Gulf of Mexico. They take an afternoon or a day or even two to fix in place again, and once you have marshaled your patience and have given up the idea of doing whatever else it was you had to do, it is wet work but not unpleasant, except in cold weather. There is no point in doing it any better than will suffice to contain your beasts, for sooner or later it will be there to do all over again; in such work a slobbish approach serves best. You salvage bits of old wire and spate-scoured stays, and splice and weave them with new stuff, and you walk away with torn fingers and wet feet and not much pride from something that will probably hold till washed out once more. At the worst places I have strung permanent cables between stout posts or trees set high on the banks, from which the things can be suspended in rebuilding, but the cables themselves occasionally hang a big drifting tree and go out too. To the sort of landowner who is enraged by any arrogance of the Way, watergaps are a special challenge and there are hence some ingenious contrivances around. The fanciest in our county, marvelous hinged steel affairs with huge buttresslike concrete supports at the ends, installed by the rich contractor on whose ranch they stood at a reputed cost of $2,500 each, ended up in the tops of some downstream pecan and cottonwood trees during a series of big storms a couple of years ago.

Fences, yes. Steel line posts have their partisans, but so do the traditional cedar ones, and creosoted pine. Different people like different wire-stretching tools, and—but fencing is a wide subject, spawned of the Syndrome's needs. . . . Rest in peace, wide subject, not that you will for long.

As for agriculture, the forage farming intended to make optimum use of the place's forty or fifty acres of manageable, generally deep field soil, it would be pleasant to be able to set down here a crisp clearminded plan that I adopted and the steps by which I carried it out to the Bromfieldian accomplishment of an ideal set of green, weedless, brushless, stoneless, rich meadows nestled along White Bluff's picturesque course. The trouble is that it hasn't gone just that way. . . . A certain Bromfieldian ideal exists and there has been progress toward it, but there has been nonprogress too. I did not even get hold of a tractor with some beat-up implements until about 1966, by which time some of the fields that had been bulldozed clean had grown up thickly again in the small hardwood brush that comes back unbelievably fast on such land. And since then, nonrural commitments and construction and thoughts of a golden time, among other things, have often gotten in the way of my doing things when they should have been done, so that the upward path of farming on the place has been quite fitful, with occasional largish setbacks. Nor has it all been expertly done. . . .

("You know what's the best thing about you being stuck way back here in the brush?" a visiting farmer friend once asked after watching some of my efforts—fairly successful, but sweaty—to harvest sweetclover seed with a doctored-up old grain windrower, a rusty monster with a flailing paddlewheel reel, known to the children as the Robert E. Lee.

"Privacy, I guess," I said.

"Maybe so," he said. "But not just the way you mean. The best thing is there can't nobody else see what a damn idjit you're making out of yourself.")

With the time and equipment I have had and necessary preliminaries like getting diversion terraces built above fields vulnerable to runoff from the hills above, it has been possible to tame only one or two patches at a time, and some of the taming is still going on. For early plowings, with all the brush and stubs and stumps and rocks and roots and old barbed wire and mason jars and barrel hoops that remain in evidence of the Way's ancient power and of men's not quite so ancient presence, you need something that will slice and chop the earth and lurch over or past immovable objects without tearing itself to pieces. Such qualities exist, more or less, in an old heavy Alamo triple disk plow that "came with" the Ford, which in low gear can barely pull the thing and even then not fully sunk. It staggers along behind, grating and rocking and occasionally leaping horribly upward and left, the weighted rear wheel leaving the round-bottomed furrow entirely, when its disks collide with an impossibility like a set of established shin-oak roots. There is no way of doing a trim job with it; just about the only route you can follow is counterclockwise round and round the unrectangular field, plowing out the corners at the end, and in the process leaving big ditches and humps that will still be jolting you three or four years later as you work that field with neater and more civilized tools. But the Alamo does roll out its great triple slice of sod and earth and debris, and severs the roots of most small brush, and only occasionally does anything on it break badly enough to have to be detached with huge wrenches and carried off to town for welding or replacement. In the early phase of re-civilizing such soil, it is a rough and battering weapon.

After that you smooth the mess as best you can with a disk harrow, and perhaps strew manufactured fertilizer before sowing whatever you are going to sow first, unless you are in an uncompromising Old Fart mood and are determined to go "organic." This praiseworthy approach is a rather slow go, however, on land where cotton exhaustion still lingers like hostile fate. Potassium—the "K" of the "NPK" on fertilizer sacks—is not usually short in our soils, and nitrogen can be built up over time through the use of legumes, whose symbiotic root-bacteria seize it from the air. But P-for-phosphorus is a problem, and there is in our region no commercial source of "natural" forms of it—ground phosphate rock is the main one—in farming quantities. So that in the Nation even a convinced O. F. is likely in the beginning to weigh the welfare of his earthworms and other soil organisms against the matter of time and expediency, and to end up laying down bought acid granulated stuff, whose dust makes him sneeze, for a year or two or three until his crops grow lush.

Then perhaps he can back off from such heresy and bring the land into a nearly fertilizerless routine of legumes and small grains and forage sorghums, with "trashy" farming techniques that work thick plant litter into the surface of the soil and help it turn to humus. And the earthworms and other organisms return in augmented billions, forgiving all, and the cows grow fat and drop calves and large brown patties everywhere, and richness begets richness. Ideally, that is, if the rains come right and you stay with it as you should, neither of which is always the case . . . For the ideal *is* organic, natural, however fitfully and impurely carried out. Because, quite aside from the question of food quality that is stirring such Counterculture passion now, only through natural replenishment can the soil hold its own and even grow better with use, and only thus therefore can there be harmony between farming and the Way.

(Precipitate descent of impure O. F. from soapbox, pelted with overripe organic fruit and vegetables by purists and jeered by well-dressed advocates of chemical factory-farming, who wave Green Revolution banners . . .)

Much of Hard Scrabble's field land is "ungrateful," in the old phrase, responding with grudging slowness to efforts to bring it back to health. Occasional long dry hot spells during which soil-improving biological processes go dormant enter into this, but so does a sort of built-in, sour, Tonkish resistance to having anything more to do with human projects and purposes. . . . Yet it is hard, looking back over the period of its use by white men, to find anything this land ought to be grateful for, and despite everything it does respond a little year by year and the feel of that is good, as is the feel of working it. Which may be partly why I have been slow about putting the fields in fancy permanent grass, heavily dosed each year with NPK, the usual practice on stock farms now.

I think I like the early fall part best, the preparation for sowing winter grain and legumes or sometimes for winter fallow to catch moisture for sowing in spring. If you are working land for grain and the soil is moist and soft, you can often make do with only a weighted tandem disk harrow, steering a curving course along the contour and setting the throttle medium slow in third and spinning along without a bounce, lifting the tool at the field's end and turning to head back alongside your last swath with a new one. Days are generally still warm then but often there is a northerly wind with an edged shove to it that belongs not to summer but autumn. Turning in the seat occasionally, you watch the shining cupped revolving disks as they slice through surface trash, flipping brown dirt up and sidewise and mixing it with the chopped stalks into a compound that will make the soil lighter and richer and moister and better to work in the years to come. Ahead of you doves and small finches rise in flocks from where they are searching out seeds among the cow-trampled forage growth, and behind you three crows strut as they look for plowed-up grubs and worms, and buzzards ride the breeze overhead against blue cloudlessness, and as a true happy poor relation of Lord Turnip Townshend and Louis Bromfield and all other triumphant returners to the land, you break out above the tractor's roar with a howling verse from "Pretty Frawlein." A tractor is much like a shower stall for singing; you sound good to yourself.

And on rough rocky land there is bulldozing to be done, and permanent range grasses to be sowed, and always more good dark soil showing up than you would have thought, enriched by its long rest under the cedars and by their shed rotting needles. And the little returning hardwood stuff has to be controlled there too—if you can—and piled brush has to be burned and the charred stubs restacked and then burned again, and all the rest. . . .

For the goals of the Head Varmint, and for his herbivores. I have read, among other vegetarians and humanitarians, the Nearings on the subject of keeping animals for exploitation and/or slaughter, and I find it possible to respect their purity. Yet I am not of their persuasion, being a longtime enthusiastic participant in what they call "the human practice of eating the dead bodies of fellow creatures," as well as in other impurities. Nor am I able, for perhaps wrong reasons, to envision a full country life without a good many domestic animals around, neighing and braying and lowing and bleating and crowing and quacking and making their other sundry noises at dawn and through the day, and existing more or less contentedly under man's loose dominion and exploitation, without which they wouldn't exist at all.

Our herbivores, besides a couple of horses, are at present cows and goats, for like old August Schraeder I am no hog man, and though I have intentions concerning sheep, I haven't yet managed to navigate my way past a mild distaste for them, based partly no doubt on the ancient West Texas prejudice, but also on some slight direct experience with their proneness toward all manner of snot-nosed, pus-dribbling, and parasitic afflictions. ("A goat," says the worn adage, "is looking for a place to get out; a sheep's looking for a place to die.") In my time, there have never yet been enough animals on the place to make full use of its range forage and its field production; during the absentee years it was safer during drouths or bad winters to have the land lightly stocked, and since we moved down, other things, mainly high cattle prices and a shortage of disposable cash, have kept us from moving toward capacity stocking except at the rate of the number of heifer calves born and kept each year, less cows that are culled for birthing troubles or age or an occasional one that dies. For that matter the place is not ready for full stocking; both it and its owner lack (as the businesslike reader may already have discerned with disgust) a surging inclination toward speedy attainment of useful goals.

The cows are still grade black Angus, unregistered but growing a bit more "typy" as successive purebred bulls leave their marks on offspring. I don't have any strong feelings about breeds of cattle and seem to lack entirely whatever drive it is that makes people want to own a current, premium-priced, "in" variety. Angus had a brief vogue among such folks in the fifties through their presence on Eisenhower's Gettysburg farm, and then (in our region at least) for the stockman desirous of status there were Santa Gertrudis after the King Ranch people first released some breeding stock, and more lately big pale Charolais, with other exotics in the wings preparing for their moment of modishness, like new Ferraris and Mercedes-Benzes waiting to show up on country-club parking lots. . . . Having known mainly the old honest horned Herefords when young, I started out with Angus because some friends who knew what they were doing ran them and spoke well of them, and because of all cow work I have truly disliked only the one job of gouging or searing or otherwise mutilating a screaming animal's skull to kill out the roots of its horns, and wanted a hornless breed.

Like all other breeds, they have a set of their own special flaws. They tend to mate much too early if given the chance, with resultant obstetrical uproars. And though all cattle can kick pretty well, as the prevalence of missing front teeth throughout the West bears witness, Angus have a special swift talent in the use of their hard sharp hind hooves on human bones and flesh. Nor are they easy to tell apart, particularly for an amateur stockman. Close up, I can usually identify most of mine through some quirk of countenance or stance or neckline or teat or navel. But as the purebred bulls leave their blocky, straightbacked stamp on new generations these differences grow less emphatic and there is need for aids like numbered eartags—which, however, are no good at a distance, as when you are wondering what cow it is that holds herself apart on the hill and is maybe considering dropping a calf. Nevertheless, though I have it vaguely in mind to play with some crossbreeding sooner or later, probably with Brahmans, in pursuit of "hybrid vigor" and easier calving and other qualities, I imagine that over the long haul I will stick basically with the hornless blacks, if only because I am now used to them.

I am no cowboy, nor ever was except in fancy when young, standing with a bit of sashcord on the curb at home and roping passing cars' headlights (they stuck up separately then, as other O. F.s will recall), or running a pony in someone's father's South Texas pasture in forbidden but joyful harassment of calves—which we sometimes caught and rode for three or four jumps till tossed—or occasionally being allowed to help with things like throwing calves and holding them down while an adult did the essentials with knife and iron and hypodermic. Some friends I had in those days grew up to be real cowmen like their fathers and grandfathers, casual in all of *vaquería*'s ancient skills. But I lost touch with all that fairly early—even with horses, never getting to be anything but a mediocre rider, and no rider at all these days. There not being anywhere near enough room in a life for all that you know is worth doing, and how to God could anyone ever be bored? . . .

Fortunately for people like me, though, under stockfarm conditions with a limited number of cattle, cowboying is seldom necessary now, and the happy loud chousing and running it often entails can make cows wild and hard to handle. Mine will nearly always come lowing to a corral in response to a howl and the rattle of a bucket of range cubes, and once there, can be immobilized in a chute for any needed work. And if occasionally an animal or so goes rogue and refuses to be tolled in, amateur cowboys abound and are glad of a chance to come and rope it out for you—if they can, in the cedar where it is apt to sull. Before quite so much bulldozing had been done in the region, one professional with a horse and a rope and a couple of good Catahoula Leopard cow dogs used to make a fair living by catching brush-happy bulls and steers and cows for other people, at ten dollars a head.

In one way or another the work with them gets done, most of it on time, and if Madame, being Eastern-bred, knows of many things she would rather be doing than standing astraddle a chute and pulling up on a headgated bellowing bullcalf's tail to keep him from kicking, while he is subjected to villainous surgery at the hands of the Head Varmint, she will nevertheless do it if nobody else is around to help. At cow obstetrics, except where main strength is called for, as in tugging a reluctant calf from the womb with a chain looped around its front feet—she tends to be more cool-headed than the Varmint. But so are numbers of his neighbors and friends —difficult birthings, like fires, being times when willing amateur help pops up all around. This is fortunate, for vets are far between and overworked and expensive these days in the country, profitable dog-and-cat practices having lured most of them to big towns. So that if at some point you get into real trouble with, say, a bred heifer whose calf is too big to be born at all and dies in place—the souvenir, perhaps, of someone's big-boned Charolais bull's visit to your premises despite all those nice fences—you need a friend like one of mine, who can deliver it by dissection. . . .

(Yes, such matters are bloody, and more or less brutal, and necessary, and in the end exhilarating if they come out right and you save a mother and calf or maybe only a mother, though some people are immune to such exhilaration and ought to stay away from cows. A psychiatrist I know, who did his residency at a big mental hospital in Galveston, had as one patient the scion of an old South Texas ranching family, a sensitive youth with a heavyhanded tough father and a host of related symptoms, among them an aversion to cattle, which gave him the total horrors. One day when the psychiatrist was making his rounds he came to this young man's room and found him on knees and elbows on the bed, arching his back and straining every tendon.

"Baw! Baw!" he cried. "Baw!"

"What's this?" the doctor said. "What are you trying to do?"

"Baw!" screamed his patient. "I'm having a calf! . . .")

But crises come only now and then at odd long intervals, and births usually take place without any need for human intervention. Most work with the cattle consists of occasional, simple, known things—castrating and branding and ear-tagging and vaccinating and small doctoring from time to time, and shunting your animals to different pastures as the state of the grass requires, and segregating heifers and so on, with a little feeding in winter. There is not much to it except keeping it in mind, and the big stupid black pretty creatures are friends, regardless of the fact that you are going to sell or eat their male progeny and will haul the cows themselves off to auction if they fail in their main function. With a small group of known animals, it is not possible to avoid some personalization, even if you see them clearly enough as beasts and not as imitation people. For you have gone through things with them and most of the older ones have names in your mind, as do others who have departed.

There was, for instance, Nutty Johnson, who found new motherhood so shocking that she refused to have anything to do with her first calf and, in the absence of any real corrals then, had to be chased around a big hillside lot and roped inexpertly twice a day for a week or so and snubbed up to a tree or post while the starved thing sucked, before she finally took it to raise. (During one of those ludicrous ropings, serving as my own horse, I hit an armadillo hole while running and cartwheeled and came down flat, which jarred some gallstones loose that had been nicely Chinese-puzzled together till then, and led to surgery. . . .) And the Little-Headed Cow, who was a runty heifer and had afterbirth trouble on the first calving and should have been culled but wasn't, so that on the second one she died miserably straining in a rock-bottomed draw, with no one around to help . . . And, still with us out of the original batch, the Big-Navel Cow who has the best bullcalves of all, and Roy's Mother who will run at you wild-eyed and maybe butt a bucket of feed out of your hand if you aren't pouring it fast enough to suit her, and High Shoulders and the Other Lean Cow and the rest, all in their more or (often) less placid bovine ways individuals, and the main point of Syndromish work about the place.

15 ≈ *Interlude: Our own Pippa passes at the age of seven or so—a sop for those who would have preferred a happy homestead sort of book...* ≈≈≈≈≈≈≈≈≈≈≈

The goats are down in their Pen,
I can hear a little wren.
She sings a beautiful song,
Through this day; and all the days On
Hi Ho, Hi Ho, another day to Go!
We'll play tomorrow, Work today.
Hi Ho, Hi Ho, another day to Go!

16 ≋ *The War Resumed* ≋

Goats, if of much less importance than cows, take a greater rather than lesser amount of attention at times. But unless you are truly bogged in an economic view of country life, they are probably worth it except when occasionally they get to be worry enough to make you swear to get rid of the whole damned herd for good. During the absentee time but after most fences were in, I put fifty Angora wethers on the upper Booker, but they had predator troubles and shearing crews had become hard to find when needed and the mohair market had collapsed in the face of synthetic fibers and cheap South African production and changing fabric styles (it has since resurged a bit), so I sold off what was left of them before we moved down to stay.

What we have now is a breeding herd of the tough scrub goats known generally in Texas as Spanish, because they came out of Mexico and trace back to old Murcian stock, with some admixture of mohair and North European milker blood picked up along the way. Colored and patterned in hundreds of ways, horned or hornless, slick or shaggy, large or small,

flop-eared or fox-eared, they are the raffish proletarians of the
domestic animal world, and association with them brings you
kinship with earth's most hard-scrabble herdsmen, for whom
they have long furnished meat and milk in places where few
other tame beasts furnish anything at all. They resist disease
and the intestinal parasites that play hob with sheep and
Angoras, have few obstetrical complications, often kid twice
a year and with a fair proportion of twins, and can find a living almost anywhere a blade or stalk of anything green will
sprout from dirt or rocks or sad rain-eaten subsoil.

In the steep or hot or semibarren lands where they find
most use, such as highland Mexico or the Mediterranean's
islands and rougher shores, they have been saddled with much
blame for the old and continuing deterioration of the soil and
the vegetation. But it is not certain this is fair, for as that most
civilized and whimsical of livestock authorities, the late
David Mackenzie, has noted convincingly in his *Goat Husbandry*, it was logging and bad farming and sheep-grazing on
erodible soils over long centuries that did the chief damage in
the Mediterranean region and the Middle East, making the
land unfit for any livestock but scrub-eating goats, and now:
"Being found beside the corpse, the goat is accused of the
murder."

Clearly enough in Somervell County, Texas, goats can't
yet be blamed for much of anything, for there were few
around before the fifties of this century, by which time extractive cash farming and heavy grazing by cows, over just a
few decades, had produced if not a corpse at least a landscape
that was very tired and sick, economically extinct. At present,
used well, goats can do much good by controlling small hardwood brush on land lately cleared of cedar, during the period
when grass is coming back to strength. After that, used
heavily, they might well help to make a Middle East or a
highland Mexico out of us, but it would take a long time and
probably several more cyclical repetitions of the old destruc-

tive frontier crops-and-cattle pattern—which, if you go by the past history of practically all marginal land, may well come about some day, if in other Somervellian eras than our own. Many of the limestone ruins that goats now deck with their ovoid droppings around, say, the Aegean's rocky coasts must once have gazed out on country as least as pleasantly productive as what the Tonks and the Comanches and the first whites knew here.

A man who doesn't get all his kicks from totting up probable gain may well find goats the most interesting of usual livestock to have near him day by day. They have good whole life in them. Not only the raffish Spaniards, but to a lesser extent Angoras and even the upbred dairy Nubians of which we have a handful that started out with one pet kid, have a spirit and a perverse intelligence and an instinctual self-sufficiency that modern breeds of cows have mainly lost and sheep haven't had since prehistory, if then. A goat flock is a sort of active, inquisitive, flowing force, finding out avenues to stored feed and forbidden plantings, alert for gates left ajar or new holes in fences, and in a rough natural pasture prone to revert occasionally to wild herd ways—staring with prick-eared suspicion from a hilltop at their kindly master below, unresponsive to either his seductive goatie-goatie call or the rattled bucket of corn to which he has believed them by now addicted. If, as often, his aim is to get them to a pen before dark and out of reach of night-wandering fanged things, his seductive call may soon turn to shouted obscenity, which will do him no good at all. What he needs at such a time is a good herding dog, or failing that a willingness to trudge up the hill and toll his goats penward with dribbled handfuls of grain, though grabbing the head billy by an ear or a horn and dragging him with you will often bring his harem and his multicolored get along behind.

Generally, though, they are more or less manageable, especially if among them there are two or three senior does that have learned to like petting and tidbits of Tinsley Natural Leaf Yours for Good Chewing and such things. They are rather mercurial beasts, able to go from head-butting king-of-the-mountain play (perhaps on some visitor's new car), to panic, to belly-full contentment, to vigorous browsing, to sullen hunched disgust with bad weather, all in the course of a couple of hours. Individual variance among them is strong, not just in color and shape and size but in intelligence and outlook as well, so that one small flock will nearly always contain mischief-makers and placid cud-chewers, fighters and victims, comedians and sages and dullards and amiable idiots and shy spooks, good mothers and prima donnas, gluttons and picky ascetics. . . . These differences create a pecking order which is, however, not static, for bright younger animals are always trying to shove up through the ranks. The differences also create names, especially if you have children around, and great is the gloom when the high Booker's wild things gobble up Redlegs and Rumpelstiltskin, or Wattle Baby goes to auction with a pickup-load of his half-siblings, or another wether kid known as the Blue Goat's Little Boy turns up marinated and barbecued and delicious on a platter. . . .

The billy or two or three that a small herd needs are fairly superfluous during most of the year—sturdy, smelly, suspicious, ineffective, pompous herd-guards who maintain an appearance of authority while the older does run things. They come into their own only in breeding season, which in our latitude is an orgy set off ordinarily by the first cool spell in August or September, with often a secondary uproar after kids arrive in late winter. At these times the bucks go crazy with unesthetic lust night and day for a couple of weeks or so, stinking and fighting and braying and yodeling and urinating on their own faces and grunting and nudging and chasing unrelentingly after the moment's demurely fleeing victim. No one who has watched this, I think, will ever again feel quite comfortably humorous about the nymph-and-satyr paintings on randy old Greek pots in museums. For the Greeks not only knew goats but knew also human kinship with them, and how to set down parallels and implications. . . .

The kids that all this joy engenders in a mass January or February birthing—generally it seems to come during the year's prize spell of foul cold weather—are among the Nation's most vulnerable meat products, magnetically attractive to all sorts of varmints down to and including, I'm told, an occasional large coon. Since the Nation has plenty of varmints, kids born in a rough wild pasture have a hard go in their first few tremulous tottering days of life, for the squeaky hunger-bleats they launch from hillside tall-grass nooks may bring the loving mothers who stashed them there, or may reach the ears of things with sharp, rending teeth. . . . As many a happy-go-lucky owner has found, after deciding that good tough foragers like goats need little watching over, it is possible to lose a whole kid crop thus within a very short while. And on the hills the red foxes and the bobcats thrive while generating and gestating their own spring young, maybe grateful to the scheme of things if not specifically to the happy-go-lucky owner, for that is usually a leanish time of year to be a varmint.

Close care of the sort given sheep at lambing time works poorly with half-wild pasture goats, leading often to numbers of disowned kids and total wailing chaos. They need to be watched, but not too hoveringly. If you live on your place, you can usually arrange for kidding to take place on more or less open ground close by the house and barn, where watchdogs and the sounds and stinks of man keep wise varmints at a distance. Within short weeks after birth, the kids are big and agile enough that foxes will not bother them, and if cats are scarce as they have been around Hard Scrabble in the five years or so that we have had goats, all you have left to worry about are the sorts of predators that can kill goats of any size. And if, like us, you seem not yet to be blessed with the hybrid "wolves" that range more open parts of the region, then all you really have to watch out for is Man's Best Friend, the dog. Not that he isn't enough.

Few if any of these raider dogs are "wild" in a true feral sense, though people sometimes describe them so. Among the native hound-dog men who know this region more intimately than just about anyone else, there are some whose eyes miss very little in the way of tracks or signs or furtive creatures—fit descendants of the old bear-hunters and Indian-fighters from whom lore came down to them. One of the brightest, a friend of mine called (here, anyhow) Evetts Gilliver, remembers one pair of border collies that for two or three years or so maintained themselves without help from man in a cedarbrake up near Chalk Mountain, wary as any wild thing. But they managed to raise no young and finally disappeared, and Evetts says he has never seen any other dogs gone really wild. Those that raid one's goats have homes and names and owners, if maybe several miles away from where they run at night.

This being so, and the race we belong to being a sentimental one, raider dogs constitute a touchy subject. I myself still have a fair measure of bourgeois soupiness in me toward good dogs, but have come in the past few years to look at spoiled and uncontrolled members of the species with much slantwise skepticism and no sentimentality at all. The damage they can do among goats and sheep and calves and turkeys and such things, mainly at night and usually in haphazard pairs or trios or packs that assemble for the purpose, is far more infuriating than the damage wild things do, as well as more extensive. For wild things generally kill to eat and have a sort of right to do so, even if you believe you have a right to stop them as best you can. But dogs for the most part kill to kill, not out of hunger but out of a lingering instinctive aggressiveness that anyone who owns a dog has an obligation to control. So that from one point of view what predatory dogs really are is other people's slobbishness moving in on you, upsetting the order of your little venture in using the land, making you know that isolation, however much you may think you want it, is nearly always illusory in a world thickly sprinkled with men.

Most countrymen come to see the unwisdom of personalizing range livestock, especially the perishable kinds like goats. Yet you know them as individuals, and in the knowing there is bound to be some attachment. Even a bunch of Angora wethers—dimwits among goats, compared to the quick and curious Spanish does—make a place for themselves in your mind. In the flock I ran here for a while, there were such individuals as Rags Ragsdale, a sickly friendly creature with the face of a querulous, not-very-bright old man and a tattered ear and a taste for tobacco, and the Dog-faced Goat and the Sheepish Goat and Harry S. Truman and the One-Horned Cripple and Alexander Graham Bell and a good many others that had some trait to make them more than just a set of hairy white anonymous browsers. . . . So that when dogs running in the night begin to slaughter such known beasts by tearing their bellies open and running on to tear another, and then another, and in the morning you find maybe six or eight dead or dying in gullies and fence corners and clumps of brush along the route of destruction, their feet tangled in their own spilled pink-white-and-blue guts, your feeling about those dogs is not at all bourgeois.

If, improbably, you get a good look at one of the marauders and recognize him, you can pay a visit to his owner and state your problem, whereupon the country code requires that he either disprove your claim or else get rid of his dog and pay you for lost stock—in theory, anyhow. In practice, what such reasonableness usually leads to is a flat indignant denial on his part that Old Speck ever leaves the yard, and some enduring hard feelings, for he is probably convinced of his own rightness, since by the time he gets up each morning Old Speck has bidden farewell to his buddies and returned from his bloody gambols and in his Dr. Jekyll aspect is resting among tomato vines and horehound weed and old tires behind the house, a prized noble guardian of the homestead. The country code is therefore not much help except when you're dealing with people whom you know well and trust and who feel the same way about you, and even then not always. What you most often have to do is to catch Old Speck on your own place *in flagrante delicto* and to make sure he stays there as fertility for the soil, and afterward to speak very little if at all on the subject. ("He come around a day or two after that," a small-rancher said to me once in concluding a killer-dog tale. "We was good friends—still are. He said that old chow dog of his had done got lost and it was the best dog he'd ever had hold of, and had I seen him anywhere. I was standing there by the barn right about exactly on top of where I'd buried the big red son of a bitch and I said, 'Shoo, Charlie, that's a shame. I sure will keep an eye out for that dog.' Them sheep he'd killed I just wrote off. . . .")

In other words, the dogs being sneaky you have to try to be sneakier, and the whole subject has that tone. The sneakiest and easiest and perhaps most effective countermeasure against Old Speck and his kind is to get hold of some strychnine and some frankfurters or summer sausage and to put out poisoned baits around the troubled pasture. It is standard enough practice. I admit to having been tempted in that direction a time or so, but thus far have resisted and probably will never succumb. Not from any sense of fairness toward the dogs in question, but because poison inevitably kills a lot of creatures I'd much rather not see killed, and for that matter, scattered and dragged about by wild things, the baits can constitute a danger for a long while afterward to your own dogs and to the native fox-hunters' "goat-broke" hounds. If you are built differently from me, I suppose you can do without dogs of your own and tell the hound-dog people that you're using poison, which makes them avoid your neck of the woods from then on out. But you lose some helpful friends if you do that, and lose some pretty music at night.

Steel traps have been known to catch outlaw dogs, but generally catch more foxes and armadillos and things you don't want to catch, and sometimes your own goats. And in the lore of the subject, which is a central and absorbing one wherever sheep and goats are raised, you can find other suggested techniques ranging to complexities like live-trap pens whose bait is a bitch in heat in an inner cage.

Generally, though, what you do is to pen the goats at night when and if you can, and carry a rifle in the pickup as you ride about the place, with a spotlight and a full-choke twelve gauge full of OO Buck near your bed at night, awaiting a chance which may or may not come. Raiding dogs are man-shy, and even if the wind is right for you to hear them at their killing, in rough country like ours by the time you have reached the scene of carnage—preferably on foot, for the sound of a pickup alerts them—the damage is likely to be done and the surviving goats scattered and the dogs headed on toward wherever they decide to go next. And since they hit usually at irregular intervals, sometimes letting your flock alone for two or three weeks at a time while they maraud elsewhere, it seldom helps to camp up near the goats with a sleeping bag and a gun, as I have sometimes done for nights on end. The best hope is to find them at work in the daytime, as may happen sooner or later, especially if you have managed to keep the goats penned up at night.

It is an odd intense sort of hunting, filled with purpose and often with moral anger of a sort I have never felt toward any wild animal, even when for good reason I wanted to get rid of him. It is a bit like war, though on your side of the lines the threat is not to you but to your goats. . . . You come to know the unseen enemies' tracks and even voices, for most are happily loud at their work. I remember one trio, made up of a big dog and two smaller yapping feists, that ravaged the high Booker's Angoras intermittently for three months once, staunch against my part-time absentee wiles and those of the other ranchers who must have been after them too. The big one was the leader, and at each foray's end he would call the others to him with a queer short ascending howl that never failed to raise the hairs across my neck. By then I would usually be on that side of the creek and would work toward him in darkness through the brush, but he was sharp, and I never saw either him or the feists until the decisive Battle of the Sumac Patch, when on a bright November afternoon I caught them in a frost-red thicket with three goats down and others cornered, and extracted an eye for an eye. . . .

After you or someone else manage to get rid of one batch of such dogs, there comes a period of peace that may last for months, but what is certain is that in time others will show up, similar in their purpose. The toll they take is fairly. costly, and they make it hard to do what needs to be done on the place. The two hilly rough pastures across the creek, for instance—about 230 acres in all—badly need heavy browsing if small brush is not to take over entirely from the grass on cleared ground and in the glades and openings where cedar has not been dozed. A shredder-mower can't function in most parts of them. They could sustain at least two hundred goats for three or four years and would be better off for having done so, much closer to what they were like when white men started using this land. Goats, in fact, are worth more for that than for anything else, even though the salable kids they bear—or the Angoras' mohair when the market is decent—can bring in more each year than your total goat investment. . . . Yet those pastures are the farthest land from the house, and to put that many goats in them without being willing to poison everything carnivorous in the neighborhood would mean embarking on a more or less continual war, for which my time at present—crammed with a good many other things besides goats—will not suffice. Nor with increasing years do I find exhilaration in scrambling through dew-wet thorny brush at three o'clock in the morning with a shotgun, half-dressed and wondering where the nearest rattlesnake lies waiting to be stepped on. . . . Therefore for now I have sold the Spanish herd, once eighty or ninety strong, down to about twenty of the healthiest and best mothers and am running these in a smaller pasture near the house, corraling them at night and watching the Booker scrub grow lush across the way.

In essence, maybe, the problem is a more or less modern-American one, sprouting from the economics and sociology of our time, and from our penchant for doing traditional things in untraditional ways. Herding people since the dim red dawn of animal domestication have known that vulnerable small stock needs to be guarded closely in rough country. Through Spanish America and southern Europe and Africa and Asia, tough children and leathery old men perched on rocky hillsides and watching flocks of goats and sheep, controlling them with whistlings and gestures and thrown rocks and vigilant dogs, are a fixture of the landscape. Clearly enough, they are available for such work because they're stuck in a social order that makes them glad of any activity that feeds their mouths. Our own social order, for the moment anyhow, is no longer like that, and we tend to be proud of that fact. But herding of that watchful sort is a longtime proven adaptation to the Way's harshnesses, a sort of stand-off arrangement that holds damage on either side to a minimum, whereas our contemporary insistence on a God-granted right to run small stock loose in wild or half-wild marginal country protected only by net fencing, if that, puts us as usual in direct gory conflict with the scheme of things and leads to such pleasant spectacles as the Northwestern sheepman who had hundreds of eagles shot from planes. . . .

The fact that on Hard Scrabble just now the fight is mainly with domestic dogs rather than wild creatures is only incidental. If in one sense the dogs represent human slobbishness, in another they are part of the Way—an inflow of medium-sized predators, albeit perverted ones, into a vacant niche. Sooner or later the region's hybrid "wolves," part dog themselves, will likely adapt to rougher terrain than they seem to favor at present, and the niche will be chock-full and the fight will have a new dimension.

I have lately read about an admirable man named Lasater, who started ranching in South Texas and since has moved to Colorado. He originated a respected, big, hardy, part-Brahman breed of cattle called Beefmasters and has improved them over the years through application of a simple rigorous Darwinian selective principle. Like other men, he culls his cows for failing to bear a good calf every year, but he culls them ruthlessly too for failing to rear that calf to weaning age, for any reason. On his ranch no predators are shot or trapped or poisoned—even rattlesnakes are let alone—and if coyotes gang up and kill a baby calf the only retribution taken is against the calf's mother, who is hustled off to auction for not having fought them off.

If such an attitude seemed likely to take hold among the run of American farmers and stockmen, there would be a better prospect of having a decent world a few decades hence. But in truth it is a hard pure path to follow, and though the principle seems to have worked beautifully with Lasater's Beefmasters, it is impossible not to wonder how it would work if the old natural scheme of things were still entire—if, say, there were still numbers of Plains grizzlies and cougars and lobos around. . . . And how you could go about applying it to animals like goats is a puzzler indeed. If you bred super-goats agile or fierce enough to cope with dogs and wolves, you surely would have hell coping with the goats yourself.

The wisest approach at Hard Scrabble may well turn out to be to quit trying to keep things like goats and sheep except on a small scale, as I am doing at present. But it is hard to have to admit it if so. Not only does the Tonk Nation more or less need goats during its rehabilitation, but they seem to fit its landscape, to belong here. . . .

Nothing else on the place generates quite as much friction with the order of things as goats do, though nearly all the Syndrome's activities generate some. Chickens are proverbially attractive to carnivores, but ours at present, a hen house and yard not having yet been built, are scrub games, true Darwinian fowl that roost here and there in the barn and get along without even being fed anything except what they can steal by pecking holes in sacks or can glean from larger animals' feed. Sneaking nests in cubbyholes, chasing grasshoppers far out into the pastures, they have managed to raise some chicks and to increase a little every year despite the good red-yolked brown eggs the children find by searching and bring to the house, and the young roosters we take for meat, and an occasional specimen grabbed and eaten by a gray fox that lives up the horse-trap's fenceline. I have intentions of doing battle with this fellow if I ever get the chance, but I rather like him too and somehow never have a gun around when I catch a glimpse of him. For that matter his toll is minimal; the games can fly like quail and even the cockerels I kill for the table have to be shot sportingly in the head from a distance, with a twenty-two. . . . They could probably cope with hawks too, for when buzzards fly over low they give the hollow hawk-warning call and dart for cover. One man I used to know had a gamecock that would fly up in the air to meet and fight a diving hawk, which I daresay the hawk found disconcerting. . . . But sadly hawks are not much of a problem these days, DDT and other sweet agents of profit and progress having decimated their numbers in a brief few years, since in the late fifties I saw that great "hawk storm" on White Bluff. I miss them and am glad to see the few that still show up, nor would I shoot one now if he killed every chicken I have.

Deer love the winter grainfields and graze them hard at times. Here on the creek there aren't yet enough to worry much about, and an occasional loin or haunch of venison is recompense for what damage they do. But at the Soft Scrabble place a few miles south, near big ranches where the current deer explosion is centered, they are already making it nearly impossible to raise certain crops. Though I leased the tract for hunting to friends last winter to hold down depredations a bit, the hunters' light legal take affected them not at all, and at the height of the season a neighbor counted fifty in one bunch amid the ruined oats and vetch I had sowed to make spring hay. . . .

Rabbits have sometimes been rough on the vegetable garden's lettuce and things, but a good tight poultry-wire fence now keeps most of them out, and predators hold their numbers down, so that maybe by not shooting the gray up the fence I am just swapping an occasional fowl for lettuce and cabbage and greens. Coons, barred access to our garbage by dogs at the house, climb over that garden fence at the wild end, and for two or three years made it impossible to harvest any sweet corn—ripping it off the stalks just before it was prime, eating some ears and discarding others scornfully on the ground. I tried lanterns and ticking clocks and cans of urine and other O. F.–recommended techniques but they did no good, and at last I put a sheepdog bitch down there one night, which led to a fine, squalling, barking battle at four in the morning, three grown coons and the bitch and the bitch's big son Blue, and me dancing around in my shorts with a flashlight and a club.

But I don't really dislike coons that much—not at all, in fact—and when the big tough boar specimen that did not survive the battle had been buried shallowly amid my ravaged corn (where he would be, like Old Speck the erstwhile goat-killing dog, a fertility in the soil, a dying and reborn god), I found by accident what seems to be a peaceful solution for the problem. As the smell of coonish mortality seeps gently roundabout in that area of the garden, it serves as a reminder to other trespassing coons of their own mortality. Like their human brethren they appear not to care for such reminders and thenceforth stay away, at least till the smell dies out. Nor do you have to resort to further coon-murder to get hold of a corpse to bury; a stretch of morning highway will often yield one or two, freshly slaughtered by last night's passing cars.

(There is perhaps a problem about what to say to acquaintances who may come along and catch you scavenging dead things from the roadside, but an O. F. learns furtive swooping skill in such activity, and a certain amount of shamelessness. He finds it possible to feel not only unashamed but proud of something like a heaped pickup-load of chicken poot. . . .)

The Way's real Sunday punch at vegetable gardens, though, is delivered by bugs. Squash bugs, stink bugs, cabbage loopers, hornworms, cutworms, army worms, nematodes, grasshoppers, crickets, cucumber beetles of two sorts, aphids of a dozen, leafhoppers, corn earworms, pill bugs, Colorado potato beetles, root maggots, and any number of other such skillful and hungry destroyers . . . All true O. F.s distrust poisons, and hence from year to year we base new hopes on Rodalian "organic" approaches and concoctions—ladybugs and mantids, fireplace ashes, garlic-and-pepper water, companionate plantings, compost and mulch and garbage and manure to firm up the plants' resistance, mineral oil, salt water, beer. . . . Some work surprisingly well at times, and at other times none seem to do much, and impurity invades the O. F. and maybe he guiltily slathers some poison around, but even then of nonresidual sorts, preferably the old botanicals like rotenone and nicotine and sabadilla dust. Or maybe at such times he just lets the bugs take over, or replants enough stuff for them and him both. The garden's dark deep soil, used by the old ones and the cedar people for vegetables long long before our days here, does grow looser and better each year, though, with the various forms of richness we heap on it, and the plants that grow there do seem to stand up better to insect attack. Fall is the hardest time. We usually have a fine growing season with good rains after the worst summer heat and before frost comes in November, but September and October bugs are very well developed and hungry and can often wipe you out, except for mustard greens and okra and a couple of other items they flatly abhor.

One potent force to keep an O. F. more or less pure in the matter of poisons is the presence of creatures he likes. These include birds and toads and lizards, and predatory insects like ladybugs and polistes wasps, and sacred earthworms, and the miraculous tiny organisms that pull nitrogen from air and turn organic matter into mellow humus. They include too the O. F.'s most diminutive livestock, his bees. We have ten or so hives at present in an apiary just beside the garden, and I could not begin to count the times when, disgusted with stinkbugs or grasshoppers, I have been held off from chemical revenge by the fact that the stuff I put out might drift toward the hives or get on blooms the bees were working. In the little world of the garden the bees function much like Evetts Gilliver's foxhounds on the hills; they help to keep me honest.

Most people who interest themselves in bees got the infection from some older relative, and I suppose I did too. My maternal grandfather, a farmer, kept an array of box hives out behind his house, but he died when I was quite young and I doubt that memory had much influence on me. Paradoxically, though, the kinsman from whom I suspect I did get the idea was one whom I never knew at all. This was my father's older brother Will, who died in his thirties in the flu epidemic of the First World War, before I was born. But the family liked to tell stories about him, and listening to them I formed quite early a sense of our soul kinship. . . . Intended by his strong father for the ministry, at the incubator for Southern Episcopalian divines in Sewanee, Tennessee, he learned mainly carousal and came down with tuberculosis. Sent therefore to stay with ranching relatives in a dry high part of New Mexico, he recuperated and took so genially to cowboying that he had to be hauled forcibly home to South Texas, where he was put to clerking in Grandpa's dry-goods store. This he disliked, and when set up in a business of his own in another town he married the prettiest girl in the county and cut a social swath. And all along the way he was seized by successive and cumulative consuming passions for unuseful activities and things, or when useful they had little to do with what he was supposed to be doing at the time.

He raced pretty horses, he fought dogs and cocks, he fished and hunted (my long-tom twelve, an early Winchester repeater, came down from him), he did many things. . . . The last venture in which my grandfather backed him was five or six hundred acres of good grass- and farm-land stocked with big draft-breed mares from which Uncle Will was going to raise, with the aid of some Spanish jacks, large numbers of the tall strong working mules then heavily in demand. But once ensconced as a mule-breeder he got obsessed with honeybees, and spent two or three years reading about them and puttering with his apiary, and the mule project went to hell. "Bees, wouldn't you know?" or something like that, someone in the family would usually say when that particular Will story had been told. . . . It lodged in me, and undoubtedly fertilized a small determination in my own mind, which has been in its way as successively obsessed with irrelevant things as his, to find out about bees for myself when the chance came, as it now has.

Bees are worth some time and study. Complex in their governing instincts, enmeshed with human thinking about blossoms and meadows and drowsy summer days, productive of a clean healthful sweet that men have sought since there have been men . . . Once you get over worrying unduly about the loaded needle each carries in its tail (the best of all teachers it is, for it underlines mistakes on your part) you are likely to be hooked for life. For tending them has in it the pull that all animal husbandry has—if, that is, you are built to feel such pull—but the scale is small enough for a backyard. And the work connected with it, on a small scale anyhow, is light enough for many a man of eighty.

A patient man of eighty . . . The apiarist is denied those harsh violent loudmouthed satisfactions that go with the chousing and working of hoofed livestock, because if he gets in a hurry or loses his temper the mysterious hive mind is going to lose its temper too, painfully for him. He needs to acquire slow and certain motions and a willingness to examine his pet bugs hive by hive and comb by comb, if he wants to know even a part of what there is to know. Then maybe after a span of years he will be able to see at least sometimes when queens are good or defective, and how to stave off brood disease and undesired swarmings and other misfortunes, and how to count definitely on reaping a fair surplus of honey for his trouble. I doubt that I will ever reach this point in either patience or skill, for bees take time and time is always short. But the effort to get there still seems worthy.

Individual bees amount to little even in their own scheme of things, being in a sense just replaceable cells in the real biological unit, the tribal colony. When you come to see this clearly you tend to wince less at the occasional crunch of small bodies as you move hive parts about. . . . The different hives have differing moods and traits, mainly racial but sometimes less tangibly clear. Of our current group the gentlest, called Number Six or the Reynolds Hive, came from a big hollow porch column torn by house-wreckers from the doomed former home of a Fort Worth ranching family, having been living there unmolested since the nineties, a part of the family's lore. The most disagreeable is Number Two, descended from a wild swarm with possibly a tarbrush touch of the old hysterical "German blacks" in its bloodline; it produces well but has a hornet fierceness against invaders like me and so far has rejected and slaughtered the Italian queens I introduce in hope of improving its temper.

Sometimes all the hives go touchy at once, from rain or chill or wind or sultriness or some unfathomable itch, or worst of all from the raiding and honey-robbing that can get started among them when nectar is short—for bees give the lie to those who claim that man is unique in his penchant for war and thievery and murder aimed against his own sweet species. . . . And they despise small noisy stinking engines of the sort that propel lawnmowers and garden tillers, bulleting themselves against the offending contraption's highest point, its operator's head. There they turn somersaults in his back hairs while singing a little hate-song ("Me, me, me, me, me!" is the way one bee man I know renders it) and ram home their sting when they reach bottom, unless their victim before then has managed to land a good killing swat. I have also seen a wild colony, their hollow-tree home bumped and shaken, chase a bulldozer man from his high howdah and run him frantic to the woods.

But most of the time, if you have the hives pointed elsewhere than directly at your yard and garden, and fence cows and other large blunderers away from them, bees go their hardworking ways without paying people any mind. And if you pick good bright calm weather for your intrusions in their affairs and use your smoker right, they seldom get much riled. Management of them, like most other things worth knowing, involves a lot of "feel." With time and effort one's feel improves somewhat, and this past summer for the first time we had a colony that yielded a more or less book-standard surplus, either because I somehow did the right things with it or, more likely, failed to do the usual wrong things. It started strong in spring, built up to a three-story brood nest without swarming and weakening itself, and on spring flowers and sweetclover alone (it was a poor year for sumac) made fifteen gallons or so of good honey beyond its own winter reserve, about half of what we got from all the hives together. The harvest time is pleasant—trundling the heavy, sticky, white supers full of laden combs on a wheelbarrow to the screen porch where questing bees can't get in to dispute your possession of them, uncapping the sealed combs with a hot knife over a strainer tray on Papa's old redwood table, whirling them centrifugally in the extractor's shiny drum, filling the jars and random bottles cleaned and lined up to receive the viscous, fragrant, jewel-bright, amber stuff.

And bees may be, I think, a good subject with which to round out a section concerned with war on nature, for they bring the war full circle back to peace. No other livestock puts you so in tune with the gentler botanical aspects of the Way, with blossoms and sun and pollen and good smells and queer plants that bloom for a week or so in early spring and start the hives to working. They demand no defense from you against any natural agencies except disease and weather, honey-loving bears having long since vanished from our hills, and the inroads of insectivorous skunks and toads and some birds hardly denting the hives' fecundity. They firm your conscience against bug poisons, and if in your choice of plantings for your fields you let yourself be swayed a bit—uneconomically—by the thought of bees and their needs, that too fits with the Way, for the flowering legumes they like so well, sweetclover and vetch and such things, are the best soil-improvers of all.

17 ≋ *What Happened to Mother N.'s Own Boy?* ≋

All right. Clearly enough, stock raising and gardening and farming—land use, the Syndrome's fruit—do somewhat taint the purity of a man's feelings about the natural earth. Woody things on soil that might be yielding grass or crops are foes. A crystal singing day in October, sheer pleasure to objective eyes, may rouse small joy in one whose winter oats need rain, and certain exquisite wildflowers can glow less bright when viewed as weeds in hay. Wee, sleekit, cow'rin, tim'rous beasties, larger ones with fangs, bugs, and even some birds of the air all at times loom sinister. . . .

Nor can the impasse really be resolved. No nation of meat-eaters is going to invite back bears and lobos and panthers in their old hungry strength; no teeming urban population such as our seems likely to swap its bread for a new chance to view millions of wild ungulates roving the prairies and plains. And no people who herd or farm for a living, now or in the past, have been able to look on all the Way's forces and creatures and quirks as beneficent, even if in other days when men were farther between and their technology less brutal they weighed lighter on the scheme of things, asking less and getting less, and alongside them and their crops and beasts the Way kept simmering along in its timid and violent, wet and dry, green and bleak, generous and cruel, inscrutable, shifting entirety. (At least it is nice to think so, though a good unsentimental look at much of the Mediterranean's shoreline and the old Aztec parts of Mexico and other marginal places may make you wonder. And did not temperate unmarginal heartland Europe manage to get rid of a whole landscape of wild things a long long time ago? . . .)

God knows we need to learn lightness again, and some people try, including such dubs as me. If much of a future remains to mankind on this planet—a good moot point, of course—it probably rests largely in the hands of Old Farts, of whatever age or size or color or sex or wealth or class or profession or level of educational bliss. For the mark and sign of a true hydrogen-sulfide Old Fart is this: that while he knows men must use the earth, he knows too that it matters for its own sake and that it must stay alive, and therefore according to such understanding as he may have he tries to keep his dealings with it right and gentle, and only thereafter reflects on fiscal gain. He is not necessarily a nice sort of fellow or in current cant a "fine human being." Besides being an Old Fart he may well also be an Old Bastard and dislike the mass of his fellow men heartily. He is not always right in his judgments, and may be capable of unecological murderous rage against rattlesnakes and coyotes and such. But after his own individual fashion he cares about the earth and earthy things and how they work.

In surviving fertile parts of the Old World many men who live on the soil and work with it are the heirs to calm, often difficult techniques of lightness worked out—because they had to be—centuries or even millennia since. Our own progenitors happily shucked most of that lore on the Eastern seaboard when they glimpsed the continent of virginity that

lay stretched before them for the raping, though some renewed awareness kept seeping in from time to time with fresh
waves of immigrant peasants who had the quaint illusion that
land was precious stuff, to be nurtured and passed on whole.
Those immigrants' children for the most part, though, came
to share the general view of a "good" farmer or stockman as
one who squeezed the most cash he could out of his patch of
dirt without fretting over its future wholeness and health,
because westward ho, was the land not bright? . . .

But that is a tale that has been told by better agricultur-
alists than I have any notion of pretending to be or any chance
at my age of ever becoming. It led of course to catastrophe—
to the gullied hill South of hookworms and pellagra and
hopelessness, to the economic extinction of marginal pockets
like Somervell County, Texas, to Dust Bowls and rural
desperation and the swelling, spraddling, solutionless, psy-
chotic ruin of cities that not long ago used to be places to
live and strive and learn what richness there was in human
variety.

Such bleaknesses may not seem to jibe nicely with the
publicized fact that in our day one hypothetical American
farmer, on land not yet wholly botched, can feed more
mouths than any farmer has ever been known to feed before,
but that too is a subject for a differently flavored, more expert
book than this, or for several of them. With an O. F.-ish sort
of growl, however, one may note briefly his (and others')
outrageous opinion that (a) this production is based largely
on a massively chemical, factory-farming technology that is
itself an extension of frontier fecklessness, since it commonly
exploits rather than nurtures the soil, (b) its energy input in
terms of fuel and all that is horribly high in relation to its
results, (c) its yield is not always as palatable as it is copious,
as witness supermarket tomatoes and corn, and cage-laid eggs,
(d) much good Old World land, tended in peasant ways for
hundreds or thousands of years, still grows more *per acre*

than ours, (e) a sizable proportion of the owners of those mouths old Hypotheticus feeds would be better off self-sufficient and self-respecting on an honestly tilled piece of ground than where and how they presently are, (f) in really practical terms, the . . .

(Soapbox collapses to splinters with a screech of straining nails, as Nobel-Prizewinning Dr. Norman E. Borlaug, knight-errant of miracle plant varieties and pesticides and manu-factured NPK, breaks the staff of his Green Revolution banner over the polemical O. F.'s skull and the Secretary of Agriculture aims a swift kick at his crotch while shouting about Gross National Product. Industrializers, urban re-newers, welfare recipients, commodity futures speculators, county agents, factory farmers, food processors, chemical manufacturers, supermarket executives, USAID muckety-mucks, and the ghost of the Baron von Liebig all loudly ap-plaud the violence. Representatives of the Third World look on puzzled: what is this fuss all about?

"How says the shabby old gringo, that they should abuse him thus?"

"*Pués*, it appears he insists that thus and so."

"But *hombre*, that is *mierda!*

"To the old one it pleases him, *mierda*. Enthusiasmed, he speaks of placing it in one's garden."

"Do we not know as fact, for we have been told, that to farm as the official gringos prescribe will insert each of us in a Cadillac, with a female of cinematic proportions making friction against his shoulder?"

"Yes, it is certain. *¡Viva el DDT! ¡Viva el NPK!*"

"Permit me as a favor to pass; I myself shall apportion to the shabby subversive *viejo* a buffet—but no! He flees rapidly down the street, clutching his eggs. . . .")

A lot of Americans over a lot of years—since before the Revolution, in places like Tidewater Virginia—have known that something was badly wrong with the pattern of unreckoning exploitation of land, though knowledge of what to do about it has not been very widespread. Once last year while I was hunting quail with a friend, we wandered behind the weaving, searching dogs along a broad-topped ridge, old cotton land once black but mainly water-gnawed now to pale subsoil and in places gullied to bare ledge rock six feet below the surface, worse than any erosion I have on Hard Scrabble. It was furred patchily in feather bluestem and three-awn needlegrass and other unpalatable inheritors, with tangles of scrub oak and cedar here and there. At the bottom end of one of the biggest gullies we came on a thick stone retaining wall, forty feet long and tumbled down in spots, with the gully, once briefly thus blocked, now crooking past one of its ends. Armed with a little hard-way knowledge of masonry, I could see how angrily and long whoever it was had labored many years ago in an effort to stop the washing of his field. The great sadness—it really was a sadness, like empty vanquished faces in old brown photographs—was that he had attacked the symptom, the gully, and not the cause, which was stormwater sweeping across the naked land from higher up. . . . Sour and whipped, his shade still puzzled there on the place where he had used out his manhood, wanting to do right but not knowing how. You could feel it, with the quality of its despair.

The big head of such despair that had built up by the dead-end 1930's gave religious force to the soil conservation movement when Hugh H. Bennett and his cohorts began to preach its gospel and its tactics, offering an out. For westward ho was finished; westward ho was owned now, and often in lousy shape too. The gospel was simple and very old, if fresh among most here: leave land bare as seldom as you can manage, control runoff and the effects of wind, be gentle. Because of the damage that had been done through three centuries, it involved massive restoration in some regions too, with sweaty hard work and in latter years thousands of huge

233

machines. A lot remains still to be done in places like the Tonk Nation where there was less left to restore and work started later, usually under new ownerships. Nor have the more subtle implications of "gentleness"—building new top-soil with green manure and legumes and trashy techniques, rotating crops on plowland, avoiding damage to natural processes and creatures that are part of the Way the world works—achieved wide acceptance except among some Old Farts, for they can get in the path of quick profit through full-dose NPK and chlorinated hydrocarbon insecticides and such things.

But what *has* been done is impressive, even if obscured by the uproar of warfare and technological boom and urbanization that churned down amongst us with Pearl Harbor. It matters far more than journeys to the moon. Fly low in a light plane from Georgia to New Mexico, seeking the rougher parts of the land, if you want to see what it means. New smoothed grasslands, terraces, stripcropping, contoured furrows, ponds and tight fences to distribute grazing better—all holding the soil that remains where it is, where it belongs . . . Even the most crabbed and misanthropic O. F. has trouble believing that utter ignorance in such matters will ever again prevail.

("He has found for himself another box, the *viejo!*"

"Yes, but he declaims less dangerously now. Observe that his pursuers shrug and turn away. They are no longer in great disaccord with him."

"Does this then signify that they confess themselves equivocated? What about the factories of fertilizer? What about? . . .")

But at this crucial point the movie star Rachel Smelch in spangled hotpants is handed forth from an orange Lincoln Continental hardtop by the public-relations vice-president of American Cyanamid and beams roundabout with teeth like white Day-Glo. Her smile and her large siliconized breasts allay all doubts. Anthems blare from loudspeakers. Cries of *"Olé!"* and *"Uhuru!"* and other expressions of delight rend the smoggy air. Bereft of listeners, abraded and disgruntled but unbowed, the O. F. slouches away toward the edge of the city, there to occupy himself with the philosophical problem of leaf-hoppers in his Swiss chard.)

Because of the labor and intimacy implicit in the O. F. approach to farming, even backsliding and part-time O. F.s tend, I believe, to feel closer to their land and its ways than any factory-farmer can. For that matter the sort of patch of ground many of them possess—rough, marginal, in need of help but resisting it Tonkishly—is more individual and quirkish and demands more learning and love than do the wide arable acreages where high-yield, high-risk, big-machine techniques can be applied. In a region like ours, which despite some moderately prosperous sandy-land peanut farms and a few fair-sized cattle operations nevertheless runs mainly to smallish rough tracts, intimately owned, the resultant identification with one's place can be extreme. In a feed store or on the courthouse lawn men may speak not as themselves but as their holdings, creating flash images that can disconcert, as when a large beefy type avers, "I got broomweed sprouting all over me this year."

So if after a rain-short spring and early summer the July sun and the hot blasting wind out of Chihuahua burn grasses brown and bake the soil dry three and four feet down, they burn and bake your spirit too. And if in, say, September you have gone ahead and gambled—worked some fields and dusted in seed of wheat and oats and vetch and things on faith and not much of it—and one morning in the gray predawn a fine big crack of thunder sounds close by and raises you jumping out of sleep on the screen porch, and more resounds with lightning striking somewhere on the Booker through heavy air, the thunder is not around you but inside, echoing in your bowels. And when the rain starts—hesitant spatters of big drops at first, ungenerous, making you push with your stomach muscles for more—then thickens and turns to sheets and wind-driven walls of water so that you know you've caught the middle of a strong good storm and the rain will be real rain, not just a shower to sprout crops and let them die, it is raining on the place all right but it is raining on you too, even though you sit there pleasantly dry, wrapped in your sheet beneath the roaring metal roof. . . . It is raining on your dark cracked fluffy soil and filling it and waking its microbes and fungi and worms, and raining on your hills and soaking into grass and running down rocky draws to brim your tanks, and sending its excess from ten thousand acres of Tonk ruggedness to make your creek run strong, and rousing life in seeds and roots to carry your cows through winter. All this you feel, being yourself the land, owning it not merely on paper but inside your hard-way head and your guts.

And being that close to the land you are close to the Way itself, in spite of the Syndrome's sway, or maybe because of it. . . .

Nor does it often seem to matter much any more, with such closeness, that while usefully tending crops and beasts you are seldom in danger of imagining yourself in some Upper Paleolithic hunting-and-gathering paradise, or of recapturing the feel of an interim time of your life that was not meant to last. As owner and user and family man you have moved up (or is it down? or does it make any difference which?) the scale of human ways and farther from kinship with sinewy men who lounged in sunlit glades among great Old World oaks, and flaked flint points and tools, and spoke to one another of bloody holy encounters with great cave bears and mammoths. Or kinship with old Indians who brewed spells and visions and cures from this region's roots and leaves. Or

with that lesser man who, landless and glad of it, wandered
the unregenerate Tonk hills alone with a shotgun and found
a winter stream running clear over ledge rock with ice along
its fringes and brown leaves drifting down, and someone's
old garden in the cedar, and an elm tree full of squirrels, and
owned them in his head. . . .

He pops out still at times, though, that fellow, forgetting
usefulness for a morning or an afternoon or a day or so,
moving about the wilder parts of his land with gun or field
glass and a stealthy tread that does not resemble the forthright
clomp of the owner he elsewhile is. At night in bed on the
screen porch while the harried wakeful squireen of Hard
Scrabble cocks an ear toward strange dogs' distant voices and
the bawls of frustrated fence-walking bulls and heifers, that
other, calmer, more simple man is a part of the night and its
wild sounds, listening and sometimes learning. He knows
when the raccoons violently pair and mate, and maybe one
night as he drifts into sleep their nattering squalls turn into a
great spinning horizontal circle of light in his mind, with
sparks shooting out as it turns. . . . He knows the big hoot
owls' solemn bourgeois lust and territoriality, three plus two
equals five possessive notes over and over and over again,
when they set up nests in the metallic cold of still late-winter
nights. He hears the midnight rabbit's scream when caught
and the whirr of fox-flushed quail, and has listened one March
to a single unknown stolid Mesozoic thing that moved in for
a week or so and said at intervals, simply and flatly, "Ink."
(Until one night when, inconceivably, something stirred its
phlegm and for a while it exclaimed, still flatly, "Ink, ink, ink,
ink . . .") He is there in late summer when plover and
yellowlegs come through in whickering, fluting flocks low
under clouds, on their way to the far Argentine. The spring
birds sing at dawn for him, and spirits and faces and portents
shape themselves for his waking eye amid trees' leaves and
branches, and he learns in moonlight how a fox (red? gray?

young? old?) can modulate its hollow diminishing rhythmic bark close beyond the barn to quavering whines and clucks that, heard alone, you would swear came from a screech owl. He ponders such things, the muser, while his newer, useful self ponders other affairs. . . .

These days I hunt only a little, partly because of other things there are to do but mainly I think because living on the queer, half-wild, half-useful place all year, knowing its changing sounds and smells and colors and shapes and movements during night and dawn and daylight through the seasons, tending fields and garden and beasts and sometimes slaughtering tame meat, I no longer sharply need the sense of purposeful presence on the land that throughout most of my life hunting and sometimes fishing have given me more strongly than other pursuits. Because as squireen and O. F. and Paleolithic muser, I am quite purposefully present all the time. . . . Not that I have given up hunting, or that I expect I ever will, or that I am queasy about it when people do it honestly and right. A long while back I passed through whatever conscience crisis I was destined to pass through in regard to the blood sports, and unlike Henry David Thoreau I came out the other side of it as a blood sportsman still, if not a very gory or dedicated one. Nor do I intend to review the stages of that process here except to note that it has to do not only with purposeful presence but also with being, in part at least, a thing that men have always been, maybe the most fundamental thing that they still are, inside. (And if you insist that men have not always been that thing and you are a vegetarian, I will respect you while demurring, and if you insist thus but still eat flesh, I will upon demand propound for you my outrageous theory that it is more honorable and reverent and sane by far to seek and kill and dress the bird or beast or fish you eat, wild or tame, than it is to pay somebody else to do it for you. . . .)

For all us moral agonizers and pantheistic types, of

course, the subject of destroying fellow creatures is prickly with taboos, partly rational. I won't kill a wild thing that I can't eat unless it is an individual threat to my function as the stock farm's own Head Varmint, and not always then. I dislike game-hoggishness, even when legal, and the sterile technological gadgetry that has infested field sports and fishing in recent years and made them, as is often noted with pride, Big Business. In general I heed game laws on the theory that they are formulated by men more aware than I of how various species are thriving year by year, though occasionally such things as the reinclusion of sandhill cranes on the huntable list can make me doubt that. . . . And being a fairly indifferent competitor afield as well as elsewhere, I care little now about things like trophy bucks, which are apt to yield raunchy meat.

By preference I am still, as during most of my life, a shotgun hunter of doves and bobwhite quail in the company of old friends. The doves give the finest shooting, in stubble grainfields and sunflower patches and beside stock tanks where they come to water at evening, flying in low or high and up or down or across the wind, jinking in their courses and going warier as the season moves on, so that to kill a legal limit, currently ten, with a box of twenty-five shells is considered pretty fair work. (The per-pound cost of such meat, of course, comes out a trifle high. . . .) But quail are the real hunting, the plump, alert, predictable little chickens of field and pasture around whose ritual pursuit whole breeds of dogs have been built and whole human lives, very nearly, have been shaped without regret. Some uncles of mine were a bit like that, and I have friends still for whom December and January are a period to slice out of the business and professional year and to lay aside for a higher, almost religious use. Much of the rest of their year also may go in working with their dogs, ranging with them gunless before and after the season itself.

You can hunt bobwhites without dogs, especially if you live on a place and in going about your work have seen more or less where the coveys lie; they are creatures of strong habit and will be somewhere near there again when you come. But to flush them out just for shooting, like doves, is a grossness like swilling fine wine to get drunk. It turns quail into mere meat, for they are not very hard to hit on a straightaway rising shot, and it leaves out all the sharp rightness and beauty of seeing the lean swift gaudy dogs work back and forth across the wind until one swivels down to a point, and the others honoring with points of their own, and the loud heart-startling though foreknown explosion of the covey's rise and the shooting and retrieving, and afterward watching the best dogs of all search out the singles where they have scattered. It is possible to enjoy such a hunt without even carrying a gun, as I have sometimes done to friends' amused disgust. Hunting quail only a few times a year—some years not at all—I keep no bird dogs of my own, though occasionally I nurse a notion of finding a Brittany spaniel or some other little close-hunting, moseying canine with which to range the high Booker and the creekside fields in old age. . . .

On the whole, not many O. F.s are addicted to such ritualistic forms of field sport, for being practical men they tend to prefer working dirt and nurturing domestic creatures, and hunt if at all for meat and enough of it to justify expended cartridges and time. If they hunt birds, I regret to note, some are addicted to potshots, wanting more than one bird per shell. . . . Deer hunting, at least my brand of it, puts me closer to such folks. Young, I had a little exposure to the Texas deer ritual—the trip to distant limestone hills, the bourbon and banter and rough cooking of the men, the rising at three or four in the morning in a lamplit cold cabin to biscuits and white gravy and sausage, the chill lone hopeful wait in a brush-built stand for animals that might or might not show up, the fine bloody knifework later on whatever someone had managed to kill. . . . But it did not take with me somehow, maybe because my own people were bird hunters and those are two quite different passions coming on at roughly the same time of year. Only lately and on my own land have I worked up much interest in hunting deer, and that interest is rather unsportingly pragmatic: there are getting to be too many deer around, with none of the old natural predators and controls to hold their numbers in check; they are first-rate meat if you pick them right; your kill is therefore a legitimate harvest of the land, like peas or calves or wild plum jelly.

As with quail and most other game, a resident hunter comes to know more or less incidentally the habits and schedules of deer. Hence he has to bring, in honesty, not much real understanding to his pursuit of them, none of the keen awareness of deer ways that brings a real hunter success even in strange country. They haunt the winter grainfields, grazing at night when the moon is out, but during cloudy or moonless spells slipping forth at dawn and dusk from the brush and woods along the fields' edges, watching alert for a while, trotting doglike to lush spots, lowering their heads to feed, then raising them high-eared to listen and sniff and watch again. They have pecking orders, and adults will run the year's big fawns away from the choicest places. . . . Hidden downwind beside the field, a pragmatic O. F. can study them and wait his time for a clean sure shot—being oldmaidish about maiming things—at a fat dry doe or young buck, often going out several different days before sighting one that he wants.

Certainly there is unpragmatic pleasure in being in such places, especially at dawn. In cold darkness you ease to your hidey-hole and settle yourself and wait cat-silent and still for light to come, with possibly a few uncatlike soft slaps at the bass-whining Tonk winter mosquitoes that somehow survive hard frosts and come out whenever the temperature gets above the twenties, warming themselves with your blood. The creek talks to its boulders. East pales. Wintering finches and field larks chit and flutter. Quail night-scattered by predators call where-you. A mockingbird finds you and rasps officiously from a cedar. Big dark lumps materialize here and there and become your cows; smaller gray ones, nervous and shifting, turn into deer, six or eight or ten. . . . Maybe you have misjudged the air's drift or maybe it eddies and carries a whiff of you to one of the gray things, which coughs and brings them all upright, flags high, tense and ready for panic. Or maybe, unpanicked, they sense unspecific danger on your side of the field and keep three or four hundred yards away as through a glass you watch them feed and play and bully one another. Such mischance, though, matters little against the privilege of being there; on occasion I have had my rifle's sight centered on a fat deer's foreribs, then have flicked the safety back on, unwilling to break the morning's crisp brightening peace. But sooner or later, on that morning or another or in some softer dusk, one does break the peace and the end result is good loins and roasts and sausages and chops in one's pragmatic freezer, and a pretty hide upon which one's younger daughter scrapes with squaw patience for a full day, though we have not yet managed to tan anything right. . . .

I suspect most real deer hunters know and prize that sort of peace far more than do quail men, who are forever on the move, scurrying to come up to a pointed covey before it busts, yelling to one another and to dogs, shooting fast and often. Unhappily, though, a certain other proportion of the big-gamesters are not at all peaceful types but frustrated infantry heroes or something, for whom the possession of a hunting license and a high-velocity rifle is a stimulus to barge about the hills regardless of property lines, karawhocking away at anything at any range that resembles a deer and some things that do not, such as goats, cows, wheeling buzzards and hawks, jackrabbits, varmints, watertroughs, distant barn roofs, and recently emptied bottles. They can rouse fierce territoriality in O. F.s like me who try to maintain the illusion that they have some say about the harvesting and welfare of the wildlife on their places, and about their livestock's safety and their own. Things are fairly quiet in the neighborhood just now, most hunting being done by neighbors and their friends and kinsmen, who know the lay of things. But a while back, a couple of places nearby used to take in day-lease deer hunters, which meant just about anyone who showed up and plunked down his fee, and great was sometimes the uproar. . . . At such times an O. F.'s adrenaline squirts very readily. The sound of a shot that may or may not have been fired on some far corner of his land will send him leaping toward his pickup, and often without hearing anything at all he embarks on dour patrols.

On one such outing, three or four years ago, I met across my Booker boundary fence a homely palefaced fellow with buck teeth who had somehow the look of a man privileged to bolt one part onto a complex machine, over and over again all day as machines passed down the line. I returned his greeting without much warmth, for though he was on legitimate ground, having paid my neighbor to be there, his field of fire included a lane through my brush, perhaps not accidentally. But he had a sort of open unrebuffable quality, and we ended by talking a while.

He said, "Hell, I been hunting deer since I was sixteen and I ain't ever killed one yet. Don't know why I keep on trying."

I said something profound like well, getting out was a good part of it. . . .

He said, hefting the antique Austrian military firearm he bore, "Had two good rifles and sold them both for eighty-five bucks last spring, to pay a damn baby-doctor bill. Wasn't going to hunt any more. Then hell, here come November and I scooted off downtown and bought me another gun. . . ."

Admirably, this unwoodsy man—who must nevertheless have relished the lone watching and waiting and being that deer-hunting entails, having never gotten anything else out of it—had seen but not shot at a magnificent big fox that I too had glimpsed at times on that side of the place and once had watched drink at the tank. It would be pleasant to note that he had recognized its wild beauty and its rightness and hence had spared its life, but the fact is he had thought it was someone's bushy-tailed red dog. . . . Later that day I heard a shot from his direction and hoped he had at long last killed himself a deer, but somehow doubted it, for it seemed uncertain that he really wanted one. . . .

The Tonk hills' legitimate native hunters are the hound-dog men, and there are not a good many of them, with fewer still who are young. It takes a degree of rare country sophistication to keep on knowing that to be in the hills at night and to hear your dogs' clean music where they run is a far more worthwhile thing than watching defunct movie stars in the Late Late Show on the tube. And a degree of rare country toughness to follow the hounds all night and go home to a day's hard work . . . Then too the hunters themselves are territorially jealous of the stretches of country where they have what amounts to an ancestral claim to range, and discourage interlopers in ways they do not discuss, which I have not explored. Most of the lower Nation "belongs" in this sense to Evetts Gilliver and a handful of his fox-hunting friends, who nearly always hunt together, and to a similar but less active group of coon-and-cat-hound men.

Most of what friction existed between average new-style landowners and the hound people evaporated a good while back, after the dogs learned to jump net fencing without thinking twice and their owners learned to "goat-break" as well as "deer-break" them by raising kids in the pens with them and rubbing nasty stuff on their noses. Of late in parts of the region favored by the new hybrid wolves, use of poison has interdicted considerable areas to such hunters, but mainly along White Bluff they still run much as they did, and for people like me they are pleasant and often helpful to have around. Occasionally at three o'clock on a night after slogging work, when a fox or a coon goes to ground in a cranny beneath the ledges on the branch seventy-five yards from the house, and twenty big hounds converge to squall and bellow there, with your own dogs screaming in territorial rage beside your bed, you may feel slightly otherwise, but the feeling does not last. . . .

The fox hunters are not very bloodthirsty, being happy enough with a kill now and then to keep their dogs from discouragement, and satisfied the rest of the time if a fox gives them a long far-ranging run—whose sounds they interpret minutely and with passion from where they listen and cry the avid hounds on—and then makes good his escape. One dew-spangled morning early last spring I was waked at dawn by hounds close by, running along the creek. I rolled out and put on pants and a flannel shirt, quieting my sheepdog Blue, and went out to watch as they cast about with confused sporadic roars, having lost the scent, leaping through the brilliant green oats and sweetclover in the little West Creek field and among the cedars that line the creek itself, sun-fishing back and forth across fences as though they were not there. One sounded a hopeful note on the other side and the rest went to join him, and shortly the whole melodious turmoil passed up and over the old moonshiner-snipers' steep eastward hill, muffling in thick cedar.

I saw something moving toward me along the fence that leads from the creek toward the house and guards the green field's edge. It was the fox, a gray, probably the one who envies me my game chickens, for he was clearly on home ground now, nonchalant with having thrown off the hounds, trotting without haste, looking back now and then past his flank to the high dog-loud hill. At the field's near corner, before reaching the branch, he slipped through the fence wires and vanished into the cedar of the low rocky nose that pokes out there.

Came the swift hounds anew with great clamor in his tracks, and exploded sheepdog Blue again, desiring combat with all seven. . . . I hushed him and watched and listened as the little pack followed scent up the cedar-clad nose and out of sight, and heard them grow eagerly loud and then, inexplicably, fall to fighting among themselves, with silence afterward and a few snarls and puzzled whines. . . .

Across the bright still air, tires crunched gravel on my northern neighbor's place and a pickup's door slammed as someone got out to open my gate, and I knew it would be big Evetts, who prizes his dogs and begins to travel about looking for them if they haven't all come in to the horn's note by daybreak. He drove up to the house in his old green truck with the dog-cage in the back, nearly full, and beside him in the front his frequent companion Crockett Tyler, an ex-cowboy who does plowing and other tractor work for absentee owners at seventy or whatever he is, being a bit stove up for much cow work or even for chasing after hounds at night, though he likes to sit in or near the pickup and hear them run. He is a good man, Crock, usually taciturn but full of fine tales if he thinks you want to hear them, many from the time of his father and uncles, who hunted wild hogs on the tall-grass prairies in fall and rode with trail herds up to Kansas. A long time back, they say, Crock was a hell of a bull rider in the rodeos, and worked on ranches far away, coming home between jobs.

"Hey, there," said Evetts, and I said hey, and Crock grunted genially sidewise. Evetts asked the question I knew he would ask, and I said yes, I had heard them and seen them too, and pointed to where they had gone, remarking on the squabble that seemed to have ended the chase.

Evetts frowned. "I ought to known better," he said. "It's

that damn old Joanie bitch. When a fox holes up she jams her old nose in there and then she chews up any young dog that tries to get close for a smell. Going to ruin them. . . ." They had been a couple of miles up the creek after a night's hunt, the hounds all loaded and the truck pointed home, when the gray ran across the road, and unable to resist he had turned out the six young dogs to run, with the bitch to keep them steady. "You turn too many dogs loose on a gray, you mess him up," he said. "A red, you turn loose everything you got." When the chase had moved out of earshot down the valley, which has no road along it, they had had to drive fifteen miles around to catch up with the dogs. . . .

While Evetts went to find them, I talked a little with Crock. Like many old cowboys, despite their breed's fabled antipathy toward farming, he likes gardens and pretty crops and such things and he complimented me on my oats and clover, which had been wintergrazed only by heifers and were coming on strong for spring. He remembered when a tenant family had raised a big lucky crop of sweet potatoes in that little field; unable to get much for them in a glutted Depression market they had given away hundreds to people who came with baskets and boxes and tubs. Some folks had shared like that then, Crock said. . . .

He said, "You talk about hounds. . . . Old Man Bill Lee that used to own lots of land in here—this place too, I think."

"Yes, he did," I said.

"Him and my Uncle Jim, when they were young they kept wolf dogs," Crock said. "Big wolves there was back then, killed lots of calves. Uncle Jim lived three miles down Paluxy and some pretty morning real early he'd saddle his hunting horse and ride up on the ridge behind his house and blow on his old horn, and Bill Lee he'd ride up on that hill right yonder and blow his back, and they'd bring their dogs and get together and sometimes they'd run a wolf plumb to Walnut, fifteen miles south, grass all the way and nary a fence in sight except rails around somebody's corn patch. Uncle Jim he told me about it, plenty of times. 'God Almighty, the way the country was then,' he'd say."

Evetts came back wet to the knees from dewy grass and bushes, the dogs leashed on a rope strung through all their collars. He had found them around the entrance to the gray's impregnable rock den, the Joanie bitch still crabbily calling it hers. He needed to get them home and penned, he said, and eat some breakfast and then go chainsaw and deliver a promised load of posts, without as far as I knew having had any sleep at all. He being, as they say in the county, much man . . .

Close enough, most of the time . . . Shut off by the Syndrome and by temperament from the intelligent almost nonparticipant purity of a Thoreau, the Head Varmint nonetheless tries in his way to do things right, without ever quite succeeding all the way, but in the trying itself becoming a part of the land and the Way it works. So that he can no longer truly find the dividing line between his more or less useful country self, who plows and sows and builds and fences and worries and wades through frigid poot and mire while hauling feed to black cows in January, and that other less pragmatic self, older in time but younger in spirit, who sips with bees and envies trumpeting cranes, and is restless when the plover flute from beneath low clouds on their way to the distant pampas, and runs in his mind with Evetts Gilliver's hounds and with the fox they chase as well as with all honest chasers and all chased beasts now and in all times past, and waits catlike in winter dawns beside green fields, and has kinship with unknown night things that go Mesozoically, "Ink."

Queerly, they are the same man.

18 ≋ Reality as Viewed Darkly Through Old Snuff-Bottle Shards ≋≋≋

Although his cage of gold be never so gay,
Yet hath this brid, by twenty thousand foold,
Levere in a forest, that is rude and coold,
Goon ete wormes and swich wrecchednesse.

G. CHAUCER,
The Maunciples Tale of the Crowe

Queerly too, Hard Scrabble examined as an economic whole is solvent, though not for the right reasons. During its restoration to some slight degree of usefulness and its preparation as a place to live, it has cheerfully gobbled up what money I have been able and willing to shovel into it, and seems likely to gobble more. As a stockfarming endeavor it has not yet shown a profit in any calendar year since belatedly and without great urgency, a few years ago, I began to aim it in that direction. In the most slapdash accounting terms, annual calf and kid sales and such things usually now amount to more than expenditures for feed and seed and tractor fuel and all that. But if one cranks in his own time at even very slim wages and then, through application of the low cunning

249

forced on us all these days by the tax system, takes cognizance of depreciation on his machinery and livestock and improvements and of similar indirectnesses, he is faced with the sticky fact that as an agri-businessman he still has quite a way to go. Not that this comes as much of a shock.

The reason the place is solvent despite an operational deficit is simple. Land in the past couple of decades has been inflating in dollar value faster than almost any other commodity save maybe computer stocks. Except around the fringes of cities and along the shores of new reservoirs and in other speculators' paradises, the sort of land that has been appreciating fastest in Texas is marginal, varied, difficult, private, "pretty" terrain such as the tracts which, out of a nomad's happy ignorance that the Syndrome was lying in ambush for me, I bought along White Bluff Creek. The why of this lies perhaps mainly in the sort of buyers who have been running prices up—city people almost entirely, reacting to jammed urban ugliness as well as to anxiety about the future. And the irony it adds up to here is that Hard Scrabble, for all its rocks and brush and ungrateful Tonkishness about production, is currently worth per acre on the market not only a lot more than I paid for it but also more than much of the state's best farming land in regions like the Blackland Prairies and the flat rich plains along the coast.

In honesty, I would much rather this were not so. Land ought not be a commodity, and I dislike the swirling disorderly economic and physical and social pressures that the land market exerts on the region and will exert even more in years to come. But it *is* so and—in honesty too—if it weren't, I doubt I would have felt justified in ramming quite so much money and time and work into the place as I have. I probably would have gone ahead and done it, but less complacently. . . . For I grew up in hard times and I have a bred-in, self-defensive if latent streak of Hibernian economic wariness, a survival instinct adapted to a money world, and though I have no present intention of cashing the whole thing in and possibly never will, the streak shrewdly insists that if I did, I ought not come out loser.

Suppose that while waxing practical (it will not last) we cast a cold Hibernian glare on the potential operational economics of a place like Hard Scrabble. It could show a profit, and will before long. That it has not thus far done so is due partly to the fact that I have had to keep on trying to make a living in ways that I know better and have sometimes, when a specific thing badly needed doing on the place, been as much as fifteen hundred miles away, which has led to heifers dead in calving, and untilled unsowed fields whose lost production has meant big winter feed bills, and other diseconomies. More to the point, though, the place has not been ready for full use, and still isn't. In a sense, what you are doing when you feed money and time into an economically extinct piece of earth like this, to bring it back into function, is ransoming it out of the limbo into which cotton and open-range grazing had thrust it long ago. If you push the land too hard, asking from it production it is not yet ready to give, you are forfeiting the ransom and repeating old blunders, and it will slide quickly back toward limbo. This happened on the Booker, which was cleared of cedar and then overgrazed before I bought it and is now in many places an incipient brake again. And it does not make any kind of sense, economic or otherwise.

But there is room for hope (let's assume so here anyhow) that before too long I will have managed to clean up and regrass as much of the rough rangeland as warrants the effort, and to bring the arable fields not only along White Bluff but also on the Soft Scrabble tract—which counts as part of the "unit"—into steady production for supplemental grazing and enough hay to ease us through drouth periods and rough winters. At that optimum stage, the total holding will (or would) consist of at least a hundred acres of old established cedar on land too rough to be worth clearing but good for wildlife and posts, another hundred or less of field land, and the rest—say 280 acres or so—in reasonably good range grasses. Irrigation of the field parts during dry spells—the only way to achieve really intensive use of the land either as a stock farm or otherwise—would probably not be economic on either tract. Without it, in this climate, the unit would safely maintain perhaps forty-five or fifty mother cows with their offspring and a varying number of goats and sheep, year in and year out. Some people with old West Texas habits might argue that it could carry twice as many cows as that, and so it could. For a while . . .

With fifty cows and a ninety percent crop of calves selling weaned for say $225 each—more or less the price lately, though as everyone knows that market too has been wavering mainly upward—you could gross per annum on the cow operation a bit over $10,000. Add to this no more than a thousand to be realized from kids or lambs and possibly a harvest of surplus hay or seed or something, and subtract from the total gross a conservative $5,000 for operating expenses, depreciation, and so forth, and you net, from a year's fairly steady work and worrying, maybe $6,000, barring disasters of the sort that abound in agriculture. Counting on such disasters from time to time, it might be saner to expect a diligent man to average $5,000 a year. With luck.

Though such an income will not cut much of a swath for you in an affluent boomtime society or put your progeny through college or permit much saving against old age, it can be considered a "living" even now, especially under country conditions where the land can furnish much of your family's food and you are free from a good many nuisance and status expenses common in town life. But it depends heavily on your good health and more or less constant presence, and in shrewd Hibernian terms it is not much of a return on land whose current market value, invested wisely elsewhere, might earn twice five thousand bucks a year without any need at all for work on your part. A real agromaniac, a glutton for peasant pleasures but with a little logic lingering in his brain, might even while the market is suitably queer (it will not be so always; the practical world generally gets its own back) swap his rocks and brush for an equal acreage of good deep unscenic soil in a richer and better-watered region, and with considerably less labor than the Tonk Nation demands of him earn quite a lot more money.

That neither I nor very many other owner-users of marginal pretty places seem eager to make such shifts is evidence that land ownership, except of the speculative sort, is not a logical thing. You don't really own a place till you own it in your head by watering its soil with your sweat and seeking out its crannies and plants and creatures, and by that time the place comes in a way to own you too. . . . Though your shrewd Hibernian self may be aware of its lousy operational economics, he does not weigh very much against that Resident Peasant and O. F. who dreams on ways to whip the little brush in the Waterfall Field and likes to see his morning sun rise over Snipers' Hill rather than across some flat rich prairie landscape.

Aroint thee therefore, shrewd Hibernian, and in thy secret counting house concern thyself with land-value appreciations, gloatingly. . . . The fact is that if a man feels affection for his rough piece of terrain and has some way of eking out a money living through other activity, he may be better off asking from the place only enough profit to keep the IRS off his neck, if indeed he wants to fight that battle at all. Besides making life easier and giving him a little spare time for reflection and for scratching himself where he itches, light use will let him keep on improving his land, and if ever times come when a "living" means something more basic than it does just now, the place will be ready to yield. Even today Hard Scrabble, for all its tough ungratefulness, is far enough along toward health to furnish a family—several of them, conceivably—with a solid living of that basic sort if called on for it. Meat, milk and its products, vegetables, honey, wine, fuel, soap, candles, hoofed transport and draft power, even clothes with a bit of spinning and weaving . . . Many of these things we get from it already in token or larger amounts, and a shift to heavier dependence on the place would involve a good deal more hard steady work but not any great confusion.

Economic reasons, of course, are not the only valid ones for sometimes questioning your relationship to a difficult tract of land. There is the matter of being a writer of sorts as well as a Tonkish peasant, and how much writing you expect to get done in the years perhaps left to you, and the fact that country tasks are often at odds with the sedentary concentration that writing requires, as well as with the travel it sometimes calls for. There is also the question of approaching decrepitude. . . . "Good shape for age," a pleasant young doctor scrawled at the bottom of his report on a physical I had to take for some reason a few years back. It struck somehow as a hard truth, a sudden view of myself from outside, nor have the strings of awareness it fingered in me altogether stopped quivering since. Friends of one's own vintage start dying roundabout, and in thinking back over their least healthful habits and excesses, one often recognizes his own as equally bad or worse. Friends not many years older, hale enough till now, abruptly wither to fragile codgerliness:

> The flesh is bruckle, the Feynd is slee:—
> *Timor Mortis conturbat me*. . . .

Though in truth the point is not so much fear of death, which is another bone to gnaw, as fear of the bruckle flesh's dwindling, of noncompetence, of losing the illusion that one can cope. (And I wonder if any imaginative family man past forty, in disarrayed times like these, has failed to see at some point a flash vision of himself as sick and old and exhausted in a ditch, unable to defend himself or his own, while on the road above him the arrogant catastrophic young armies stride by? . . .)

Not that I dwell on these sobrieties much, or that I yet feel myself to be in full and fragrant decay . . . But Hard Scrabble is not the sort of place that once in reasonable shape is going to function placidly through the years without care, while its aging owner sleeps late in the mornings and rises to putter benevolently, appreciating bird sounds and shades of hillside green. It will be easier to handle, but even if it gets good gentle use for another twenty or thirty years, brush is going to keep trying hard to come back on hills and fields, and distant folds in the land will still lure surly or ailing live-stock into hiding while the aforesaid aging owner seeks them. The ten or so watergaps will go on washing out with big rains, and the good tight fences will sag and rust and need attention, maybe replacement. Garden johnsongrass will still have to be fought back in the midst of heat-pulsing, locust-droning July if it is not to be let make seed; goats will still be getting their stubborn horned heads fish-hooked in fencewire a half-mile from the house, starving there if not found in time. And even if you achieve—as you must, and I already partly have—an efficiently sloppy attitude that takes care of the crucial things and gets to the other ones when and if it can, the place itself will always be a bit ungrateful, visiting its grudge against old cotton and swarming longhorns on who-ever happens to own it, remembering with implacable re-sentment what it was when Tonks and Comanches knew it, and the intrepid ranger Buck Barry, and even later Bill Lee and Jim Tyler whooping exultant behind their wolf dogs south toward Walnut Springs and not a fence in sight. And in fact I would not like it half as well if the memory of all that were not here. . . .

I have no sons coming on to take up the slack with time, even assuming that such sons as I might have would view that prospect with joy. And barring large shifts in the direction our world has taken, no supply of good-humored hard-slogging hired help seems likely to turn up, grateful for wages the place could pay or for a share in its meager production. Hence sometimes when approaching brucklehood forces itself on my mind, I muse on alternatives. Stake out a homestead patch close around the house for intensive use, and let the rest go back to brushy somnolence, a hunting ground and insulation for one's privacy? Sell Hard Scrabble while prices are fat and on part of the money build a home on the Soft Scrabble hundred acres, a civilized rectangle of mainly good land with scenic rough hills in view but not inside its fences, where an aging owner could indeed rise late and putter, checking his livestock and crops through the bedroom window? . . . Cash in all your holdings, and with what you get haul your long-suffering womenfolk off to live for a few years in some quiet ancient cragged place beside the Mediterranean, owning little but your clothes and books and typewriter and trinkets and bank account, watching complacently as other men fight an even more resentful soil, sailing a small boat across blue water to rocky coves, with baskets of wine and hard sausage and olives and bread?

The chances are that we will do none of these things very soon if at all, but that I will add more rooms to the helter-skelter house here on White Bluff, and build more outbuildings and erect more fences, and fight the brush and nurture the dirt, and remain obsessed with the potential wholeness I can feel in the place as a stock farm, if less certain than a few years ago that by myself I can bring that wholeness to full flower and fruit, and less anxious about it too. But I *could* walk away, and not look back, even feeling closer to this bit of land than I have ever felt to any spot on earth before, even belonging on it as a bumbling part of its Way. . . . For better or worse, its hold on me is not unbreakable, as it was for some of the old cedar people, and is for the golden-cheeked warblers in spring and for the cedars and oaks and elms.

Because you do not really cease to be what your young years made you, nor do you really want to. And if I am in part a peasant belonger on the land and all that, having earned the right to be, I am also in large part still that detached and bookish moseyer and sojourner and watcher who during much of forty years moved on from place to place and did not want to own anything that could not travel with him in his baggage or his head, or that he could not walk away from, and who needed to move along every now and then from whatever he had or was, to make certain he still had free will. Or at least the illusion of it.

Sooner or later, I suspect, most such moseyers lose the real push and need to move along. For sooner or later if you prove something to yourself often enough you come to believe it, or maybe what you do is grow up. To stick in one place and to own things and to be in some sense owned, you finally see, does not necessarily smash free will (which may, for that matter, have been smashed to start with), and can lead to knowledge and satisfactions you could not otherwise have. But the other thing is a very irrational and solid comfort to have far down deep inside, and once there it is very hard to lose—the flat nomadic conviction that you can always walk away, if you damned well please.

It is also very American, that conviction, based in habits that for three centuries the virgin land allowed. It may be one of the big things wrong with us in a world no longer virgin. But if so it is wrong with me too.

And if you did? Sold out, packed up a few portables, and moved yourself and your ladies along to some other spot, urban or rural, foreign or domestic? Turned over your slice of the Tonk Nation to new and fresher peasants, and the house and barn you built, and the fenced grassed pastures and still unvanquished brush, and the mellowing garden and fields, and all that dried sweat and hope? . . . Would to walk away thus mean confessing that you had pounded ten or twelve years of sporadic but hard work and focus down a rat-hole, and writing it off? Would you then just be another man the rough Tonk hills had whipped, in retaliation for old longhorned cows and cotton?

Maybe, or again maybe not. There are things a man needs to learn before he dies, for fullness, and these seem to have been such things for me. It might be better to have learned them early, but I didn't, at least not in an understanding way. Earlier there were too many other things to find out about as they came along, so many of them that there was never time for all, nor any chance to be bored. So that only when past forty—in a period when by rights a man ought to be using what knowledge he has already acquired, toward writing his best books, painting his best pictures, arguing his best cases before a jury, snipping out his best carcinomas, or whatever—did I start consolidating a store of rare knowledge concerned with putting threads on pipes and stones on stones, with making a show in carpentry, with fences and humus and stumps and bugs, with the smell of rain on dung and drouthy soil, with how goats bleat when frightened and how when only alone, with strange fox sounds beyond the barn at night and the comical anger of bulls, with plows and seeds and cement mixers, with fields that are green and why and what flowers the bees work in August in the third-smallest county in Texas. . . .

But having learned these things by now, if most of them inexpertly, and the other things that go with them and make

258

up a sort of whole, I own them in my head, which is the only place you can ever own anything. And if tomorrow I had to be carted off, a physical wreck, to eke out long death in some bleak and cheery rest home, I would be carrying away with me more of Hard Scrabble than by leaving I would lose. Though it would all be here in the land still for the next man to learn for himself and to own, if he had the same sort of compulsion as I. . . .

As for whether it is really worth owning, this stuff that I have in my head, God knows. Clearly enough, I think it is. Clearly enough too, many other people don't. They show up now and then, some of them good friends, and look about with alien curiosity, and go away fortified with relief that they aren't stuck in such a place, and that their own metaphors for eternity, whatever they are, are less arduous ones than mine. Because unless we have gone dead before our bodies, eternity is what we look for, one and all.

(Marginal graffiti by an unpantheistic subself:

GOD IS NOT DEAD, HE IS ONLY HIDING IN THE DIRT.
MASSA'S IN DE COLD, COLD GROUND?)

To claim that all who have worked and lived on the land have felt strong appreciation of it, whether or not mystic in thrust, would be of course sentimental nonsense. The earth can be a rough sort of mistress, and social and economic pressures can be even rougher, and responses to such roughness have varied wildly since before any words were written. Perhaps especially in this country and especially during the first third or half of our century, there has been a great deal of articulate revulsion against rural things and ways. Not many years ago nearly all American towns and cities teemed with people whose general optimism and drive were fueled by vast joy at having escaped "the farm." Sensitive youths fled from the plow and from brute earthbound fathers and migrated to the great world where, sometimes as writers of books, they spent much of the rest of their lives looking back in relief or fascinated rage at the numbing labor and sloppy manure they had left behind. Negroes up into our own day have thronged cityward out of the sourness of rural tenantry and sharecropping, and women of all hues have spent a lot of time hating country life and the toil and isolation it has often meant for them; even now, remembering—or maybe only remembering their mothers' memories—they are often the stoutest force against their men's impulse to get back to the land.

Such bitterness has had its ample causes. Maybe Walter Prescott Webb, an unbitter man who knew whereof he spoke from a dryland-farming childhood—not very far west of our county—caught in the 1930's, in *The Great Plains*, the flavor of the background that produced it about as calmly as anyone has:

. . . . There is for us nothing new on the farm. We know it all intimately—the long hours, the sweaty, stinking, heavy underwear, the debt and the mortgage, the way it feels to drag in at twilight after a day in the field and to sit on the doorstep and pull from our aching feet our brogan shoes before we eat the coarse evening meal. That is the common heritage of the majority of American people.

For my own part, I doubt I would have felt very differently from that, under like conditions. Had I grown up, for instance, in these hills during the period of their decline, helping unhopefully to sow and tend cotton in little fields of moribund, powdery, shallowing soil and then to hand-pick a scrawny crop of it in lucky years when the drouths or the bugs didn't get to it first, living with parents and siblings in a cramped and drafty shack, learning of wider things only what could be absorbed in at most five or six years in a one-room, one-teacher school—if I had been stuck with all that, I expect I would have hauled out like a scorched bat when the first

opportunity came, and would seldom have looked back thereafter. Because that is where the hatred and revulsion were
born, partly perhaps in toil, which most men since the lazy
golden time have never truly loved, but mainly in hopelessness. . . . And hopelessness was the dead-end corner into
which cash-crop monoculture and frontier ignorance of what
land was and could do, among other things, had shoved much
American small farming. Farmers had turned into serfs, not
under the rule of some rough hairy baron but under an economic system.

But let us escape from this treatise into which I seem
unawares to have led us, even as, say, embittered Hamlin
Garland escaped agricultural life. . . . I have no large personal theories about the future of the American family farm.
It may well be doomed, as some say, by the curse of our continuing worship of bigness and profit, or through more
sensitive and comprehending use of the land it may become—
as the hopeful organicists, may their tribe increase, foresee—
the main highway to a better and wiser way of life. The
subject may not seem to have much relevance to the problems
of a largely urban nation and time, but I suspect it may have
a great deal. . . .

What I do know is that there is a gulf of difference
between using the land in that old extractive hostile way, and
trying to use it right. It is not the same thing to "drag in at
twilight" having done just another day's dull brutalizing field
work for mere cash or the hope of it, as it is to drag in
equally bushed but with the conviction of having made your
patch of earth a shade better than it was before, even if that
too may feed you or earn some money for you. As a countryman I may be, I know full well, a bit of a dilettante, not
chained to the land but free to leave when and if I want,
undependent on its yield for survival or even for the means to
keep on trying to ransom it out of limbo. But I am a fairly
hardworking dilettante at intervals, and I have experienced

both those kinds of dragging tiredness in my lifetime, and the second kind is usually clean and good, and causes you to bathe at waterfalls at dusk and to muse back with satisfaction over the day behind, while also looking forward to tomorrow.

If, that is, you are built to think the land and such things are worth owning in your head. . . .

In philosophical terms of "being" and "becoming" there is not much question that life at Hard Scrabble, with so much always still to do and the problem of whether it will ever all get done, has leaned strongly toward the latter, kinetic state. Unstatically, the house sprouts new rooms, barns and sheds grow out of nothingness, fields change from briery tangles to expanses of worked soil furred with tame greenery, and grassed stretches of new pasture lie where only a year or so ago old cedar used to brood on past human error.

Yet now that there is a house which though small can shelter us through the year, and some growing sense that the place is moving toward function, life here has a tinge of "being" too. The seasons roll by toward wherever it is that they go: tawny wind-fanged winters give way to long lush springs, and summers with (perhaps) small sheeplike clouds riding above the southwest shove of searing Chihuahuan air finally yield to moist and melancholy and exultant falls with northers and high skeins of big birds trumpeting overhead. New generations of cattle and goats appear in their time, and frolic in fresh life-joy and are admired and sometimes named, and the recurrent work with them and with the soil takes on a known and welcome pattern. Children find out for themselves, rummaging afoot or horseback, the cedar's secret places and what kinds of birds build what kinds of nests and how dark hills nose out into green and winding valleys when viewed from the high Booker, and by finding out these things they take on ownership too. Seeding and harvest, heat and cold, rain and drouth, birth and death, lushness and dormancy, earth and air and fire and water are with us closely all around, year by rhythmic year.

That this is an archaic and sideline sort of existence in a pulsating technological time is obvious. That it bespeaks no hot noble desire in the Head Varmint for immersion in twentieth-century humanity's rub and stink and clamor, the Varmint readily admits. This is not, however, sour Weltschmerz. I have moved about a good bit in the world, if in an uncontemporary sort of way. And while finding much that seemed sorrowful and wrong and reaching stout disaccord with some main forces of the age, I have been barred always from glumness by the rather ridiculous fact that I've liked so many people I've known and have always been so bloody glad to be alive. The only truly philosophical question, as Camus noted, being suicide. . . .

But it strikes me as more than a possibility that archaism, in times one disagrees with, may touch closer to lasting truth than do the times themselves—that, for instance, the timbre and meaning of various goat-bleats may be at least as much worth learning as the music and mores of the newest wave of youths to arrive at awareness of the eternal steaming turmoil of the human crotch. Therefore, having at least the illusion of choice, one chooses for the moment at any rate isolation and an older way of life.

Not that isolation itself is more than relative now, or that we have sought it fully. Like most other people these days, we have in us much that is urban, and contemporaneity comes at us through sometimes complex kinships and friendships in cities fifty or eighty or two hundred or two thousand miles away, through magazines and newspapers and electronic boxes in the helter-skelter house, through influences on children in school, through the fact that both Madame and I have work we do and like that relates to the world outside, through highlines and fuel companies that feed energy to the machines and gadgets on which we depend in lieu of the hired help and draft animals another age might have required for the less than truly simple life we lead, through raiding dogs and sonic booms and cruising helicopters and the faint groan of big trailer trucks fighting a grade on U.S. 67 two or three miles away, on quiet nights with a slight drift of southerly air. . . . Most of the time at Hard Scrabble you can feel yourself remote from the world and its moil if you want to, and one city friend of ours says that on getting out of his car here he always experiences "culture shock." But isolation and simplicity are not what they used to be.

Other prospective intrusions loom. A nuclear power plant is scheduled for construction on Squaw Creek a few miles east, with whatever titillating possibilities for malfunction and dire leakage there may be inherent in the state of that art. Its output is intended to satisfy new demands to arise in the 1980's in a "metroplex" of losangelization on erstwhile excellent farmland between Fort Worth and Dallas, sixty miles from us, which speculators and other boomers are prophesying will grow up in the environs of a new regional airport. . . . And the indefatigable Army Engineers, rumor says, keep nosing quietly up and down the Paluxy valley with some sort of big dam in mind. I am told that outcrops of the porous Trinity Sand upstream would prevent a reservoir from holding water, and hope this may be so, for otherwise we might end up either submerged or part of one of the shrill suburban playgrounds that are promoted around such lakes.

Isolation, indeed . . . Bells still toll for one and all—and, God knows, for the land.

Relative isolation, then . . .

There is always the question of whether or not you are doing your children a favor by shielding them even this much from the world as it is—whether you may just be setting them up for trauma when they barge out into its jostle, as barge out they will. I tend to think otherwise. Anyone who has been shown clearly that natural and rural basics contain a good measure of irrationality and violence and injustice and pain and lust and greed has at least a start toward comprehending adult social and professional life when the time comes to face it. And even if it does turn out that the world as it is gives them some knocks, as the world as it is surely will, who would want to cheat them of someone to blame for trauma later, when it hurts? . . . At any rate, life at Hard Scrabble is providing them with some time to build up strength, some responsibility for living things, some awareness of biological and natural truth—and, perhaps wrongly, I suspect that these are among the more meaningful things you can furnish a child in any era.

If this were a different sort of book, the reader would have been getting warm glimpses along the way of the Happy Homestead Family, of John and Jane and Helen and Sally and dog Blue and cat Kitty and goat Door Bell and ponies Ladybird and Penny and the other personified members of the place's population, laboring and playing and producing in honest rustic joy and fulfillment. Well, we do so labor and play and produce, more or less, and we do find rustic joy and fulfillment, but somehow in the process we do not manage greatly to resemble the families in back-to-the-land magazines and books or to exhibit constant hearty unison in regard to our common goals, if indeed they are common. For just as the world is often with us, so is individuality, and the voice of genial Lord Hard Scrabble is sometimes heard to swell quite loud in speaking of such matters as whose turn it may be to feed the horses, or who left what gate open endangering the heifers' virtue, or what set of small hands and feet shall go forthwith in search of kindling wood, or how he intends callously to carry the beloved pet Nubians off to auction at Meridian if someone doesn't get hot and clean their shed. . . .

But it isn't that sort of book. . . .

If it fitted into still another category, that of Triumphant Returns to the Land, now would likely be the time for a few wind-up pages of ringing affirmation and a proud recital of the universal principles symbolized by one's years of labor and rumination amid the Tonkish hills. But when you come down to it, the main idea in truth seems to have been not so much triumph as comprehension, though I suppose there is a certain minor degree of triumph in what little has been accomplished here and in the fact that it all still seems worthwhile. And if some universal principles are truly very much involved—how could they not be, with the land?—I am sure I have pointed a bony finger toward them a bit too often already. . . . .

You have the power to make a choice, or at least from long habit you think you do. And when the time comes to choose land you choose, against all good sense, a patch of rocky rough cedar hills with a few tired little fields and pretty water flowing past them over ledge limestone. In the short, disastrous, backwater history of its use by men of your race, its swift decline from primal richness, you come to see that there is a summary of the relationship between men and land on all parts of this planet, in the ages succeeding a golden time or harmony between men and the natural order that may or may not have ever been, anywhere. Because there is in you a need to know certain things—though why the need is there you do not at first discern—you undertake this bit of land's uneconomic restoration to what you hope is gentler human use, with no certainty at all that those who come after you will be gentle with it too or that in long time what you do here will matter a mote for good or bad, these being needful illusions as is land ownership itself, existing only in your head. . . .

Yet out of the work and the illusions come in time some scraps of understanding—tardy and incomplete perhaps, but there were other things to do before, and maybe for that matter it was only now time to learn about scrub brush and rhizobia and goat-bleats and all those other things. And through the understanding comes abruptly and at long last a glimpse of old reality, indestructible, hiding among the creatures wild and tame and the stones and the plants, and in the teeming dirt. Without having known fully till now that it was what you sought, you see it there as clearly as does any battered ancient pensioner who leans on a hoe and picks his nose beyond the fringes of suburbia, contemplating the rituals of bantam hens that are not even all the same color, uncontemporary, at one with vanished medieval peasants in his fundamental thrusts and rhythms, at one with Sumerian farmers working in fields beside the Tigris and hearing from far off the clash and clang of mad kings murdering one another.

You see it and it sees you. Old reality survives, blinking at you there, lizard-eyed. Survives and will prevail.

That is perhaps enough to know. Yes.

A NOTE ABOUT THE AUTHOR

A Texan who has lived much of his life outside his native state, John Graves grew up in Fort Worth, was educated at the Rice Institute (now Rice University) and at Columbia University, and during World War II served in the Marine Corps. His short fiction and articles have been published in *The New Yorker*, *Town and Country*, *The Atlantic*, *Holiday*, *American Heritage*, *Esquire*, and elsewhere. After returning to Texas in the late 1950's he wrote *Goodbye to a River*, a personal and historical book centered around an autumn canoe trip down a part of the Brazos long familiar to him. Since then he has taught college English, done a stint of conservation writing for the Department of the Interior during the Udall years and a second for the Sierra Club—*The Water Hustlers* (1971)—continued with his own writing, and occupied himself with the rough country place he calls Hard Scrabble, the first part of which he acquired in 1960. He lives there now with his wife and two daughters.

A NOTE ON THE TYPE

This book was set on the Linotype in Janson, a recutting made
direct from type cast from matrices long thought to have been
made by the Dutchman Anton Janson, who was a practicing
type founder in Leipzig during the years 1668–87. However, it
has been conclusively demonstrated that these types are actually
the work of Nicholas Kis (1650–1702), a Hungarian, who probably learned his trade from the master Dutch type founder Dirk
Voskens. The type is an excellent example of the influential and
sturdy Dutch types that prevailed in England up to the time
William Caslon developed his own incomparable
designs from them.

Composed, printed and bound by
The Kingsport Press, Inc., Kingsport, Tenn.
Typography and binding design by Virginia Tan.